St Antony's Series
General Editor: **Richard Clogg** (1999–), Fellow of St Antony's College, Oxford

Recent titles include:

Elvira María Restrepo
COLOMBIAN CRIMINAL JUSTICE IN CRISIS
Fear and Distrust

Julie M. Newton
RUSSIA, FRANCE AND THE IDEA OF EUROPE

Ilaria Favretto
THE LONG SEARCH FOR A THIRD WAY
The British Labour Party and the Italian Left Since 1945

Lawrence Tal
POLITICS, THE MILITARY, AND NATIONAL SECURITY IN JORDAN, 1955–1967

Louise Haagh and Camilla Helgø (*editors*)
SOCIAL POLICY REFORM AND MARKET GOVERNANCE IN LATIN AMERICA

Gayil Talshir
THE POLITICAL IDEOLOGY OF GREEN PARTIES
From the Politics of Nature to Redefining the Nature of Politics

E. K. Dosmukhamedov
FOREIGN DIRECT INVESTMENT IN KAZAKHSTAN
Politico–Legal Aspects of Post–Communist Transition

Felix Patrikeeff
RUSSIAN POLITICS IN EXILE
The Northeast Asian Balance of Power, 1924–1931

He Ping
CHINA'S SEARCH FOR MODERNITY
Cultural Discourse in the Late 20th Century

Mariana Llanos
PRIVATIZATION AND DEMOCRACY IN ARGENTINA
An Analysis of President–Congress Relations

Michael Addison
VIOLENT POLITICS
Strategies of Internal Conflict

Geoffrey Wiseman
CONCEPTS OF NON-PROVOCATIVE DEFENCE
Ideas and Practices in International Security

Pilar Ortuño Anaya
EUROPEAN SOCIALISTS AND SPAIN
The Transition to Democracy, 1959–77

Renato Baumann (*editor*)
BRAZIL IN THE 1990s
An Economy in Transition

Israel Getzler
NIKOLAI SUKHANOV
Chronicler of the Russian Revolution

Arturo J. Cruz, Jr
NICARAGUA'S CONSERVATIVE REPUBLIC, 1858–93

Pamela Lubell
THE CHINESE COMMUNIST PARTY AND THE CULTURAL REVOLUTION
The Case of the Sixty-One Renegades

Mikael af Malmborg
NEUTRALITY AND STATE-BUILDING IN SWEDEN

Klaus Gallo
GREAT BRITAIN AND ARGENTINA
From Invasion to Recognition, 1806–26

David Faure and Tao Tao Liu
TOWN AND COUNTRY IN CHINA
Identity and Perception

Peter Mangold
SUCCESS AND FAILURE IN BRITISH FOREIGN POLICY
Evaluating the Record, 1900–2000

Mohamad Tavakoli-Targhi
REFASHIONING IRAN
Orientalism, Occidentalism and Historiography

Louise Haagh
CITIZENSHIP, LABOUR MARKETS AND DEMOCRATIZATION
Chile and the Modern Sequence

Renato Colistete
LABOUR RELATIONS AND INDUSTRIAL PERFORMANCE IN BRAZIL
Greater São Paulo, 1945–60

St Antony's Series
Series Standing Order ISBN 0–333–71109–2
(*outside North America only*)

You can receive future titles in this series as they are published by placing a standing order. Please contact your bookseller or, in case of difficulty, write to us at the address below with your name and address, the title of the series and the ISBN quoted above.

Customer Services Department, Macmillan Distribution Ltd, Houndmills, Basingstoke, Hampshire RG21 6XS, England

---

Colombian Criminal Justice in Crisis

Fear and Distrust

Elvira María Restrepo
Research Associate of Fedesarrollo
Bogotá

palgrave macmillan in association with St Antony's College, Oxford

First published 2003 by
PALGRAVE MACMILLAN
Houndmills, Basingstoke, Hampshire RG21 6XS and
175 Fifth Avenue, New York, N.Y. 10010
Companies and representatives throughout the world

PALGRAVE MACMILLAN is the global academic imprint of the Palgrave Macmillan division of St. Martin's Press, LLC and of Palgrave Macmillan Ltd. Macmillan® is a registered trademark in the United States, United Kingdom and other countries. Palgrave is a registered trademark in the European Union and other countries.

ISBN 0–333–92163–1

This book is printed on paper suitable for recycling and made from fully managed and sustained forest sources.

A catalogue record for this book is available from the British Library.

Library of Congress Cataloging-in-Publication Data
Restrepo, Elvira María, 1965–
The Colombian Criminal justice in Crisis: fear and distrust/Elvira María Restrepo.
p. cm. – (St. Antony's series)
Includes bibliographical references and index.
ISBN 0–333–92163–1 (cloth)
1. Criminal justice, Administration of – Colombia. 2. Judges – Colombia. 3. Colombia – Politics and government – 1974 – I. Title. II. St. Antony's series (Palgrave (Firm))

KHH5404.R47 2002
345.861'05—dc21 2002026947

10 9 8 7 6 5 4 3 2 1
12 11 10 09 08 07 06 05 04 03

Printed and bound in Great Britain by
Antony Rowe Ltd, Chippenham and Eastbourne

Contents

List of Tables, Figures, Maps and Appendixes

Tables

Figures

Maps

Appendixes

Acknowledgements

The Political Map of Colombia on p. x is © copyright 2002 Lonely Planet Publications. All rights reserved. Used with permission www.lonelyplanet.com.

Maps 4.1 and 7.1 on pages 115 and 165 are reproduced by permission of their author, Professor Camilo Echandía Castilla of the Universidad Externado de Colombia, previously published in 'Manifestaciones de Violencia en las Regiones de Colombia' (1999), reproduced by permission of the Republic of Colombia Presidency.

Other Tables and Figures reproduced in the book come from the public domain unless otherwise stated.

Political Map of Colombia

Preface

This book is the development of my DPhil thesis 'Corruption and its Judicial Control in Modern Colombia, 1980–1995', which I completed at Oxford University in 1998. At the beginning of 1999, Laurence Whitehead, one of my thesis referees, recommended its publication for the St Antony's /Macmillan series (now Palgrave Macmillan). He suggested placing a greater emphasis on the general issues of the system of justice – hence widening the original focus from that of judicial corruption – with the eventual goal of understanding the place of the judiciary in the Colombian state. This book is the product of that endeavour: it analyses the general issues of the administration of justice and its place in the state, focusing primarily on the capacity of the system to administer criminal jurisdiction in modern Colombia. This focus on criminal jurisdiction is the product of the internal and external perceptions of the Colombian system of justice. Internally, the judicial crisis has been blamed on the high level of impunity in criminal jurisdiction throughout the past two decades. Although the situation is not much better for civil jurisdictions, internal concerns about crime and violence have focused significant attention on criminal jurisdiction. Externally, Colombia has been thought of as representing a special case of crime and violence in Latin America.

Although this book focuses on Colombia, I believe that the general themes are relevant to the entire Latin American region, particularly since most of these countries have recently undergone comparable processes of criminal reform. Moreover, the sustained expansion of crime, in particular organised crime, has shown that most countries in the region have similar types of problems. However the Colombian case seems to be the most critical – hence its analysis is of huge importance and its understanding should in turn provide a greater regional awareness of the medium and long-term effects of prolonged judicial crisis.

Since the advent of illegal drug trafficking in the 1980s, the Colombian criminal system of justice has suffered from the most dramatic crisis in its history; however, many of its structural problems actually preceded the consolidation of organised crime and were aggravated by it. As a result of this crisis, judicial reform in 1991 introduced a sophisticated set of judicial institutions and mechanisms that have empowered the judiciary, and the criminal jurisdiction in particular, making it more independent of the executive and the legislative.

This analysis of the performance of the criminal jurisdiction system covers the period 1958 to 1998. There have been some suggestions that judicial performance was critical even earlier than this, but I have chosen to begin the story in 1958 because the statistical data, and indeed most analyses of justice, show that it was in this year that the performance of the criminal jurisdiction system started to deteriorate. Moreover, 1958 is the year when the most reliable statistics on judicial performance became available. Since the period under review covers a transition between two Constitutions, those of 1886 and 1991, which contain structurally different criminal justice systems, this book analyses the evolution of the criminal jurisdiction performance in these two periods. Particular emphasis is placed on the effects of the 1991 constitutional reform.

The book focuses on the capacity of the system of justice to administer criminal jurisdiction in modern Colombia and on the system's prospects in the reconstruction of society and its institutions. To reach this objective, I use three theoretical frameworks: one framework to analyse the main features of the Colombian state and its political system; a second framework to discuss the characteristics of the system of justice, briefly reviewing the historical origins of the judicial power since the colonial times; and a third framework to define and understand the nature of judicial corruption. Statistics, surveys, press reports, magazines, judicial proceedings and personal interviews are used widely throughout.[1] The statistics that are discussed comprise most of the available institutional data for the period of study as well as data from private research. Survey data includes polls relating to the public perception of the administration of justice from the 1980s up to 1999. Some of the judicial proceedings were difficult to access, mainly because of the level of distrust emanating from some members of the judiciary; this is in spite of the fact that the proceedings relating to finished cases are officially in the public domain. In the case of personal interviews, it is worth mentioning that most interviewees preferred to remain anonymous (or found it hard to speak frankly about certain issues) out of fear. Fortunately, several did eventually speak out, and their revelations represent valuable tools for the analysis of the issue of criminal justice. Indeed, while this book reveals that the system of justice is driven at a fundamental level by fear and distrust, it also acknowledges that there are many anonymous heroes, clerks, judges, *fiscales* (agents of the *Fiscal* in charge of individual prosecutions), witnesses and others, who have impeded the collapse of the system and who, more importantly, are now struggling for its reconstruction. These people clearly see some hope for the future. As a parallel goal, therefore, this book has attempted to reveal the 'human face' behind Colombia's criminal jurisdiction.

The original manuscript was read in its entirety by Malcolm Deas and his comments and suggestions led to significant improvements in both the substance and organisation of the book. Mark Philp, as my thesis supervisor, provided full guidance on the initial research and very lucid suggestions throughout its preparation. He also reviewed a few chapters of the manuscript. Julio Faundez made crucial suggestions that helped turn the manuscript into a book and were fundamental to its general improvement. I am very grateful to him. Andrés Hoyos carefully reviewed the introduction. My parents, Fernando and Elvira Carmen, helped me make this book a reality with their valuable comments and constant support. My husband, Neil, encouraged and helped me throughout these years, giving me emotional support to finish this project. Finally, all the members of the judiciary and other state institutions who helped me with their valuable experiences, and provided first hand information on issues that I would otherwise have ignored. I am very grateful to all of them for helping to bring this book into being. Any remaining deficiencies are entirely my responsibility.

I hope that this book encourages the international community to reflect on the huge potential role that the system of justice could play in reducing violence and crime in Colombia.

[1] *A note on translations*: most interviews and testimonies quoted in the book were originally in Spanish. Where the translator's name has not been given, the translation is my own.

E.M.R
Oxford

List of Abbreviations

ANC	National Constitutional Assembly of 1991 (Asamblea Nacional Constituyente)
ACCU	Self-Defence Organisation of Peasants of Córdoba and Urabá (Autodefensas Campesinas de Córdoba y Urabá)
ACDEGAM	Association of Peasants and Ranchers of Magdalena Medio (Asociación Campesina de Agricultores y Ganaderos del Magadalena Medio)
ANAPO	Popular National Alliance (Alianza Nacional Popular)
ASONAL	National Association of Judicial Workers (Asociación Nacional de Jueces y Empleados judiciales)
AUC	United Self-Defence of Colombia (Autodefensas Unidas de Colombia)
CAJANAL	Social Security for Public Workers Agency (Caja Nacional de Previsión)
CP	Criminal Code
CPP	Criminal Procedures Statute
CTI	Technical and investigative body of the *Fiscalía* (Cuerpo Técnico de Investigación de la *Fiscalía*)
DAS	Department of National Security (Departamento Administrativo de Seguridad)
DANE	Department of National Statistics (Departamento Nacional de Estadísticas)
DPN	National Planning Department (Departamento de Planeación Nacional)
DIAN	Internal Revenue Services and National Customs (Dirección de Impuestos y Aduanas Nacionales)
EEB	Energy Agency in Bogotá (Empresa de Energía de Bogotá)
ELN	National Liberation Army (Ejército de Liberación Nacional)
FARC	Revolutionary Armed Forces of Colombia (Fuerzas Armadas Revolucionarias de Colombia)
FECODE	Colombian Federation of Teachers (Federación Colombiana de Educadores)
INPEC	National Prisons Directorate (Instituto Nacional Penitenciario y Carcelario)
ISS	Private Workers Social Security (Instituto de Seguro Social)

MAS	Paramilitary wing of the Medellín cartel (Muerte a Secuestradores)
M-19	April 19 Movement (Movimiento 19 de Abril)
MRL	Liberal Revolutionary Movement (Movimiento Revolucionario Liberal)
NGO	Non-Government Organisation
PSJ	Policy of Compliance with the System of Justice (Política de Sometimiento a la Justicia)
SIC	Colombian Secret Services (Servicio de Inteligencia Colombiana)
SIERJU	Statistical System of the Judiciary (Sistema Estadístico de la Rama Judicial)
SINEJ	National System of Judicial Statistics (Sistema Nacional de Estadísticas Judiciales)
UP	Patriotic Union (Unión Patriótica)
UNIJUS	Universidad Nacional Centre for Socio-judicial Studies (Unidad de Investigaciones Jurídico-Sociales 'Gerardo Molina', Universidad Nacional)
USO	Oil Workers' Union (Unión Sindical Obrera)

Currency Conversion

Years	**Average exchange rate per year (Col$ = US$1)**
1980	47.28
1988	299.17
1992	759.29
1993	803.53
1994	829.19
1998	1 350.06

Introduction

This book focuses on the system of justice in modern Colombia: in particular on its capacity to administer criminal jurisdiction, and its prospects with respect to the reconstruction of society and its institutions after prolonged civil strife. It has commonly been held that Colombia's criminal justice system is weak, inefficient and corrupt. This book delves beneath such beliefs to reveal a criminal system which is fundamentally driven by fear and distrust. Consequently the first part of the book analyses the origins of these two recurrent features in their historical, political and legal contexts, in order to understand the failures, achievements and future prospects of the criminal jurisdiction. Since the judiciary is a subsection of the political system, Chapter 1 starts by addressing the issue of whether the Colombian political system is capable of providing a framework for ensuring efficient and impartial criminal justice. With this purpose in mind, I examine whether the state is autonomous and also whether the political system commands enough legitimacy to be able legitimate the criminal system of justice. The chapter shows that the political system is unable to act authoritatively over a range of forces within the country. As such, the Colombian political system is not capable of sustaining politics as the main source of social exchange – it must contend with guerrillas and paramilitaries, drug trafficking forces and other non-political forms of exchange. Thus, the state has an elusive legitimacy and is dangerously weak, and its crumbling authority – whose decline preceded the outbreak of drug trafficking but became obvious as a result of it during the 1980s – further undermines both its legitimacy and that of its associated institutions, in particular those of the system of justice. Consequently, the inefficiency and lack of impartiality of the criminal system of justice are to a great extent symptoms of the weak legitimacy and lack of autonomy of the whole political system, rather than the cause.

Chapter 2 provides an overview of the system of justice's essential features and institutions. I first discuss the judiciary's historical characteristics: those inherited (as in most Latin American countries) from the colonial and post-colonial period, in order to determine the weight of this legacy in the problems faced by today's Colombian judiciary. I show that some of the problems of the Colombian system of justice which have recurrently limited the judiciary's capacity and determined its poor outcomes throughout the period of study, are clearly related to inherited historical characteristics. Such problems include clientelism, the judiciary's fiscal dependence, excessive reformism, exceptionalism and judicial self-restriction. The recurrent problems of the criminal jurisdiction are subsequently examined.

Chapter 2 also focuses on the present-day potential of the main institutions of the system of justice; these were strengthened after a process of constitutional reform in 1991. Particular emphasis is placed on judicial independence, which was enhanced by the 1991 Constitution. The contradictory degrees of judicial independence introduced at that time, and the sometimes inconclusive character of the reform, depict some of the frailties of Colombia's political system. A democratically elected national assembly reformed the Constitution; however, the democratic debate was permeated by the absence of clear-cut ideological proposals from the main political forces represented in the assembly, by some authoritarian executive impositions that filled the political vacuums, and by the interests of the illegal forces that pervaded the institutional debate in the period. As a result, technical debates and juridical principles were so tightly mixed with institutional and political interests as to make it difficult to determine where one began and the other ended.

In spite of the new constitutional constraints, the evidence shows that judges are more powerful and independent today, as a result of the 1991 constitutional reform, than in the period 1958–91. This judicial empowerment is demonstrated by the increasingly prominent role assumed by the judiciary, particularly with the Constitutional Court and the *Fiscalía General* (a form of Attorney General's Office). A good example of this new strength is the recent increase in prosecution for political corruption at the senior government level – for example, the presence of drug money in Ernesto Samper's Presidential campaign in 1994 (known as *Proceso 8000*), and in the investigation and prosecution of major corruption in state contracts and congressional activities which had been ignored for decades. Members of organised criminal groups, who were previously untouchable, have also been prosecuted, condemned and imprisoned – these include the leaders of the Cali Cartel and other leading drug traffickers and some important members of the paramilitary as well as guerrillas. It is also now possible judicially to control some of the violations of human rights by serving members of the military. While this possibility has only recently been introduced, it represents important progress in a country where such abuses had previously been dealt with internally, via the military's own jurisdiction system.

I also draw particular emphasis to the fact that the new Constitutional Court, the *tutela* (a form of writ to protect specific rights), and to some extent the *Fiscalía General*, have exceeded most expectations – this is mainly because they have managed to transcend some of the structural problems of the state, and hence these institutions have acquired a certain legitimacy and autonomy of their own. However, I view progress with caution. Several decades of low commitment to regularity, together with exceptionality and other forms of authoritarianism, cannot be removed by a finite package of constitutional reforms and isolated judicial action, though they are a step in the right direction.

Part II of the book discusses the crisis of criminal justice. Chapter 3 starts by examining the performance of the criminal system of justice by reviewing factors such as the judicial backlog, the length of proceedings, the atypical ways of deciding criminal cases, the level of impunity and the degree of judicial enforcement. These variables all reveal a high degree of inefficiency in the criminal jurisdiction and large levels of judicial impunity. I argue that a great part of the inefficiency results from the fact that the executive has used the criminal justice system to bolster its fragile autonomy, to help stabilise weak political administrations or to consolidate military efforts in the prolonged armed conflict that characterises modern Colombia. For decades the executive extensively used and abused state-of-siege decrees or exceptional legislation, and arbitrarily imposed 'duties' on criminal judges, often forcing them to work in ways which subvert the course and fundamental purpose of justice. The results of such exceptionality have not been successful in general.

The judges, overburdened with huge backlogs since the 1960s, were compelled to undermine their own institutions so as to sustain weak incumbent administrations. One result is that the great majority of disputes and crimes which do not directly threaten the stability of the incumbent regime or the security of the state, have been ignored or left unsolved. Due to this failure, people have tended to take justice into their own hands, generating violence and further increasing distrust in the administration of justice. The inefficiency of the criminal justice system is compounded by its failure to deal with equity and impartiality with many of those cases it does prosecute. Conversely, the criminal jurisdiction also suffers from a perverse degree of accessibility where only the few – who can afford a proper defence or 'arrange' a way out – have the privilege of obtaining prompt or impartial justice. In contrast, approximately 50 per cent of those imprisoned have not been convicted. Within this 50 per cent, the great majority are petty criminals coming from the less well-to-do sectors of society, revealing a class system where punishment has generally been for the poor and justice or acquittal for the privileged few. While these features of the criminal jurisdiction started to change in the mid-1990s following the 1991 constitutional reform, the changes are barely perceptible at the statistical level – the existing historical institutional weaknesses of the state are still present, hence progress in the judiciary is necessarily slow. Although the system of justice is not entirely responsible for its own inefficiency and high level of impunity, such poor performance clearly undermines the already fragile legitimacy.

The inability of the system of justice to resolve most crimes resulted in a situation whereby the formal institutions of justice administered by the state became increasingly displaced by 'private justice' administered through fear and violence. Those perpetrating the violence were mainly, but not exclusively, drug traffickers, paramilitaries and guerrillas. The capacity to intimidate through violence guarantees that the 'requests' or impositions of these groups are effectively and rapidly carried out. The constant competition between these groups and the increasing inability of the state to control them have meant that 'private justice' is now available as any other market commodity – in particular, it can be bought by most ordinary people, not just by those who are involved in armed conflict or drug trafficking. 'Private justice' produces a sense of fear that comes from a reign of execution, yet for many citizens its effectiveness is in sharp contrast to the inefficiency of the state's administration of justice, thereby making it a preferable option for some of those who are desperate to settle disputes both at the criminal and civil level.

'Private justice' further inhibits or corrupts the state's system of justice. The capacity of intimidation possessed by the drug traffickers, the paramilitary, the guerrillas and other armed actors is such that it can also impede or corrupt the process. This reached its worst levels when drug traffickers almost paralysed the criminal administration of justice during the 1980s, with the infamous 'option of the two metals: *plata o plomo* (silver or lead)'. A judge was thus faced with two options, to become a villain by being an accomplice to corruption, or a hero who risks sacrificing his life and tranquillity in the name of justice and the common good. The heroic option is still commonly chosen, judging from the numbers of assassinated judges and clerks and the high incidence of threats received; however, justice cannot operate wholly on the basis of individual acts of heroism, particularly when the political system itself typically provides no safeguards or protection for the majority of its judges.

Clearly, accusations are also inhibited by fear. Many crimes are never reported: for those that are, the level of fear is such that witnesses, victims and their relatives don't dare to speak up against the perpetrators.

The issue of judges' and witnesses' security was partially resolved during the 1990s with the introduction of *Justicia sin rostro* (faceless judges and secret witness legislation); however, since its abolition, most judges currently dealing with dangerous criminals, together with the corresponding key witnesses, still remain completely unprotected. Consequently, this book emphasises that the problem of impunity in criminal justice and corruption in the judiciary should be discussed in the context of widespread fear: fear to accuse and fear to prosecute. Chapter 4 explores the obviously high degree of impunity resulting from fear: the fear of the victims to accuse, the fear of the witnesses to testify and the fear of the judges to prosecute. These fears originate from the fact that the state, essentially, has no control over its territory and therefore has allowed for the existence of powerful armed actors that can easily subvert it. Even where the state has a degree of autonomy, it is unable to remove the sources of fear from these overwhelmingly powerful actors.

To finalise the discussion on the crisis of the criminal jurisdiction, Chapter 5 discusses the extent of corruption in the judiciary and tries to determine whether the lack of impartiality in the criminal jurisdiction is the result of judicial corruption. It is very difficult to assess the general level of corruption from the existing judicial statistics. This is partly as a result of the high level of impunity and an incomplete set of data, and partly because corruption in Colombia seems to prevail in the form of threats and pressures – both of which are invisible. Surveys, interviews and case studies provide a deeper insight into the problem. They show that in spite of the fact that there appears to be a high level of judicial corruption, it is not systemic. They also reveal that much of the existing judicial corruption is the product of the intimidation of judges – which brings us once again back to the issue of fear. In addition, the weak control exerted on the judges is partially responsible for the perversity of judicial corruption. The lack of control of corrupt judges is mainly the result of corrupt and inadequate laws that fail to ensure the impartiality of judges' decisions. A system of justice that has *carte blanche* to apply hard or soft laws, breeds corruption. Particular emphasis is placed on the fact that the legal possibility for controlling judicial corruption does exist, yet the state is either too embattled to secure the protection of its judges or too instrumental in terms of legal and illegal interests to provide for the impartial judicial control of the corruption of its judges.

The third and final part of this book delves into the origins of fear and distrust in the criminal jurisdiction. It reveals how and why fear and distrust are the direct result of the weak autonomy and elusive legitimacy of the state. Chapter 6 examines the impact of drug trafficking in the judicial institutions. The political and judicial crises of Colombia have been associated with decades of endogenous and decentralised forms of violence. As mentioned above, these have fuelled the growth of different forms of illegal 'private justice'. However, I show that none has used fear against the judges in a more successful way than drug traffickers, relegating the system of justice to a state of semi-paralysis for almost a decade. In Chapter 6 I illustrate the extent of the power of fear instigated by the most pervasive actor of intimidation existing in the country. In contrast to other illegal forms of 'private justice', which simply ignore and seek to supplant the formal system of justice, drug traffickers also subvert and corrupt the formal adjudication process, often with some degree of success.

Fear became a way of subverting the criminal jurisdiction with the advent of drug trafficking – yet it is presently used by many other actors who wish to take advantage of the precarious autonomy of the state and its elusive legitimacy. While many of the problems of the criminal jurisdiction come from the past, it is fair to claim that drug trafficking has notoriously diminished the autonomy of the state, either because it has paralysed its capacity to realise its goals (the embattled state) – as in the case of specific periods examined in Chapter 6 – or because the state is used by drug dealers to fulfil their own interests (the instrumental state), as demonstrated by the Policy of Compliance with the System of Justice (PSJ) and the abolition of the *Justicia sin rostro*. In order that the state recover part of its lost autonomy, it had to resort to extreme measures: in particular, it had to resort to exceptionality and authoritarian institutions (justice for war mechanisms) such as the *Justicia sin rostro* or special justice as well as mechanisms out of the reach of drug traffickers' control, such as extradition and extraordinary powers for the police. This would suggest that the judicial solution against such a powerful criminal 'enterprise' is only possible when the system of justice borrows authoritarian or arbitrary elements of 'private justice', or when the state displaces part of its sovereignty to another state, as in the case of extradition.

Yet these are dangerous solutions for the consolidation of Colombia's democracy. For example, in Chapter 6 I argue that justice for war creates even more arbitrariness, and its success is usually short lived – this may be either because of the judicial activism showed recently by the progressive Constitutional Court or because for the most part these mechanisms only control drug trafficking in a temporary and limited way while their effects are long lasting and extremely pervasive. The drug traffickers' diminished use of violence since the end of the 1990s appears to be linked with changes in their organisation – in particular, that they are no longer organised as powerful vertical cartels. There is also a perception of drug traffickers' decreased used of open forms of corruption, thanks in part to the existing legal loopholes (many of which are their own creation). This, together with the 'new' state priorities in the armed conflict, has 'relegated' justice for war against drug traffickers so that it is less visible, and consequently the threats to the system of justice have also decreased. In the long term, however, the judiciary and the state cannot fight this global criminal multinational alone. Sooner rather than later this issue will have to be resolved with international cooperation in all fields, possibly via the legalisation of psychotropic drugs and their traffic.

The final chapter of this book deals with the role of criminal justice in a country where there is an irregular war. Before turning to the prospects of justice in the construction of much-needed lasting peace, I start by exploring the role that justice has historically played as an instrument of war. I show that excessive recourse to exceptionality for consolidating the state's military efforts or justice for war – for example, military justice for civilians from the mid-1960s until 1987 – was particularly dangerous since it often interfered in many other conflicts which were not political; these were mainly common crimes and social protests with no criminal connotations. It is true that although the use of exceptionality in Colombia has been lengthy, it never reached the levels of arbitrariness of Pinochet's Chile – instead, rather like the situation in Northern Ireland, large sectors of the population rarely experienced any abuses. Ironically, the Colombian military justice's own inefficiency substantially lessened the effects of its arbitrariness.

My main claim in this book is that exceptionality became a frontier mechanism between democracy and authoritarianism, between the Constitution and the irregular war. This frontier location of exceptionality made it possible for the executive to oscillate from one side to the other according to its strategic necessities. The nature of Colombia's irregular war involves a blurring in the distinctions between political war, organised crime and large-scale violation of human rights. In this regard, many governments justified a degree of state arbitrariness through the use of exceptional legislation by the executive. As discussed earlier, exceptionality alienated the judges from the resolution of those ordinary conflicts which do not interfere directly with the security of the state. However, such alienation increased violence. I argue that exceptionality multiplied the causes for war; hence, although Colombia's irregular war often seem to justify this recourse, exceptionality allowed the executive to legislate most aspects of the criminal statutes, limiting due process and the fundamental rights and liberties of individuals, so undermining the legitimacy of the system of justice.

My final aim is to show that the present judiciary in Colombia has the potential to contribute to peace and to the re-establishment of state legitimacy. It is indeed true that since 1991 the new limitations to exceptionality introduced by the Constitution, together with a very active constitutional control, have been in place and have been able to strongly limit, although not altogether eliminate, further executive abuses. But if we eventually want to restore trust in the judiciary, the system first needs to solve its other crises in order to limit future interference. The role of justice as an instrument of peace, even bearing in mind that the criminal system cannot by itself resolve essentially political problems such as the peace of the country, is essential. Criminal justice can boost state legitimacy and contribute to the institutionalisation of a fair solution to a long and devastating irregular war. This reinforcement and institutionalisation, however, can only occur if there is a general degree of trust in the system of justice, something which can only be attained if the system of justice fulfils three main tasks. The first task is to significantly improve the adjudication of the existing (repressed) litigation. The second relates to the armed conflict: a lasting peace can only result if a certain degree of judicialisation of the war occurs. By judicialisation, I mean the inclusion of the minimum international human rights guarantees in the peace process, such as the creation of a truth commission, the imposition of sanctions to some of those responsible for the most atrocious crimes, and reparation for some of the victims of the war. A third task is to enhance military accountability and improve the military's human rights record. I need not stress that these apparently simple tasks have proved very difficult in the aftermath of most recent irregular conflicts.

The judiciary in Colombia is still in crisis. Thus, claims for progress must be tentative: the strengthening of judicial institutions is still not reflected in changing statistical trends and the signs of progress are very recent. One could even claim that new problems have been created, such as collusion between key institutions within the judiciary. More judicial reform and review are undoubtedly needed; however, the current judiciary has increased its independence from the executive and it has more power over Congress and the military than its predecessors. In terms of criminal justice, the judiciary now has more effective institutions and mechanisms, offering it a better chance of completing a given criminal investigation. Particular progress has also been made recently in the provision of justice for the less well-to-do sectors of society as a result of the creation of the *tutela* instrument, which has helped to bring to justice a number of cases that would otherwise never have reached the courts. The *tutela* – which has the capacity to stop or prevent state encroachment on an individual's fundamental rights and liberties – has the virtue, if well adjudicated, to remove the need to seek a violent solution and has broken the monopoly of lawyers in the resolution of conflicts.

Although important problems still persist, it is essential to publicly acknowledge the progress obtained if the judiciary is to begin to rebuild public confidence in its operation and trust in its members. In the end, a stronger judiciary can certainly help to reconstruct legitimacy in the state and thereby to re-establish some of the necessary conditions for a lasting peace, such as an important degree of state autonomy. Finally, to refer to the title of this book, only an autonomous and legitimate state can remove the causes that exist for fear and distrust in the criminal system of justice.

Part I

Overview of the Political and Judicial Systems

1
The Political Background

> The political domain is responsible for the legal formulation, adjudication and enforcement of society's rules, and thereby legitimates all other social powers.
>
> Beetham

> When people do not trust the institutions, democracy becomes simply a label used to protect the interests of minority elites who manipulate the rules in order to preserve themselves in power.
>
> Cuellar

This book focuses on the capacity of the system of justice to administer criminal jurisdiction in modern Colombia and on the system of justice prospects with respect to the reconstruction of society after prolonged civil strife. With this central idea in mind, this opening chapter examines certain aspects of the Colombian political system which affect the operation of the system of justice. In particular, I shall address the issue of whether and to what extent the Colombian state functions autonomously or whether it is a system controlled by the private interests of politicians or by other powerful forces such as the major economic conglomerates, drug cartels, guerrillas, the paramilitary or international forces. I also propose to discuss whether the political system commands sufficient legitimacy to enable it to endorse or deliver an effective and impartial administration of justice. The autonomy of the state and the need for it to possess a certain legitimacy are both necessary conditions for the administration of justice.

I shall first discuss the characteristics of the Colombian political system from a historical perspective. I then review the theoretical framework of state autonomy and state accountability with the aim of gathering data on the basis of which to analyse the Colombian state. Finally, I examine the issue of legitimacy both from a theoretical and an analytical perspective. The evidence strongly suggests that the Colombian state lacks autonomy and commands an extremely fragile legitimacy. This lack of autonomy, together with the insufficient legitimacy of the state, have led to the illegal usurpation of some of the state's functions, in particular the administration of justice and the provision of security.

The political system: a brief historical overview

Since 1958, when the National Front came into being, most analysts have viewed Colombia as a qualified democracy, using adjectives such as 'controlled' (Williams, 1976; Bagley, 1979); 'oligarchical' (Wilde, 1978) or 'traditional bipartisan elitist' (Cardoso and Faletto, 1979). The Colombian regime has been described as an 'elitist rule' (Berry, 1971) or as a 'near polyarchy' (Dahl, 1971). Others have characterised the country, from the other side of the democracy-authoritarianism continuum, as 'inclusionary authoritarian' (Bagley, 1984) or, simply because of its National Front[1] electoral restrictions, as 'authoritarian' (Huntington and Moore, 1970).[2] These qualifications on democracy continue today, the most novel being the procedural definition of democracy.[3] Irrespective of these qualifications, the evidence indicates that Colombia does have a democracy, though still an imperfect one. Its imperfections stem from several facts: the country has a good record on national elections and a good degree of contestation. However, at the local level, in certain areas of the country, electoral opposition is sometimes limited. Political parties exist and compete but they do not harbour the popular demands and anxieties of some sectors of society and, in some cases, they over-represent others. There are formal checks and balances, but many are inefficient. Finally, state accountability is still weak. Based on these imperfections, and using Laurence Whitehead's distinction between consolidated and viable democracies, modern Colombia is clearly in a process of consolidating its democracy, a situation which depends heavily on the outcome of the current peace process between the Pastrana administration, 1998–2002, and the FARC,[4] as well as with the ELN.[5]

The mainstream literature converges in its view on four of the main characteristics that define the character of the Colombian political system and how it functions. These four characteristics are based on the idea that although Colombian society has transformed and modernised itself very rapidly since the 1950s, the institutional apparatus of the state has remained weak.

1. The Colombian political system is often exclusive, clientelistic and alienated from large sectors of society, thereby making it unable to cope with the conflicts arising from modernisation: 'A fragmented State that is unable to use the political potential of its institutions'.[6] Clientelism has co-opted the opposition but it has been unable to cope with the rapid changes in the Colombian society or to democratise it. In other words clientelism has to some extent been exclusive also. In fact, since the 1980s, widespread clientelism, sometimes in dubious forms, has contributed to the lack of legitimacy of the system.
2. The widespread level of violence in Colombia is the most dramatic manifestation of the weakness of the state.[7] Violence has been used both by legal and illegal opposition groups as well as by reactionary sectors of society; by the former as a mechanism for opening up opportunities for political participation, and by the latter as a way of defending acquired privileges which the state is unable to protect.
3. The state has lost the monopoly on coercion. New armed protagonists – guerrillas, the paramilitary and, now, organised crime – have entered the political arena, challenging the traditional actors, the political parties. The state is also very inefficient.
4. Finally, since the beginning of the 1980s, drug trafficking, mainly in cocaine and heroin, is a factor which aggravates the weaknesses of the institutions and acts as a catalyst for all the conflicts mentioned above. Drug trafficking has, in fact, reduced the autonomy of the Colombian state through a process of deinstitutionalisation that has curbed the capacity of the state to control or reverse the process.[8] The evidence also reveals that drug traffickers and other actors, such as guerrillas or the paramilitary, have introduced alternative orders which coexist with the formal political order.

At the end of the 1950s, the two main parties, the Liberals and the Conservatives, ceased to be the exclusive actors organising and promoting the Colombian people's interests. Paradoxically, both the representation of social interests and the role of the parties as the main political agents were reduced at the same time as the country was rapidly modernising, at least from an economic and social point of view. Since these two political parties are formative in Colombian history, it is necessary to explain how they function in order to understand how the political system operates.[9] Leal claims that the Liberal and Conservative Parties were, from the mid-nineteenth century until approximately 1958 – when what was for Leal the most important political change in the history of Colombia occurred with the introduction of the National Front Pact[10] – the only national social organisations in Colombia that channelled the needs and aspirations of the emerging civil society.[11] In other words, most of the civic engagement of the people was, until the middle of the twentieth century, controlled by, or dependent on, the two political parties. Together with the Catholic Church, until recently the traditional ally of the Conservative Party, these two parties defined the political order of the state. In the 1960s, the two political parties lost their traditional dominance – other actors, for example, economic groups and some unions, gained greater prominence in the political arena – yet the parties continued to act as channels for the political expression of civil society. It is also worth noting that in the 1960s the Colombian state became much richer: urbanisation increased, the middle classes expanded, power secularised and society in general changed a great deal. Consequently, 'old fashioned' social controls – a reduced elite, fewer and more visibly rich people, smaller state contracts, and even the prevalence of *noblesse oblige* – were weakened. According to Leal, the already clientelistic system became more exclusive in 1958 as a result of the National Front Pact; that is to say, the participation of other political parties or movements was deliberately excluded from the institutional arrangements of the National Front. The emergence of the independent political movement ANAPO, led by General Gustavo Rojas Pinilla, together with the virtual electoral draw with Conservative Party candidate Misael Pastrana in 1970, when the National Front arrangements were still present, might question Leal's claim of political exclusion. However, ANAPO's effective exclusion showed otherwise: ANAPO was far ahead of the Conservative Party according to the live radio broadcasts at the time, and yet Pastrana was declared the winner very soon afterwards. This chain of events raised questions as to whether ANAPO's alleged victory was suspended fraudulently in order to sustain the National Front agreement. (This agreement implied that in the 1970 election the Presidency should fall to the Conservative Party.) In spite of all this, the sectarian violence that characterised the operation of the Liberal and the Conservative Parties, in particular during the period of *La Violencia*, ended with the National Front agreement in 1958. 'The National Front divided all government jobs "equitably" (50 per cent to each party) and alternated the presidency between Liberals and Conservatives for 16 years. It also depoliticised the two traditional parties (Leal, 1989; Leal and Dávila, 1990), which have always been associations of local political leaders (*caudillos*) (sic), and converted them into electoral machines whose main purpose was to distribute the public bounty, which included government jobs, the *situado fiscal* (sic) (budget funds assigned to each congressmen to distribute at will), and the "commissions" on government investment projects and purchases.'[12] Consequently, clientelism was constitutionally institutionalised: 'After all, why should members of one party shoot up a neighbouring village of opposite political persuasion when each party was guaranteed 50 per cent of the patronage jobs no matter what, without even taking risks?'[13]

The evidence shows that the two parties were hierarchically structured patronage parties in which the subordinate classes were organised by politicians. This clientelistic role assumed by the two parties limited these parties' actions to responding to social demands that could be transformed into votes for the next elections, and hence particularistic benefits rather than the general interest tended to prevail. Any other interests of civil society which could not be channelled through votes were rejected. The state acted as a clientelistic agency run by the two parties. Popular social organisations that were not endorsed by one of the parties tended either to disappear or to be treated as subversive. Powerful commercial or industrial organisations succeeded in entering the political scene without the intervention of the two parties, mainly because of a capitalist rationale that has traditionally dominated the macro-economic policy of the Colombian state.[14] The evidence also reveals that this clientelistic political system served the interests of the dominant sectors of society (economic conglomerates and the two political parties) for such a long time (in spite of its inefficiency) because it made for prolonged institutional stability and served to defuse potential party conflict. The relative stability of the Colombian economy, added to this institutional steadiness, lent a certain legitimacy to the political system, at least until the 1970s. However, this imperfect legitimacy started to crack with the perpetuation of the habits imposed by the National Front beyond the stipulated legal limit, that is, beyond 1974,[15] and with the economic problems which arose at the end of the 1980s, that is to say, internal issues combined with the international fall in coffee prices as well as the effects of the 1980s' Latin American debt crisis.[16] In a society which had been transformed dramatically and rapidly since the 1930s, the existing political underdevelopment led to a new form of violence, orchestrated initially by emerging leftist guerrillas.[17] Bushnell, referring to the left, embracing both the guerrillas and the minority Communist Party, has argued that 'The splintered Colombian left was perfectly correct in arguing that the rules of the political game – referring not merely to the mechanisms of the National Front but to all the built-in advantages enjoyed by the government in power and by the economic owners of the means of production – were stacked against the proponents of radical transformation'.[18]

The political costs of the guerrilla warfare have been twofold. First, a gradual erosion of governmental legitimacy because of the government's inability to remove the sources of social discontent or to crush the military power of the guerrillas. Second, because of the guerrillas' terrorism, there has been an institutional tendency to regard some stances of legitimate peaceful protest from the left as expressions of 'guerrilla terrorism'.[19] However, Bushnell argues that the dominant groups in society – the large-scale owners of means of production and the main political power brokers – have always been open to new blood from outside, or from below, and that they have been steadily growing in size, especially in the last 50 years. These new forces, however, have obtained limited although not insignificant gains. For instance, the inclusion of the M-19 former guerrilla leader Antonio Navarro Wolf in Gaviria's cabinet as Minister of Health demonstrates that the political system is not closed to other forces outside the two traditional parties, although Wolf eventually left voluntarily to chair the tripartite Presidency of the ANC (National Constitutional Assembly) which reformed the old 1886 Constitution. However, the evidence of other emerging forces which had relatively short lives – for example ANAPO in the 1970s – suggests that political movements or parties other than the Liberals or Conservatives or their dissidents, have either not lasted long or have been co-opted or absorbed by the two main political parties.[20]

A number of things gradually led to the illegal usurpation of some of the state's functions in some areas of the country: the weakness of the Colombian state and its incapacity to maintain public order; and its overall lack of autonomy, together with the almost insignificant popular support for the guerrillas[21] as the main form of sustained opposition during much of the period under consideration. This was the case in particular with the administration of justice, with a wide recourse to 'private justice', and the provision of security, with the emergence of self-defence or paramilitary organisations.[22] Some of these self-defence organisations began as legal entities. Their legality was first established in 1966 under the Guillermo Valencia administration, but they were later banned in 1989, legalised again in 1994 and banned once more in 1997. Their coexistence with illegal paramilitary organisations has called even further into question the state's capacity to hold the monopoly in terms of enforcement. This trend, which is characteristic of countries at war, is partly the result of the political power of the armed actors in Colombia. In addition, and partly as a consequence of the increase in the administration of 'private justice' and the breakdown in control of public order, there were the actions of the drug-traffickers, actions which became widespread in the 1980s. Although it is unclear how much social support the drug cartels have in Colombian society, their corrupt practices have pervaded most spheres of society. With drug trafficking, which has played an enormous role in the expansion of guerrillas and paramilitary forces, the state's weaknesses have become even more evident, and this situation has exacerbated all the other inadequacies of the system. As a result of all these factors, most contemporary literature in the subject has argued that there was a political and structural crisis in Colombia during the 1980s,[23] and present-day evidence suggests that the crisis will continue.[24]

State autonomy and state accountability

State autonomy and accountability require more precise analysis in order to establish the extent to which the Colombian State is capable of sustaining politics as the prevalent mode of social exchange. Since the system of justice is part of the political system, this will also enable us to gather some additional data on which to base our later discussion of the extent to which the Colombian political system is able to provide for the effective and impartial administration of justice. Politics should ideally be the salient mode of social exchange in most modern societies.[25] In this sense politics can be understood as '... offering an alternative to the dominance by one or more groups or classes over others, by providing a political realm in which political norms, referenced to the common good or the public interests, displace sectional interests'.[26] Viewed from this perspective, politics requires a certain type of state, essentially one that is to a significant degree autonomous. Following Offe, Przeworski and Philp, I define an autonomous state as one in which state managers, politicians and public officials are able to choose the main policies to be followed and in which these policies or objectives can be realised;[27] in other words, a state that is able to choose its policies and realise its goals – see Table 1.1.

According to Table 1.1, an instrumental state is one where the objectives are set by interests and groups within society (extra-state goals) and the state merely acts as an agent. In an embattled state, on the contrary, the state chooses its policies but is unable to realise its goals. As Philp has

Table 1.1 State autonomy

	Chooses policy	
Realises goals	Yes	No
Yes	Autonomous	Instrumental
No	Embattled	Irrelevant

Source: From M. Philp, in S. Kotkin and A. Sajos (eds), reproduced with permission.

Table 1.2 State accountability

	Public accountability	
Hostage to sectional interests	No	Yes
No	Authoritarian state	Constitutional state
Yes	Class state	Façade state

Source: From Mark Philp's seminar on 'The Autonomy of the State', Oxford University, Trinity Term 1994, reproduced with permission.

argued, an embattled state is unable to act hegemonically and is incapable of establishing its legitimacy in such a way as to be able to control its actions and command sufficient support to rule society. In neither case are instrumental or embattled states capable of sustaining a unique and distinct political domain.

There is a further dimension of state autonomy which is essential for sustaining politics as the salient mode of exchange: the accountability of the state, that is to say the responsibility of a state for its actions and omissions. This accountability is twofold: first it limits the justifications that the state can use in the formulation and implementation of policy, and secondly, it establishes a set of norms for public legitimacy which condition the demands presented to the state. Under these premises a state can be publicly accountable or hostage to particular or sectional interests. Again we can tabulate this data to state the case better – see Table 1.2.

Fragile autonomy and poor accountability of the state

The evidence presented above shows that the Colombian political system has had a tendency to neglect or absorb political forces or movements – other than the two traditional parties. In fact, apart from the

Liberal or Conservative Parties, no other political or social force strong enough to represent the interests of society has managed to survive long enough to challenge the bipartisan system, a situation that continues up to the present. Moreover, the general failure of any form of official opposition to the existing bipartisan regime has left a vacuum for any social interests that do not translate into electoral assets for these two parties.[28] This situation would not have proved to be serious if the parties had represented the interests of broader sectors of society, or if their interests had reflected the common good. However, as explained, this has not always been the case in Colombia where, in the period under review, both the Liberal and Conservative Parties have traditionally represented sectional, class or even illegal interests which in turn have helped them to retain their power. Under these circumstances, public accountability has been fragile since the bipartisan dominance of the political system is guaranteed without it, and also because, since 1958, there has been little competition between the parties. Even though there are some autonomous state institutions, such as the Banco de la República (Central Bank), the Colombian state has oscillated between a constitutional, a façade and a class state as defined in Table 1.2, above.[29]

However, at the end of the 1970s, following the dramatic socioeconomic changes in Colombian society discussed earlier, this sectarian system became explosive in political terms. The traditional weakness of the state's authority – mainly a consequence of the widespread perception of a class state and hence the generally fragile state autonomy – made it impossible for the state to realise its main goals and objectives. By the beginning of the 1980s the Colombian state had become increasingly embattled. Excessive state-of-siege legislation, enacted exclusively by the executive, made the state look even less democratic and public accountability under these circumstances was very patchy. In the eyes of a growing majority of Colombians, most of whom were located in the urban areas of the country and did not even enjoy some of the basic public services, the political system was seen as distinctively imperfect. Worst of all, the state was generally failing in the provision of two of its most fundamental responsibilities: security and justice. The violence among Liberals and Conservatives during the *Violencia* period (1945–65) had been effectively annulled by the formation of the National Front, but violence continued in the 1960s and 1970s when left-wing guerrillas emerged as the main form of opposition (however illegal), which has endured.[30] The guerrillas initially challenged the autonomy of the state and that of the two political parties which, during the National Front, became, from an ideological point of view, in effect one single party, sharing the state bureaucracy equally between them. The state's legitimacy entered into a serious process of 'delegitimation' which Barco's and Gaviria's reforms of the 1990s (in particular the 1991 Constitution) tried legally to reverse by opening up the system and ending almost three decades of *de facto* National Front domination.[31] With these reforms and the effects of a partial process of modernisation, clientelism declined as a principal mode of social exchange, particularly in the main urban areas of the country. Clientelism, however, is still the prevalent mode of participation among rural voters and in the small cities. Moreover, new forms of armed clientelism have also permeated the political system, notably 'guerrillas' armed clientelism'.[32] Consequently, political transformation in the 1990s was obscured by the intensification of the armed conflict and by the drug-traffickers' infiltration into state institutions and the political and economic life of the country. Since the 1980s, the guerrillas or at least the majority of them have become less focused on their original objectives,[33] as their economic power has increased, thanks largely to extortion, kidnappings and drug-traffic-related activities and this too has clouded the effects of the 1990s' reforms.[34] The new illegal drugs-related 'exclusivist' force has further weakened the already fragile autonomy and imperfect legitimacy of the state, both nationally and internationally, and politics has once more been bypassed as the main form of social exchange in Colombian society. The strength of this force is difficult to measure, yet its corruptive effects are evident for it is in the interest of those who sustain it to maintain the existing weak and corrupt political arrangements. The virtual lack of a legal opposition (despite the constitutional possibility for it) to act as a channel for the new emerging forces in society, has contributed not only to the perpetuation of violent opposition in its different forms and violence as a way of life, but also to widespread political corruption.[35] The state is trapped in the sense of being an instrument of the goals that both legal forces – primarily some of the most influential economic groups of the country, local political leaders, and a few strong unions – and extra-legal ones – principally the paramilitary, guerrillas and the drug cartels – have imposed. The state is also embattled in so far as it is unable to establish its legitimacy sufficiently to be able to realise its most pressing collective objective, mainly the search for peace and with it the provision of justice, security and basic public services for all its subjects. Both cases give cause for concern about the actual capacity of the Colombian state to achieve these aims.

A final issue which is worth discussing, since it relates to the autonomy of the political system, is the effect of the impositions placed on

Colombia, since the appearance of drug-trafficking, by the United States. Recent analysis suggests that, contrary to what has been perceived internally, the United States' main requests relating to drug policy have been adopted by Colombia's incumbent administrations with acquiescence, as opposed to being perceived as unilateral impositions.[36] However, a certain degree of tutelage from the United States does exist, raising questions about Colombia's full sovereignty in drug-related issues. There are some clear examples of such intervention: in 1979, the Colombian government was pressured into subscribing to an extradition treaty with the United States[37] – for reasons that are explained later, this extradition treaty did not fully operate for many years. In the 1980s and 1990s, the state policy towards drugs was more erratic and fluctuated between repression and negotiation with the drug traffickers. Following the assassination in 1984 of the Minister of Justice, Rodrigo Lara Bonilla, the Belisario Betancur administration (1982–86) implemented military justice through state-of-siege legislation, in order to prosecute drug traffickers, and revived extradition of Colombian nationals to the United States. Drug traffickers perceived the revival of extradition as a declaration of war. This was all the more relevant given that the state was at the time involved in its first ever negotiations with drug traffickers. In the course of these negotiations, various drug dealers had even offered to cease trafficking and to repatriate all their capital in exchange for the Colombian state's agreement not extradite them to the United States. However, these negotiations failed, in part because of pressure from the United States together with strong opposition from sectors of the Colombian elite who refused to accept the assassination of the Minister.[38] A third example of United States' intervention occurred during the Cesar Gaviria administration (1990–94) when, in an effort to end the drug traffickers' terrorism, he enacted the PSJ (Política de Sometimiento a la Justicia – Policy of compliance with the system of justice).[39] As discussed later in more detail, the PSJ was perceived by the United States as a soft statute – hence its approval was made conditional upon several factors, among which the most notorious was Gaviria's acceptance to support the retirement of *Fiscal General* Gustavo de Greiff, before the end of his legal term. The United States wanted de Greiff out of office after he publicly expressed support for the legalisation of drugs, and for special conditions to accompany the surrender of the leaders of the Cali Cartel.[40] Following the killing of Pablo Escobar, the leader of the Medellín Cartel in 1993, the United States pressurised President Gaviria to put aside the PSJ statute and to immediately start the persecution of the Cali Cartel leaders. A further example of United States' tutelage over drug issues occurred during the Ernesto Samper administration (1994–98). As analysed elsewhere, the Samper administration represented a period of severe political crisis owing to accusations that there were donations from the Cali Cartel to finance his presidential campaign. According to most analysts, this crisis transformed diplomatic relations between Colombia and the United States.[41] This signified increasingly direct diplomatic pressure by the United States on the Colombian state, accompanied this time by threats of economic sanctions. As a result of these pressures, the Samper administration carried out a significant police operation against the Cali Cartel during which the main leaders were captured and put in jail while others were killed. In addition, the extradition of Colombian nationals, which had been banned by the 1991 Constitution, was re-established via a Constitutional amendment. Moreover, Congress approved a statute of extinction covering drug traffickers' property and belongings, and strengthened the existing statutes related to money laundering. The Samper administration also carried out a campaign that was one of the most severe ever against illegal drug crops. There are questions about whether the Samper administration's actions and statutes against drug dealers were entirely the result of United States' pressures – however, in the period of study, it is generally the case that the Colombian state's actions against drug dealers resulted from a reaction to internal threats (usually assassinations of influential people) or pressures from the United States. In short, it is true that the United States' tutelage over Colombia's drug-related issues has induced or contributed to some positive results – such as the dismantling of the Cali Cartel. However, it has also served to delegitimise the domestic system (since people consequently perceived the state as weak, porous and easily manipulated) and has fuelled the internal strife.

An elusive legitimacy

Legitimate power or authority has the right to expect obedience from the people. Even those who disagree with a particular rule or policy have only exceptional grounds for disobeying if it is legitimate. In short, legitimacy is a concept concerning the right to rule. Legitimacy in a political system is, however, difficult to assess. Some analysts have claimed that there is still little empirical data on legitimacy, the main reason being that it is very difficult to know exactly how to measure it. It has been argued that legitimacy involves a normative orientation and that, in analysing it, one must distinguish between rulers and ruled, between political and social orders[42] and, what is even more difficult, assess the values and beliefs of the ruled.[43] Heller, concurring with Weber, argued that a social order is legitimate if 'At least one part of the population acknowledges the order as "exemplary and binding" and the other part does not confront the existing social order with the image of an alternative one as equally exemplary'.[44] This definition implies that an order will be illegitimate if the majority believes in an alternative order, not simply if they are dissatisfied with the existing one. Even though Weber's theory on legitimacy has influenced a wide range of disciplines, it seems to suffer from conceptual problems which can obscure some dimensions of legitimacy.[45] A much clearer theoretical approach to legitimacy is that followed by Beetham – at least for the purposes of analysing the Colombian case.[46] Beetham's concept of legitimacy embodies three different levels of legitimacy which are qualitatively different from each other. To paraphrase Beetham, power can be said to be legitimate to the extent that:

1. power is acquired and exercised in terms of the existing laws;
2. the rules can be justified by reference to beliefs and values shared by both the dominant and the subordinate;
3. there is evidence of consent by the subordinate to the particular power relationship.[47]

For Beetham, all three components contribute to full legitimacy. Yet he acknowledges that legitimacy is not an all-or-nothing affair. The extent to which each condition is realised in a particular society is a matter of degree. What he proposes is shown in Table 1.3.

Using the Beetham approach to legitimacy, the Colombian evidence suggests that the rulers have acquired and exercised power legally. The first prerequisite for legal validity in Beetham's theory is whether the system of justice is effectively independent from the legislative and executive powers. Since I discuss the issue of judicial independence in

Table 1.3 State legitimacy

Criteria of legitimacy	*Form of non-legitimate power*
(i) Legal validity	Illegitimacy (breach of rules)
(ii) Justifiability	Legitimacy deficit
(iii) Consent	Delegitimation

Source: 'The Three Dimensions of Legitimacy', from D. Beetham, *The Legitimation of Power. Issues in Political Theory*, copyright 1991, Palgrave Macmillan, reproduced with permission.

Chapter 5, suffice it to say here that the independence of the Colombian system of justice from the executive was very weak during the period 1958–74, relative between 1974 and 1991, and strong since 1991. In terms of Beetham's second prerequisite of legal validity, that is to say the effective subordination of the military to civilian control, Colombia has an outstanding record of civilian rule throughout most of the nineteenth and twentieth centuries, something which cannot be said of most Latin American countries. Notwithstanding the issue of the independence of the judiciary, and if we take into account that there are many degrees of legitimacy (see Table 1.3, above), Colombia's government is not illegitimate by Western standards.

However, Beetham's second dimension of legitimacy appears to be less perfect in the case of Colombia. Firstly, the kinds of shared beliefs and values that are needed to justify power have to be derived from an authoritative source of power and, secondly, the structure of power has to be seen to be serving a recognisably general interest. In the case of Colombia, formal elections take place regularly and under established rules that are generally complied with. Yet effectively the percentage of the electorate that votes is traditionally small, suggesting a lack of belief in the sources of authority among some important sectors of society (electoral abstentionism has been traditionally high in Colombia). Moreover, disruption to public-order, mainly – but not exclusively – in areas where alternative orders operate, has sometimes forced the state to suspend elections in certain areas of the country, while on other occasions these elections have taken place in an environment of fear and corruption. This has mainly been the case in some rural municipalities over local elections for mayor. To quote Beetham again: 'Naturally what counts as an adequate or sufficient justification will be more open to dispute than what is legally valid, and there is no ultimate authority to settle such questions; nevertheless clear limits are set by logic and the beliefs of a given society to what justifications are plausible or credible within it'.[48]

Furthermore, there appears to be a widespread belief in Colombia that the power structure is not generally geared to serve a recognisably general interest. In the case of the system of justice, this claim is supported by survey data and these are analysed later. The rules for resolving problems in government performance seem inadequate. This is demonstrated by the numerous reforms of the political system since 1958, most of which are symptomatic of the fact that the great majority of people did not believe in or value the existing structure. The Constitutional reform approved in 1991 was, for instance, clearly the result of the government's failure to resolve the main problems of Colombia's political system as well as being an attempt to resolve them. Thus, according to Table 1.3, above, it would appear that power in Colombia has suffered from a deficit of legitimacy throughout the period under review. The extent of this deficit has varied from one government to another, fluctuating upwards and downwards. One could say that in this panorama, the political system is not totally legitimate or illegitimate, but rather that it reflects an insufficient legitimacy.

The third and last dimension of Beetham's theory involves the demonstrable expression of consent on the part of the ruled. In Beetham's view, actions expressive of consent are important for legitimacy because they constitute an express confirmation on the part of the subordinate of the position of those in power. Consent also introduces a moral component into the power relationship. In the words of Beetham, even if consent is culturally specific. 'Actions ranging from non-cooperation and passive resistance to open disobedience and militant opposition on the part of those qualified to give consent will in different measure erode legitimacy, and the larger the numbers involved, the greater this erosion will be'.[49]

The electoral abstentionism and the absence of a fiscalising political opposition in Colombia are both clear signs of the widespread lack of consent of the ruled, manifested mainly in the form of non-cooperation. Moreover, the presence of violent opposition mainly on the part of the guerrillas, the high presence of other forms of violence, and even the drug trafficking, are all signs of a process of delegitimation which, as the evidence has revealed, became explosive towards the end of the 1980s. Such violent resistance to consent for the political system also challenges the basis of Beetham's first dimension of legitimacy, legal validity. Hence, in accordance with Table 1.3, the Colombian political system also suffers from a process of 'delegitimation' which likewise fluctuates upwards and downwards.[50]

In summary, we can say that Colombia is a paradoxical and imperfect democracy. Its paradoxical democratic nature stems from the fact that for a long time Colombia escaped the theoretical generalisations of most Latin American countries, in particular military dictatorships. In fact, Colombia experienced very few years of military dictatorship during its approximately 180 years of independence.[51] As the historian Deas has argued, Colombia has had more elections than any Latin American or even European country.[52] Moreover Colombia, in contrast to much of the region, experienced a good degree of political stability during the twentieth century, being mainly represented by a bipartisan regime whose constitutional continuity throughout this period is surprising.[53] Also in contrast with the standards of Latin American capitalism has been Colombia's economic stability, with moderate GDP growth and the absence of hyperinflation that has characterised the region. However, these paradoxes have not translated into institutional stability, or greater democratisation of Colombian society. Nor have they been able to contribute to the pacification of social relations, as evidenced by the long periods of civil war in the nineteenth and beginning of the twentieth centuries, and the high levels of violence from the 1950s until the present. Since its independence, Colombia has demonstrated a paradoxical mixture of economic and political stability, absence of military rule, one of the highest rates of homicides in the world and far more armed conflicts than the rest of the region. This paradox is even more dramatic if one takes into account the weakness and precariousness of the Colombian state.

The imperfect nature of Colombia's democracy stems from the mix of characteristics that democracy takes in the country. Colombia is a democracy and not 'an authoritarian or qualified regime' as many analysts have argued. However, democracy in Colombia is still imperfect: at the local level electoral opposition is sometimes suppressed or limited by the armed actors, the political parties that exist do not represent the general interests and concerns of many sectors of the society, checks and balances are often inefficient, and state accountability is still weak.

With the exception of the armed actors, including drug traffickers, the remaining characteristics of Colombia are similar to those of other developing countries in the region. However, what is more worrying for the consolidation of Colombia's democracy, is its extremely fragile autonomy, and the general precariousness of the state faced with such powerful armed actors. This precariousness signifies that the state is unable to sustain politics as the main mode of social exchange. On the one hand, the state has not been able to differentiate itself from the private interests of the dominant elites, while on the other it has been unable to represent the general interests of the people. Clientelism has co-opted most forms of political opposition, yet it has proved incapable of truly democratising society since it displaces politics, privatises the public and fragments power. The state often acts as a clientelistic agency of the two main political parties. Moreover, because clientelism in Colombia has remained almost unchallenged due to the absence of popular movements,[54] it is both extremely powerful and extremely exclusive.[55] Furthermore, the state has lost its monopoly of coercion, while new-armed protagonists have entered the political arena challenging the state autonomy with their alternative orders.

Since the beginning of the 1980s, drug trafficking, has further reduced the autonomy of the state through a process of de-institutionalisation which is hard to reverse. In short, the reduced autonomy, elusive legitimacy and porosity of the Colombian state signifies that it is strongly influenced and often controlled by legal forces – these include the economic conglomerates and local political leaders; extralegal forces such as guerrillas, paramilitary, or drug dealers; and international agents, such as the United States as a result of drug-related issues. Notwithstanding the above, it is also fair to emphasise that some state institutions are indeed relatively autonomous and enjoy good levels of legitimacy, as analysed elsewhere. This is perhaps what has made the Colombian paradox 'work' for so long.

As a preliminary conclusion we can state that a political system that does not command a sufficient degree of autonomy and has a legitimacy deficit is open to corruption and violence in all its forms. The problems of justice are not limited to that sector's institutions; consequently, these extrasectorial issues affect the performance of the system of justice. As Hammergren argues, 'The wider political system, and society as a whole provide the environment in which they [the justice sector institutions] operate and contribute their own influences to their performance'. This in all probability will result in the failure of the system of justice in Colombia because of the fragility and imperfections of the political system. The inefficiency and lack of impartiality of the system of justice are to a great extent symptoms both of the weak legitimacy and the lack of autonomy in the whole political system.

2
The System of Justice

The aim of this chapter is to review the main characteristics, problems and institutions of the Colombian system of justice. For analytical clarity, this chapter is divided into five main sections. The first section briefly discusses the judiciary's historical characteristics, inherited from the colonial period as in most Latin American countries. This section provides a base for understanding the roots of many of the problems faced by the Colombian judiciary. The second section analyses three of the main features of the Colombian system of justice which have greatly limited its function and led to its poor outcomes: (1) clientelism; (2) its fiscal dependence; and (3) the constant reformism and exceptionalism of the criminal jurisdiction. These features are also related to the historical characteristics of the system. In the third section, the general and recurrent problems of the criminal system of justice are discussed. The fourth section discusses the present-day potential of the main institutions of the system of justice, placing particular emphasis on judicial independence – something which was enhanced by the 1991 Constitution. Some of the drawbacks of the 1991 Constitutional reform, in relation to the administration of justice, are also examined – in particular the ban on extradition, the limited role of the National Police in the control of crime, and the excessive number of judicial institutions and their frequent collusion with one another. The fifth and last section analyses the *Fiscalía*, which is equivalent to an Attorney General's Office and is in charge of the prosecution of all crimes. This is one of the most important yet controversial institutions incorporated into the judicial system by the 1991 Constitution. An understanding of the *Fiscalía* is crucial, not only because this new institution embodies many of the problems and characteristics of the system of justice as a whole, but also because it represents the most drastic change in criminal jurisdiction in the history of the country. In these last two sections I place particular emphasis on the three main institutions that transformed the system of justice following the 1991 Constitutional reform – these are the Constitutional Court, the *tutela* and the *Fiscalía General.* These three institutions have exceeded most expectations – this is mainly because they have managed to transcend some of the structural problems of the state, and hence have aquired a certain legitimacy and autonomy of their own.

The system of justice: a brief historical overview

The origins of the institutional structure of the Colombian judiciary can be traced back to the government of the Spanish Crown in the fifteenth century, and to the colonial institutions that prevailed in Spanish America. In the fifteenth century, the Spanish territories of Castilla, Léon, Navarra and Aragón united under the leadership of the Catholic monarchs Isabel de Castilla and Fernando de Aragón. It represented the strongest period of their rule. The discovery of America and the conquest of Spanish America strengthened the power of the Spanish monarchy even more: according to the prevailing legal doctrine, the monarchs, not the state, personally acquired full sovereignty over the conquered territories. Consequently, the kings of Spain promoted the creation of a centralised and technical bureaucracy that was accountable directly to them. They also centralised the political and administrative powers without the need for precedents, giving a predominant role to the legal counsellors.[56] The Inquisition itself provided the basis for the criminal jurisdiction. This structure of power defined the institutional and organisational characteristics of the administration of justice during the Colonial period, yet some of these traits still survive in modern Latin America. For example, the Colonial 'judiciary' had a hierarchical division of three bodies with quite different functions regarding jurisdiction, methods of appointment and qualification requirements. These were established according to each body's political and administrative importance for the Crown – for instance, the lower body was composed of the less qualified and had little control over its political counterpart. In spite of the fact that the Crown tried to incorporate some of the common law of the native people into its Spanish American legislation – in particular those of the Incas and Aztecs – it was not deemed to be legitimate by the majority of the colonial population. The most 'inconvenient' laws were hence treated with the infamous phrase: 'I obey, but I do not perform' (*Obedezco pero no ejecuto*).

The post-colonial scenario was the result of the Spanish-American wars of independence. Many revisionist historians agree that, in spite of the ideological influence of the French Revolution and the Independence of the United States, the Independence of the Spanish colonies was mainly the result of the collapse of the Borbón Dynasty at the beginning of the 1800s. The Spanish American creoles who led the Independence were not actually prepared for it: they had no agenda for social and political change. This is reflected in the text of the constitutions following Independence, which partially followed that of the Spanish Constitution of 1812. In spite of the fact that the Spanish American Constitutions proclaimed Liberal regimes, significant power was given to the executive who consequently played a more important role than their corresponding legislative and judicial bodies. Furthermore, Catholicism was constitutionally established as the official religion, not only limiting the individual liberties of the people but also showing a surprising continuity with the colonial regime. Spanish-American independence, then, did not produce an institutional transformation – in contrast to the case of the United States, where absolute powers were limited through effective checks and balances of the different branches of power, and where popular participation in political and judicial decisions was crucial – for instance, in the jury trial by system. By contrast, according to Sáez,

> Latin American countries maintained, after their independence, authoritarian institutional structures, politically characterised by highly personalised power relations, and in the economic dimension by an arbitrary and interventionist bureaucracy – this generated insecurity on property rights, because patronage, political influence and family prestige ruled.[57]

In relation to the judiciary, most Latin American countries, including Colombia, adopted the Montesquieu doctrine of the separation of powers. This doctrine, a product of the French Revolution, was geared to protect executive and legislative powers from the judiciary's interference. The separation-of-powers doctrine responded to the particularities of pre-Revolutionary France – mainly the conservative (and aristocratic) hereditary judges who obstructed the real authority in Paris. However, this situation bore no relation to that of the emerging Latin American countries. On the contrary, with their extreme colonial administrative and political powers, judges from post-colonial Latin American countries were submitted to strong and authoritarian executives as well as to other restrictions in order to prevent their control of legislative or executive actions. The judge's task was reduced to that of the application of the literal meaning of the law, taking into account only the law-drafter's intention. According to Merryman, judges were forced to apply the letter of the law to the specific case and declare a result.[58]

The most profound consequence of the French doctrine of separation of powers was the generalised underestimation of judicial power in Latin America. The judicial function was perceived as 'something narrow, mechanical and without creativity ... and judges were seen as the public officials with lower prestige amongst the legal profession'.[59] Paraphrasing Sáez, the mixture of colonial legal systems – highly erudite and formal, as derived from the Spanish tradition – together with the subordinate role of the judiciary – as derived from the French separation of powers – generated a fixed and inflexible bureaucracy in these societies. This bureaucracy was consequently alienated from subsequent historical changes and from the economic, social and political institutional evolution of society. The judiciary would show virtual subordination to the predominant political forces in times of crisis or political instability; however, their bureaucratic culture alienated them from the social demands and realities of their countries. As a result, judges in Latin America have historically enjoyed very little legitimacy.

The main features of the modern Colombian system of justice

To some extent, the colonial and post-colonial historical characteristics still survive in modern Latin American judiciaries. In this section I analyse the main features of the Colombian judiciary, placing particular emphasis on the historical antecedents discussed since some analysts argue that such antecedents have driven most of the judiciaries of the region into crisis.[60]

The appointment of judges: aristocratic and political clientelism

Judicial independence – understood to be the relative autonomy of the judiciary from the rule of electoral majority and from the interference of other branches of power – derives from the role given to the judiciary to protect the rule of law from the other branches of power, and also from its social function of conflict resolution. Historically, the judiciary gained autonomy over the selection of judges in 1957 – previously, under the 1886 Constitution, judges were selected by the President of

Colombia and appointed by the Congress following the Spanish colonial tradition. From 1957, when the system of *cooptación* was introduced, and until 1991, all judges were appointed by the judiciary itself.[61] The system for the selection of judges was simple: magistrates of the Supreme Court appointed for life, elected by *cooptación*; the magistrates of the district tribunals for a period of four years. The latter magistrates appointed the judges for their own judicial district (circuit and municipal judges) for periods of two years.

Paradoxically, the organic independence of Colombian judges was not derived from judicial conquest. This independence was the result of the transitional 1957 military Junta that succeeded the fall of the dictator Gustavo Rojas Pinilla (1953–57). Prior to the plebiscite that would eventually give rise to the *Frente Nacional Pact*, the magistrates of the Supreme Court of Justice and of the Consejo de Estado were elected by Congress for 5 and 4 years respectively, their names being taken from lists of three presented by the President of Colombia. The high courts appointed the magistrates of the tribunals and the latter appointed the judges of their district. Consequently there was significant political influence by politicians on the conformation of the courts, in a similar way to other Latin American countries. Since the political parties left a vacuum in relation to the judiciary, the military Junta proposed the introduction of *cooptación* for the elections of the judges. According to the military, this was a necessary reform in order to guarantee the independence of the courts from the executive and legislative powers – especially, as argued by Charria (referring to the Violencia period) from 'a political class that had driven the country to a barbaric violence'.[62] Others claim that the independence of the courts was set by the military in order to guarantee their freedom once civil government was restored.[63] With the system of *cooptación*, the risks of a trial of the military *golpistas* were minimal, since the military Junta would elect the first magistrates of the Supreme Court. Paradoxically, the military gave the judiciary enormous independence – this independence was quite unique and, for good or bad, distanced the judges from the political class for more than three decades.[64]

If the *cooptación* system represented a great conquest for the organic independence of the judiciary, it did bring other types of problems. First, the self-integration of the judiciary generated a judicial elite with aristocratic traits since the high courts controlled the appointment of all judges but were independent from the democratic process. According to some analysts, this situation froze judicial interpretation since possible candidates who did not share the postures or ideology of the high courts' existing magistrates were not appointed. As a result, self-integration perpetuated an 'aristocratic' judiciary. A second consequence of this organic independence was that this self-integration process alienated judges from the social reality of the country. Both these factors made the judiciary inaccessible to the people and lacking in legitimacy, a situation in fact that resembled that of the colonial and post-colonial periods.

The second problem arose from the fact that this organic independence gave the district tribunal magistrates – themselves appointed by the magistrates of the high courts – the power to select all judges, with no requirements stipulated other than their own personal criteria. This, together with the absence of a judicial career, meant that the judges who were appointed had little experience and judicial professional posts were often filled using clientelistic methods and personal appointments.[65] In fact, personal appointments and clientelism are still very much the case: in 1994, only 21.9 per cent of judges had gained their posts in open competition,[66] even though a professional career structure for the judiciary had already been created. In the case of the *fiscales* (prosecuting crime since 1992, their role resembling that of attorneys) the proportion of career professionals is even smaller – the professional career structure for such *fiscales* only became obligatory in 2002. The absence of a fully operational professional career – together with the political composition of the Consejo Superior, which since 1992 has been responsible for the appointment of all judges – is likely to perpetuate the personal and clientelistic characteristics of most judges in the future. However, instead of an aristocratic nature, the clientele will now be of a political nature.[67]

The lack of an operating professional career structure for the judiciary has 'de-institutionalised' the administration of justice. Together with the selection system of judges, both before and after the 1991 Constitution, this has perpetuated the appointment of poorly trained judges. In 1987 judges and public officials in the judiciary were surveyed on how they viewed their training.[68] The majority cited lack of education and the failure to keep up to date among the main problems facing the administration of justice. Furthermore, 45.3 per cent of judges considered that their clerks needed significant additional training. Since 1988 the Escuela Judicial Rodrigo Lara Bonilla has undertaken the training of judges. Some critics have challenged the premises of the Escuela Judicial, claiming that the training that it provides is no more than that offered by an ordinary law school.[69] Additional evidence from a 1994 survey revealed that 97 per cent of judges were self-trained once they left law school, which suggests both the irrelevance of the Escuela Judicial and the judge-dependent nature of the training.[70]

A third problem of clientelism relates to the promotion of judges. In principle, promotion based on merit and special emoluments for judges existed before the 1991 Constitution (see Figure 2.1).[71] In practice, however, promotion was often granted on a purely personal basis rather than on merit, and there were a few privileges: bonuses, for instance, which were age rather than performance-related and could constitute up to 96 per cent of a judge's salary.[72] Some analysts argued that the lack of a professional judicial career structure legitimated the introduction of an 'auction' for the offices of judges and public officials in the judiciary.

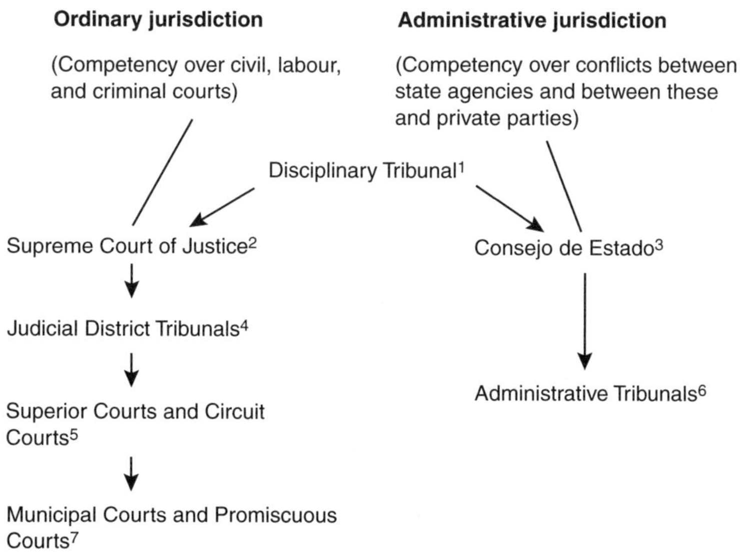

Figure 2.1 The Colombian system of justice before the 1991 Constitution

Notes:

1. The Disciplinary Tribunal decided conflicts of jurisdiction were it was unclear whether the case was competency of the ordinary or administrative jurisdiction.
2. The Supreme Court of Justice (Consejo Superior) in the second instance appeals to the Tribunal decisions. Its decisions are final and binding.
3. The Consejo de Estado (Council of State) exercises two types of functions: judicial (as the highest administrative court) and consultative (as advisory body to the executive). It has appellate but also original jurisdiction in some specific cases.
4. The Judicial District Tribunals are appeal courts of (5) and (7).
5. The Superior and Circuit Courts have original and appellate jurisdiction. They are the second instance of the municipal courts.
6. The Administrative Tribunals are the first instance courts of the Consejo de Estado judicial decisions.
7. The Municipal and Promiscuous Courts have original jurisdiction over low value civil cases and over minor crimes.

For instance, during the years of *La Violencia* (1945–65), the absence of a judicial civil service meant that the incumbent government elected the majority of the judges, who were then removed when a different government came to power. This system – virtually that of auction – was to be replaced by the clientelistic methods instituted by the National Front regime between 1958 and 1974.[73] This meant that during the National Front period, all judges were self-selected (aristocratic clientelism) – yet in the collegiate bodies there had to be equal numbers of liberal and conservative judges (political clientelism). Today the evidence suggests that most judges from the lower courts have *de facto* tenure while, the small percentage of judges who follow the structured career path would appear to indicate that promotion on merit is still a rarity. A 1994 survey revealed that 25 per cent of judges has been offered no promotion while 57 per cent had been promoted only in the previous three years: in other words, following the reforms of the 1990s.[74] Overall, the mechanisms for the selection, training and promotion of judges in Colombia have failed in that they have perpetuated a system which produces poorly trained or inefficient judges. In spite of the substantial rise in judges' salaries introduced through the 1991 Constitution, together with the Consejo Superior's new role in the selection and appointment of all judges in the lower courts (see Figure 2.2), the issue of the quality of judges remains unresolved.[75] Several testimonies from members of the judiciary suggest that the Consejo Superior's selection of judges is now more politicised than ever – a situation which *per se* implies a disregard for the professional level and qualifications of potential judges – and that training is sorely needed at all levels of the judiciary.[76] This signifies that in spite of the reforms the career of a judge is still not a professional one: there are few incentives for judges to undertake further training and the style of their appointment resembles that of colonial times.

A fourth problem associated with the clientelism of judges is that there is an enormous number of judges and clerks in the lower courts in comparison with other Latin American countries (see Table 2.1). Traditionally, the increase in the number of judges and clerks has been publicly justified as a way of coping with an increasing judicial backlog.[77] However, the evidence suggests that this increase could also be the result of clientelistic pressures by politicians, who see it as a way of creating new jobs for their clientele. As Tables 2.2 and 2.3 show, there has been a consistent trend towards increases in the numbers of judges and clerks, even since the 1991 Constitutional reform.

Even though the increase in the number of judges for the period 1990–95 partly stems from the 1991 Constitution's introduction of

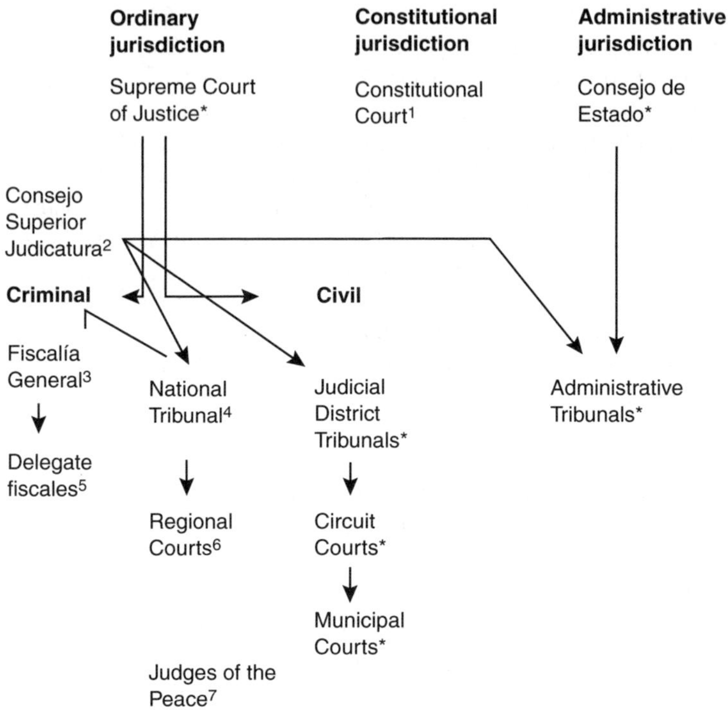

Figure 2.2 The Colombian system of justice after the 1991 Constitution

Notes:

* These courts exercise the same functions before and after the 1991 Constitution.

1. The Constitutional Court is the final interpreter of the Constitution, that is it decides legal actions filed by any individual or state agency directed to redress any violation to the Constitutional provisions. It exercises judicial review in the United States sense with the exception that there is no rule of precedent in Colombia.
2. The Consejo Superior de la Judicatura (High Council of the Judiciary) is in charge of the administration of the system of justice, in particular, the selection and appointment of all judges.
3. The *Fiscalía* is in charge of the investigation and prosecution of all crimes. Once the investigative phase is over the case is sent to the competent court for a decision.
4. The National Tribunal was the second instance of the regional courts until April 1999.
5. The delegate *fiscales* are agents of the *Fiscal* in charge of the prosecution of individual cases.
6. The regional courts had the same competency of circuit courts but dealt specifically and exclusively with crimes against the state such as terrorism, drug trafficking, extortion and kidnapping until April 1999.
7. Judges of the Peace were introduced by the 1991 Constitution to resolve conflicts between individuals or communities in equity rather than in law. However only in September 1997 (that is, 6 years after the 1991 Constitution) the Senate initiated the debate to regulate the justices of peace.

Table 2.1 Number of judges and *fiscales* per 100 000 inhabitants

Country	*Number of judges and* fiscales *per 100 000 inhabitants in 1993*
Colombia	17.1
Uruguay	15.5
Argentina	11
Greece	10
El Salvador	9
Ecuador	4.7
Chile	3.8
Spain	3
United States	2

Sources: Corporación Excelencia en la Justicia (1993) based on data of United Nations, IBD and Colombia's Ministry of Justice.

Table 2.2 Increase in the number of criminal judges, 1971–82

Judges	*1971*	*1982*	*Percentage increase*
Criminal Court magistrates (District Tribunals)	150	171	13
Superior judges	141	178	21
Circuit judges	266	323	21
Municipal judges	372	529	42
Territorial judges	18	20	11
Instruction judges	160	560	250
Total	1 107	1 781	60.8

Source: Corporación Excelencia en la Justicia (1996).

three new judicial institutions – that is, the Consejo Superior, the Constitutional Court and the *Fiscalía* – what gives rise to concern with regard to the numbers of justice personnel is the fact that historically this quantitative measure has not been successful in Colombia.[78] Clearly, the recruitment of large numbers of poorly qualified judges has proven very inefficient for the purposes of administering prompt justice.[79] Increasing the number of judges creates new posts, and thus fulfils the long standing tradition of judicial clientelism. If we compare the number of judges in Colombia with that in the United States of America in relation to the population of each country in the mid-1990s, the evidence shows that the judge–inhabitant ratio in Colombia was almost

Table 2.3 Increase in justice personnel, 1990–95

	1990	*1995*
Total number of clerks and judges	26 352	40 932
National management and administration	1 239	1 480
Consejo Superior	–	654
Courts and tribunals	17 230	17 740
Supreme Court	118	181
Consejo de estado	271	251
Constitutional court	–	115
Criminal instruction	7 494	631
Fiscalía	–	19 880
Total increase		14 580
Relative increase (%)		55

Source: Corporación Excelencia en la Justicia (1996).

five times higher than that of the United States: that is to say 112 judicial employees per 100 000 inhabitants in Colombia against 20 in the United States.[80] This is notwithstanding the fact that the number of lawsuits in the United States is far superior to that in Colombia.

Fiscal dependence?

A second historical characteristic of the system of justice is restricted fiscal independence. Fiscal independence of the judiciary did not exist until 1991. The judiciary's budget as a percentage of state spending was decided by the executive and approved by the legislature without the approval or even the intervention of the judiciary. In addition, the budget for the administration of justice in Colombia was extremely restricted until 1991. Between 1970 and 1985, for instance, only 0.28 per cent of GNP was allocated to the judiciary and from 1985 to 1993 an average of 0.66 per cent of GNP.[81] Since 1993, however, this situation has changed and the fiscal resources allotted to the judiciary were increased to 1.1 per cent of GNP[82] and to 1.4 per cent of GNP in 1995.[83] According to data produced by DANE, the system of justice received between 4.3 and 5.2 per cent of the total expenditure of the Colombian state[84] in the period 1980 to 1992.[85] In 1993, the percentage earmarked for the administration of justice was raised to 6.05 per cent of the national budget expenditure.[86] The latter signifies an increase of 105 per cent in real terms, while defence spending grew only 60 per cent in that same period.[87] One factor that was symptomatic of the inadequate resourcing of the system of justice was the poor and quite frequently degrading infrastructure of many courts (outside the high courts, that is). Court buildings today still often have non-functional facilities which are quite inadequate for the purposes for which they are intended. This situation, however, begun to improve with the reforms of the 1990s. A second factor which reflects the historic under-resourcing in the judiciary was the low remuneration offered to judges and public officials working in criminal justice as well as the disparity in stipends between those in senior positions and those lower down the hierarchy.[88] A 1994 study corroborates this historic under-resourcing by revealing that most judges come from low and middle socio-economic levels of society.[89] Furthermore, some have claimed that the low salaries earned by judges in the lower courts, particularly municipal judges, has inhibited the entry of better candidates into the judiciary.[90] As Table 2.4 shows, the salaries currently earned by magistrates in the high court are actually high compared with other Latin American countries. However, the disparity of stipends among low and high court judges is still a problem, a situation that decreases the prestige of the lower courts' judgeship (and hence the majority of the criminal justice system). As in most Latin American countries, this prestige has historically been lacking.

Another problem related to judges' salaries over the study period is that only two out of three judges had their salaries paid on time.[91] Since I could not find similar evidence for the 1990s I believe this to be no longer an issue. A third factor is the lack of provision of essential work materials, such as stationery and basic equipment such as typewriters – computers

Table 2.4 Judges' salaries in some countries of Latin America in 1993 (in US dollars)

Country	*First instance judge*	*Tribunal magistrate*	*High court magistrate*
Argentina	4 000	5 000	–
Paraguay	2 336	3 049	4 126
Uruguay	1 899	2 290	2 764
Colombia	**1 523**	**2 265**	**4 601**
Costa Rica	1 386	1 650	2 506
El Salvador	1 132	2 046	2 048
Guatemala	896	948	1 800

Source: IBD, Informes de Consultoría de Países Latinoamericanos (1994).

were almost non-existent until the beginning of the 1990s in most courts, other than the highest ones. A survey found that half the judges claimed that the supply of stationery and office equipment was bad, the judges and other parties involved often having to supply their own stationery, while 80 per cent of judges complained that the maintenance of equipment was poor.[92] In August 2000, members of the *Fiscalía* in Bogotá told me that the lack of stationery is still a common problem today. Moreover, the lack of technical tools and modern equipment for criminal investigation made proper criminal investigation very difficult. Since the introduction of the CTI, this situation is gradually changing.[93] However, there is still considerable room for improvement in the medium-sized and smaller cities of the country: here, the local *Fiscalías*, the municipal and circuit courts – which have jurisdiction over much of what Watanabe calls the repressed litigation – are without computers, which could of course help in the exchange of information for combatting crime.[94]

The deficient administration of the judiciary budget over many years has also contributed to the lack of fiscal autonomy. In 1985, for instance, the *Tribunal Superior del Distrito Judicial de Buga* (Valle) was on the point of being evicted since the *Fondo Rotatorio* had not paid the rent on the building for several months.[95] The administration of judicial resources is still problematic, even though the judiciary has in theory had fiscal autonomy since 1991[96] and was eventually allocated a significant fiscal contribution.[97] The deficient administration of the judicial budget was identified as early as 1978 when the Instituto SER demonstrated that 85 per cent of the resources allotted to the administration of criminal justice were given over to the investigation and prosecution of small-time criminals while, according to same study, the big-time criminals 'walked free' in the streets.[98] In 1989, in order to solve this problem, the judiciary was granted the administration of its own budget (Ley 38 de 1989). The *Dirección Nacional de la Carrera Judicial*, a body composed of members of the existing courts, was put in charge of managing the budget for the judiciary from that year. Some analysts argued then that the *Dirección Nacional* lacked an appropriate structure and the instruments to fulfil such a function. Others, on the contrary, considered that the judiciary was administering its own budget very effectively, a view reflected in the 1991 Constitution, which assigned the drawing up and management of the judicial budget to the newly created Consejo Superior de la Judicatura.[99] However, both the characteristics of the fiscal autonomy and the composition of the Consejo Superior, as in the case of the judges' appointments, have raised serious questions about

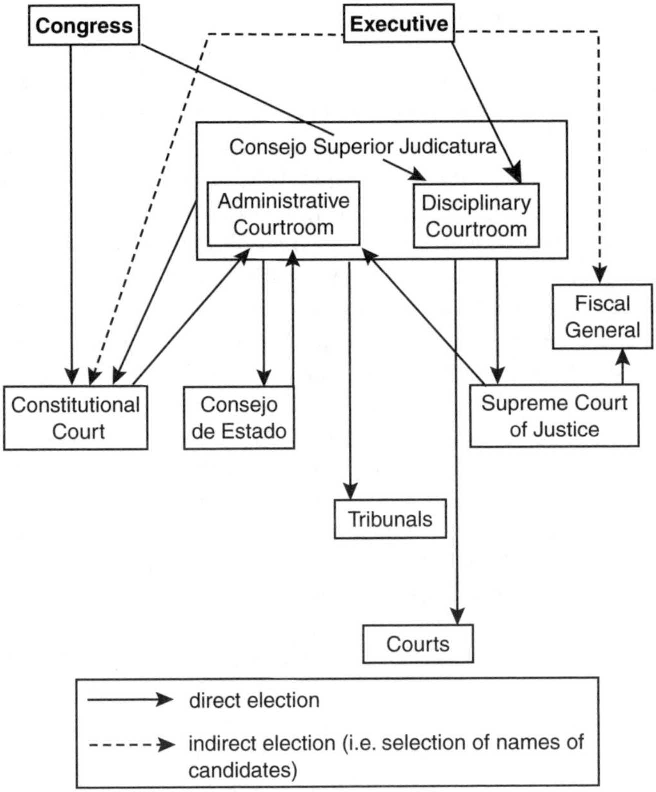

Figure 2.3 Executive and congressional interference in the functional independence of the judiciary after the 1991 Constitution

NB: Members of the highest courts are elected for 8 years without possibility of re-election.

the course that this 'fiscal autonomy' might take. The Consejo Superior has the function of planning and assigning the judiciary budget – yet it is subject to the limitations imposed by the expected national budget, and by the debt capacity agreed between the executive and Congress. Moreover, the fact that the majority of the members of the Consejo Superior are not elected by the judiciary (see Figure 2.3) raises concerns as to whether the fiscal autonomy of the judiciary is merely a convenient 'label' in order to continue a trend from the past, when the executive and the legislature were in charge of the judiciary budget percentage and its independent judicial management was purely symbolic.

Excessive reformism and exceptionalism

A third feature of the modern Colombian judiciary is the excessive reformism and exceptionalism. These have defined the operation of the criminal system of justice in the period under review, even after the 1991 Constitution. Excessive reformism reflects the lack of judicial state policy that has characterised the operation of the system of justice for decades, and exceptionalism mirrors an authoritarian executive that uses the criminal justice system to recover part of its lost autonomy.

Historically, most of the principal solutions that have been proposed for solving the problems facing the administration of criminal justice in Colombia are viewed in terms of legal reforms and the most significant reforms have been 'exceptionally' legislated by the executive. Colombia has a striking record as far as the number of reforms to the system of criminal justice is concerned. In only three decades, from 1964 to 1994, there were reforms in almost every area of the criminal justice system, as the following brief account shows. In 1964 a general reform of the system of justice as well as a drastic prison statute (Código Carcelario of 1965) were enacted. In 1968, a Constitutional reform reorganised the judges of criminal instruction; a new code of criminal procedure was enacted; a criminal code to cover misdemeanours, the National Police Code, and also a new criminal statute relating to customs. In 1969, the 1964 reform was amended again. In 1971 a new criminal procedure statute was enacted (Código de Procedimiento Penal); in 1974 the narcotics statute was enacted, while in 1975 it was the turn of the Procuraduría statute. In 1979, a Constitutional reform was enacted, aimed primarily at amending the existing system of justice, and in particular the administration of criminal justice. This reform was instrumental in introducing the accusatorial criminal system in Colombia for the first time.[100] In 1981, a new criminal statute was introduced, the 1981 Código Penal; in 1984, substantial changes were introduced in criminal procedure and finally a new code of criminal procedure was enacted in 1987. In 1989, the national administration presented to Congress a project for reform that contained most of the proposals contained in the failed 1979 reform. This reform project was approved by the House of Representatives in Congress, but ratification by the Senate never took place.[101] In 1990, the new statute for the defence of justice, Decree 2790/1990, introduced the regional justice statute known also as *Justicia sin rostro*. In 1991, Law 23/1991 relating to the judicial backlog and the current criminal procedure statute (CPP, 1991) were enacted.[102] Finally, in 1991, a Constitutional reform that was to change the organisation of the judiciary was approved for the first time by a democratically elected constitutional assembly.

The evidence shows that, with the exception of the 1991 reform, the above-mentioned reforms, which represented important changes to the system of criminal justice, were made through exceptional legislation by the executive.[103] Exceptionality is in theory limited to the control of a specific crisis or abnormal situations.[104] Yet this has not been the case in Colombia where the recent history of the country has been characterised by state-of-siege legislation. For instance, between August 1958 and August 1978, there were approximately 300 state-of-siege decrees.[105] The trend was similar between 1978 and 1984 until it reached a new peak between 1984 and 1989 when there were 139 state-of-siege decrees, most of which later became permanent legislation.[106] After the introduction of the 1991 Constitution, which itself restricted the use of exceptional legislation, exceptionality decreases, but it does not disappear. The impact of this exceptionality in relation to the administration of criminal justice is great. The evidence shows that from 1944 until 1991 exceptional legislation dominated the main aspects of the administration of criminal justice, with the formal approval of the majority of the members of the Supreme Court of Justice,[107] which is responsible for controlling the constitutionality of state-of-siege decrees.[108] This exceptionality has contributed not only to minimising justice (the minimising of justice trend), perpetuating inefficiency, increasing unpredictability (frequently resulting in arbitrary or partial decisions), but also aggravating armed conflict. The effects of exceptionality on armed conflict situations are discussed later. I also demonstrate elsewhere in this volume how reforms of the criminal statutes have minimised the effective administration of justice by forcing judges to concentrate their efforts on already 'solved' cases, in other words cases where the evidence is easily come by. Justice is also minimised when the state concentrates on the prosecution of certain crimes which it considers more important, while trivialising other crimes. According to García and Uprimny, 'Exceptionality encourages judges to take a leading role in matters to which public opinion is particularly sensitive, such as political corruption or decisions based on constitutionality. Exceptionality however does not enhance the overall capacity of the system of justice to respond to the everyday demands made on it'.[109] Exceptionality also increases unpredictability since by definition it is the result of an uncoordinated response to a particular situation. In most cases the executive has replaced democratic debate by a quick state-of-siege exceptional decree which most often than not perpetuates inefficiency and increases arbitrariness.

Many analysts have shown that excessive reformism has to a great extent contributed to the enormous judicial backlog because of the inefficiency that it generates.[110] Clearly, reformism has over the years contributed to excess legislation for activities that would best be dealt with outside the scope of the system of justice. This judicialisation has multiplied the number of cases that have to be processed by the system of justice. Similarly, the evidence shows that this constant reformism has left the courts having to deal with a whole host of statutes, some originating in the legislature, others in the executive, which often introduce contradictory principles and increase the unreliability and arbitrariness to be found in the administration of justice. An example of this is to be found in legislation that deals with drug trafficking, where soft statutes, for example, the PSJ (Policy of Compliance with the System of Justice), coexist with hard statutes, such as that providing for the confiscation of drug traffickers' property. Moreover, the excessive number of laws and reforms to the system also indirectly threaten impartiality since they may make legal procedures unpredictable, and the process of adjudication of an individual case becomes subject to the personal criteria of the presiding prosecutor or judge.

Some analysts have focused their criticism on the proliferation of extraordinary statutes which have to a great extent replaced the original function of Congress. They have argued that this abnormal situation violates such legislative principles as the representation of minorities, political responsibility and publicity in the law-making process. This arbitrariness is even more worrying since, as evidence reveals, the extraordinary statutes are usually those which produce decrees having higher economic, social, cultural and political impact.[111] Extraordinary legislation of this nature has also threatened the rule of law and people's individual rights. A relatively recent example was the legitimisation of the use of military justice to deal with civilian matters. Some go as far as to claim that exceptionalism has increased the cost of administering justice, again violating the principle of equal access to the system of justice, and that it has also reduced Colombia's economic growth.[112]

In this respect the structural reform to the system of justice introduced by the popularly elected Constitutional Assembly of 1991 is an important 'exception' to the traditional 'exceptionality' that has prevailed intermittently over large areas of the administration of justice for a least six decades.[113] Furthermore, the 1991 Constitutional reform introduced new limits on state-of-siege legislation together with a constitutional control which entails a complete revision of the exceptional decrees provisions, in addition to the existing formal control.[114] However, the 1991 reform of the system of justice still suffers from a lack of clear policy direction, with the result that, like most exceptional reforms, it combines authoritarian and democratic elements. In the words of the *Fiscal General*, the problem is that 'In Colombia there has never been a judicial policy'.[115]

Judicial self-restriction

The Roman and Canonical legal doctrines inherited from Spain introduced a prevailing formal and abstract judicial philosophy – this philosophy conceived the legislative system as a body of rules of literal interpretation. For decades, this tradition inhibited the possibility of judges moving farther away from the literal meaning of the constitutional text or the supposed intention of the author. One could argue that this passive attitude of the judiciary might have prevented judicial arbitrariness and the possibility of judge-led dictatorships – however, it generated substantial costs for the judiciary's legitimacy since society perceived it as immersed in an abstract discourse that was a long way from social reality.

In Colombia, as in most other Latin American countries, this formalism has been taken to extremes. The existing laws and consequently the judges and legal clerks who interpret them tend to favour an excessive ritualism that reduces efficiency, speed and transparency in the administration of justice. This tendency partially accounts for the heavy judicial backlog analysed in Chapter 3. However, judicial self-restriction has changed in most Latin American countries: Colombia is arguably one positive example. This is analysed below when we discuss the progressive role of the decisions of the Constitutional jurisdiction since 1991.

Overall, the aristocratic and judicial clientelism, fiscal dependence, excessive reformism, exceptionalism and judicial self-restriction are a reflection of the historical characteristics of Colombia and of the weaknesses of the state and its political system. The organic independence of the judiciary in the period 1957–91 was fortuitous and constitutes one of those paradoxes of Colombia's history. The new method of the appointment of judges, introduced by the 1991 Constitution, kept some of the existing judicial autonomy – however, it allowed for the introduction of a degree of political clientelism inside the judiciary that was characteristic of the Colombian political system. The absence of an operational professional career for much of the period of study, and its minor impact on the present day judiciary in spite of new regulations, mirrors the precariousness of the state and its general lack of institutionalisation. The factors of fiscal dependence of the judiciary: restricted budget, at least until 1991; an excessive reformism and exceptionalism, are a reflection of a dominant and authoritarian executive which has been characteristic of most Latin American countries since post-colonial times – and in addition of a weak state that seeks to recover its autonomy through authoritarian actions. Overall, the alleged dominant executive is symptomatic of weak state autonomy and a fragile legitimacy.

Recurrent problems of the criminal jurisdiction

Limited coverage and inequality of access

The preamble the Colombian Constitution of 1991 declares equality to be a fundamental value of the rule of law. Moreover, the section of the Constitution which proclaims the basic rights and liberties of the people develops this principle further by guaranteeing the basic right of equality in the protection of citizens and in their access to the authorities.[116] In spite of these constitutional dictates, the limited coverage and inequality of access to the system of justice continue to be one of the most pressing problems affecting the administration of justice in Colombia today, as it is also the case in much of Latin America. In general, the limited capability for satisfying the demand for justice in Colombia, unlike that of other countries of the region, stems from the threats and corruption on the part of powerful agents who impede the administration of justice or obstruct its impartial adjudication in areas of the country where their alternative order operates. In most cases the threats and corruption come from external actors to the state, such as the guerrillas, the paramilitary and the drug trafficking organisations, but in other instances agents of the state are involved in this unscrupulous behaviour, particularly in the case of human rights violations. Problems of justice provision also exist in parts of the country where the system of justice operates but is not perceived as being either accessible, efficient or legitimate. With regard to equal access, the evidence reveals that the system of justice is unable to cope with a growing 'repressed litigation' that mainly (but not exclusively) affects the less well-to-do sectors of society.

The amount of this repressed litigation became particularly large in the 1990s. Its growth is partly due to the intensity of violence that has forced the national administration to use the judiciary as an instrument of war dedicated to solving public order issues, to the detriment of the smaller day-to-day conflicts that affect private parties. The increase in repressed litigation also stems from executive impositions which have sacrificed justice for the sake of efficiency. Since these two issues are analysed elsewhere, suffice it to say here that both the limited coverage of justice provision and the discrimination in access to the system of justice increase the tendency to violence and encourage the use of 'private justice'. As Uprimny has claimed:

> In fact the system of justice's incapacity to resolve daily conflicts not only reduces the system's credibility, but also feeds violence, particularly among the less well to do sectors of society. The unresolved conflicts, even if they have low economic value, have a great significance for the people involved. Violence is more likely to arise from a dispute of £300 pounds among people who earn the minimum salary (and this conflict will certainly never reach the courts due to its low economic value) than among those people of high income involved in a conflict revolving around a hundred thousand pounds. A judge will undoubtedly resolve the latter conflict in a peaceful way.[117]

The unequal access and coverage of criminal justice is the result of structural problems of the state – in particular, it is related to the precariousness of a state that does not enjoy control over its territory. Even when it has this control, it demonstrates inefficiency in the administration of justice. Once again, we are led to an understanding of the system of justice's poor historical record regarding legitimacy.

Defective preliminary investigation

If access to the system of justice is limited, further problems arise once a criminal case enters the system of justice. A defective preliminary phase has been for many years one of the most pressing issues in criminal jurisdiction.[118] In spite of the fact that there are recent signs of improvement, especially since the *Fiscalía* took over the preliminary investigation function, there are still no data to suggest that the problems of deficient criminal investigation are a thing of the past. Statistics from 1982 show that 97 per cent of all proceedings in the criminal courts were cases in the preliminary phase, whereas only the remaining 3 per cent were in the trial phase.[119] A decade later statistical data reveal that the backlog in the number of criminal cases originated mainly in the preliminary phase of the criminal process.[120] As evidence analysed elsewhere demonstrates, the pattern of accumulation of preliminary phase cases continued until mid-1999, when a significant yet inconclusive recovery started to take place.[121] The main problem of the preliminary phase is that by that stage there has not been sufficient evidence to establish that there is reason to believe that a crime has been committed and that a defendant committed it, in other words, that is there is not enough evidence to carry the criminal investigation into the trial phase. Consequently, most criminal investigations simply peter out. Historically, this lack of evidence has been the result of administrative and technical failures on the part of those in charge of the preliminary phase of the criminal process, and on the inquisitorial nature of a criminal process which ignores evidence at the trial phase. In fact, most of the literature on Colombia supports the view that preliminary investigations in criminal proceedings have invariably tended to fail and that the problem has existed since at least 1926. In that year, an administrative decree (Decree 1775/1926) ordered that the handling of the preliminary (then called the investigation phase) and the prosecution (then known as the instruction) of all criminal proceedings should be a function of the national police. Since 1926, the responsibility for conducting the preliminary phase in criminal proceedings has shifted between the national police (that is to say the executive) and the judiciary. These shifts occurred in 1938, 1943, 1945, 1948 and 1968.[122] During one of these periods of judicial uncertainty, from 1948 to 1953, the *Violencia* left 140 000 people dead, the total number of victims representing 1 per cent of the national population.[123] In 1968, the executive carried through exceptional legislation (Law 16/1968 and Decree 2267/69) to create the National Direction of Criminal Instruction (*Dirección de Instrucción Criminal*). The aim was to remove any interference by the executive in the instruction phase of criminal proceedings.[124] Continuing this trend, in 1971, a criminal procedure statute (Código de Procedimiento Penal de 1971 or CPP, 1971) was enacted in order to rationalise the criminal process, which was then to be divided into three phases. First, there was the preliminary phase, a pre-judicial stage, which was to be conducted by the judicial police, who were at the time an auxiliary of the judiciary and consisted of technical personnel from the DAS (Administrative Department of State Security), the F-2, the national police (all these three being bodies of the executive) and *Medicina Legal* (the forensic institute), all under the direction of the Procuraduría General. Secondly, there was the prosecution phase which fell under the jurisdiction of the instruction judge. Thirdly, was the judgment or trial phase conducted before a judge.

Most analysts agree that the preliminary phase continued to be chaotic and inefficient at the beginning of the 1970s in spite of the reforms.[125] In 1975, responsibility for directing the preliminary investigation carried out by the judicial police was assigned to a judge (Law 17/1975, Art. 2).[126] The judicial police were still a dependent body of the Procuraduría, but administratively they were accountable to the body from which they originated, that is to say they essentially responded to the executive (the DAS or the Ministry of Defence). This administrative dependence was blamed for slowing down the efficiency of the administration of justice for, instead of there being co-operation between the courts and the judicial police, there was confusion of demarcation, and frequently operational anarchy, with two bodies or more involved in cases that required unity of direction and goals. Moreover, the Procuraduría's Office did not have unrestricted access to the judicial police since it had no hierarchical or disciplinary power over it. It was therefore necessary to go through a number of formalities to obtain the co-operation of the judicial police.[127]

In 1987, the preliminary and prosecution phases were again reformed by two executive decrees which modified the existing criminal procedures statute (the CPP of 1971). These amendments seem to have brought more problems than they resolved since they involved yet more institutions in the overall co-ordination and direction of the judicial police. This situation, it was claimed, generated duplication of function and as a result, the lack of any central authority in charge of the preliminary investigation persisted. With the 1991 Constitution, the introduction of the *Fiscalía* and yet another criminal procedures statute (the CPP of 1991), the preliminary and prosecution phases were once more partially reformed. The 1991 Constitution assigns the judicial police's function to the national police, the Procuraduría and the Contraloría Office,[128] this time under the direction and co-ordination of the *Fiscalía*.[129] In addition, the infrastructure and technical equipment for forensic and criminal research is dramatically enhanced both at national police level and, in 1992, at *Fiscalía* level. In spite of these improvements, the administrative and technical problems which have traditionally affected the national police's handling of the preliminary phase will continue, attributable mainly to the extreme limitations of the national police's system of information and intelligence, and the small percentage of national police personnel detailed to carry out criminal preliminary investigations. At the level of the Contraloría and the Procuraduría, the other two institutions in charge of the preliminary phase, the evidence suggests that preliminary investigation is still deficient owing to a lack of technical tools and able personnel.[130] At present, however, all the inadequacies found in the bodies responsible for the preliminary phase have been partially covered by the *Fiscalía*, which is indeed carrying out most preliminary investigations at the expense of an increasing backlog of its own. This 'usurpation' of judicial police functions by the CTI, the technical and investigative body of the *Fiscalía*, has led to an increase in the quantity and quality of the technical evidence available for the prosecution of crimes.[131] This represents a significant improvement for a country where in the past most of the evidence used in prosecutions was testimonial. For an investigator of the CTI, the increased use of technical evidence translates into an enhanced respect for the fundamental rights and liberties of the accused, and consequently into a more impartial adjudication. In the words of the CTI investigator: 'technical evidence replaces the old recourse to torture or other intimidating techniques used in the past to obtain criminal evidence'.[132] The most recent advances in the modernisation of the CTI were introduced by the *Fiscal General*, Alfonso Gómez Méndez, as part of the *Plan de la Fiscalía 2001*. They are aimed at strengthening and modernising the CTI by means of various measures, including the introduction of advanced systems of communication interception; the setting up of centres for the attention of the victims of crimes with facilities for medical, psychological and social assistance; the backup of modern forensic laboratories;[133] the creation of a criminal archive in collaboration with the National Registry (the *Registraduría Nacional*); the introduction of modern techniques for the identification of corpses; digital photography, modern ballistic equipment and a genetic laboratory with the most advanced equipment.[134] With regard to the technical training of personnel, there is some degree of improvement, although according to most members of the CTI whom I interviewed, there is still much to be done. So far these deficiencies are being tackled by measures such as the drawing-up of a manual for preliminary investigation, the *Manual Único de Policía Judicial*, together with isolated programmes of personnel training in specific areas of forensic investigation, some of which are sponsored by foreign countries and institutions.[135] Prominent among other programmes contained in the *Plan de la Fiscalía 2001*, is the establishment of a centre for victims of rape and other sexual offences. Apart from the victims' need for this type of centre, the ulterior objective in setting them up is to facilitate and improve the collection of evidence needed in order to prosecute successfully these sorts of crimes, crimes which in the past hardly ever appeared in the criminal statistics. All these improvements demonstrate that even if the *Fiscalía* has exceeded the powers of preliminary investigation assigned to it by the Constitution, it is actually the institution best equipped to do so. The concrete results of the *Fiscalía*'s input in the preliminary investigation phase are still difficult to measure in statistical terms, but it is probably through its efforts that the rates of judicial impunity have come down since 1999. However, the fundamental problems of the judicial police remain unsolved since there is little co-ordination between the national police and the *Fiscalía* in this area, and even less collaboration between the Contraloría, the Procuraduría, and the *Fiscalía*.

Most problems with the preliminary phase are the result of the historical weakness of the judiciary over other state powers, in particular those of the executive. These state-related problems are maximised in the preliminary phase since, historically, many state institutions have been involved in this crucial stage of the criminal procedure. However, until the CTI, they generally showed very limited commitment and co-ordination. Things have improved since 1991 and the CTI. However, most structural state deficiencies still persist, making the preliminary investigation the bottleneck of criminal jurisdiction and one of the main causes of judicial impunity. Moreover, recent executive reforms, which give many other state institutions judicial police functions, threaten to make things worse than before: there are now a myriad of other institutions, including the military, which exercise the function of judicial police. To make matters worse, they tend to carry out these functions in an unco-ordinated way, lacking both dedication and professionalism. As a result, the risks of inefficiency during the collection of evidence have increased, and there is a real danger of arbitrariness in the search for evidence.

An unreliable prison system

All the efforts of the *Fiscalía* in the preliminary investigation of crimes will inevitably increase the number of convictions. Even though the judiciary is not in charge of judicial enforcement, a credible system of justice needs a reliable prison system capable of enforcing its decisions.[136] The prisons in Colombia have traditionally presented a problem in spite of the fact that the prison population in the last three decades only represents an average of 0.085 per cent of the national population.[137] With the aim of resolving the most pressing problems of the prisons, the national administration presented a draft law to Congress and in 1993 this became the new prison statute.[138] In spite of the efforts of the administration and a few modifications introduced by Congress, the new prison statute (Law 65/1993) does not modify the substance of the former prison code (Decree 1817/1964). However, Law 65 does introduce a series of contradictory precepts, mainly relating to the rights and liberties of prisoners. According to the Procuraduría, most prisoners' complaints in the early 1990s related either to physical and psychological ill-treatment (32.9 per cent), or to unfair disciplinary sanctions, arbitrary transfers and 'taxes' demanded for obtaining favours or privileges. In general, most complaints of ill-treatment were directed against the governors and guardians of 50 of the then 175 prisons in Colombia.[139] For the most part, the traditional problems of overcrowded prisons have been left unresolved, notably in the three prisons in Bogotá, and one consequence of this is that both convicted prisoners and those on preventative detention are still given the same treatment. As a 1997 audit of Contraloría reveals, the old problems of Colombian prisons with regard to violence and human rights' violations persist, while pressing new issues remain unsolved.[140] The 167 existing prisons sheltered approximately 40 000 inmates in 2000, but have the capacity for only 28 000. For example, the Cárcel Modelo in Bogotá, which had the capacity for 1800 inmates in April 2000, had 5000 prisoners.[141] 'What can we do', asks Grimaldos, President of the INPEC[142] Prison Wardens' Union, 'with a ratio of one guard per 800 inmates in a yard?' 'The prisoners are already tired of killing their inmates. If we put 50 or 60 wardens per yard there will be no more killings, since we will then be able to control the "traffic" inside'.[143]

According to the 1997 audit, the accommodation and sanitary conditions of most prisons are inhumane. Approximately 50 per cent of the inmates are convicts, while the remainder are awaiting trial.[144] This problem, which is also common to other countries of Latin America, has been noted in the literature as a sign of a state that violates human rights.[145] The prison wardens have to work excessively long shifts, lasting from 30 to 36 hours at a stretch owing to the shortage of guards. As for violence, the Contraloría audit shows that more than 75 inmates are killed and 350 wounded every year. The reward for a killing (*chuzo*) can be as little as 15 to 30 US dollars. Vendettas amongst old enemies, such as rival drug cartels, are also carried out inside the prisons. For instance, two vendettas fought out in Bogotá Cárcel Modelo in December 1999 and April 2000, left a total of 44 prisoners dead.[146] According to the *Defensoría del Pueblo*,[147] 169 prisoners died in 1999 as a result of violence in Colombian prisons, of which 76 deaths, that is 44.9 per cent, occurred in the Modelo Prison in Bogotá.[148] While violence inside prisons is common even in the developed countries, in Colombia this violence goes beyond the prison limits as prisoners continue to carry out their criminal agendas from inside the jails. In fact, there are cases which reveal that prisons are used by some major criminals in order to escape from outside threats while they organise their new criminal agendas. Some even argue that: 'the big time criminals in jail are those who voluntarily want to be there. They can leave whenever they want'.[149] Corruption amongst the most serious offenders is also very common. Evidence of this corruption emerged clearly in 1991 with the escape of Pablo Escobar (the Medellín Cartel leader) from his 'country club prison' in Envigado, Antioquia. The type of corruption which evidently prevails ranges from bribery of prison warders and assisted escapes – as demonstrated by the recent escape of an American prisoner 1.90 metres in height, who managed to get through 9 security doors inside a mattress[150] – to the capacity of major criminals, notably drugs traffickers, paramilitary and guerrillas, to continue directing their illicit businesses from inside the prisons.[151] As far as to the judicial adjudication process is concerned, a new and worrying issue is the capacity of prisoners to make alterations to their own criminal records from within jail. This occurred in the case of Carlos Rayo Montaño, who was accused of drug trafficking and of having links with the paramilitary, and who is the first identified hacker to penetrate the system of justice data system, using a computer installed in his own prison cell.[152] These issues demonstrate not only that the prisons are not safe, but also that they do not accomplish their main functions of crime deterrence and the education and social rehabilitation of the inmates. This situation is even more worrying if we take into account the fact that only a small percentage of those convicted go to jail and that, amongst those who are imprisoned, approximately 50 per cent have not actually been convicted.

If true criminals continue to elude prison sentences, and a great percentage of those imprisoned are arbitrarily detained, there is little hope for either the legitimacy or the deterrent function of the criminal justice system in the future. The administration of the prisons has continually been in the hands of an executive that neglected its task. However, in 1998, the Constitutional Court for the first time ordered the state to develop a construction and reconstruction plan for prisons ('Plan de construcción y refacción carcelaria') which would be incorporated into the General Development Plan.[153] The Court's decision was part of its new *tutela* jurisprudence concerning the 'unconstitutional state of things'.[154] This theory, geared to protect people's social rights, recognises that the violation of people's fundamental rights can occur as a result of structural faults in state services – not simply as the product of state arbitrariness – and that the various state agencies involved are accountable to redress the violations. The latter is a demonstration of the autonomy of the Constitutional Court and a sign that the judiciary can play an important role in the reconstruction of state autonomy and legitimacy.

Armed with this historical perspective of the judiciary, we can now proceed to a more detailed analysis of the main reforms and institutions of the system of justice introduced by the 1991 Constitution.

The main 1991 constitutional reforms to the judiciary and their impact on its overall independence

The complexity of the political crisis of the 1980s, as well as the increasing level of violence in the country, led to the creation of a National Constitutional Assembly, the ANC, to reform the existing constitutional order.[155] The true aim of the ANC was the establishment of peace. Hence most of the articles of the new Constitution related directly or indirectly to this objective, as did the reforms to the system of justice. This section discusses the 1991 Constitutional reforms to the main institutions of the system of justice and their effects on its overall independence, with the purpose of showing the institutional capacity and potential of the present-day system of justice.

According to one of the promoters of the 1991 Constitution, the main purpose of the reforms to the administration of justice was to strengthen the power and autonomy of the judiciary.[156] Evidence shows that the Constitution of 1991 introduced profound modifications to the Colombian state, among which was a re-structuring of the administrative and functional organisation of the judiciary. In particular, a 'semi-accusatorial' criminal system was introduced, based principally, but not entirely, on the Anglo-American system of criminal administration of justice. In addition, the *Fiscalía General* was created (an office that is akin to the Attorney General's Office in the United States), a Constitutional Court was established with extensive judicial review powers similar to those of the United States Supreme Court, and a Consejo Superior de la Judicatura (Higher Council of the Judiciary) was set up to be responsible for the administration of the judiciary (similar to the French Conseil Supérieur de la Magistrature). More powers were given to the existing Procuraduría (Procurator's Office) and Contraloría (General Comptroller's Office – see Figure 2.4).[157] Important mechanisms to 'democratise justice' were also introduced, the most important being the *acción de tutela*. The 1991 Constitution also imposed a controversial ban on the extradition of Colombian nationals and limited the powers of the national police in the control of crime.

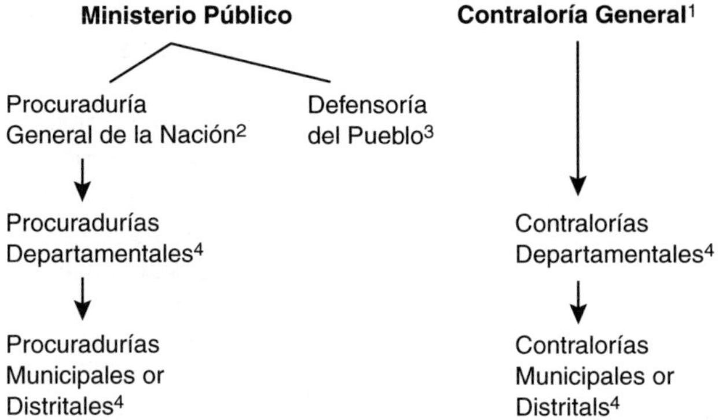

Figure 2.4 Control agencies linked to the judiciary

Notes:

1. The *Contraloría General* (General Comptroller Office) controls the fiscal resources of the state. It controls the finances of public and private institutions that administer public funds.
2. The *Procuraduría General*'s (Procurator General Office) main function is the disciplinary control of all public officials, including members of the Judiciary or popularly elected officials, i.e. congressmen. The control over members of the Judiciary overlaps with the more direct disciplinary control that the *Consejo Superior de la Judicatura* has over all public officials of the Judiciary generating tensions between these two institutions.
3. The *Defensoría del Pueblo* (similar to the Scandinavian Ombudsman) is in charge of the information, promotion and protection of human rights.
4. The *procuradurías* and *contralorías departamentales* and *municipales* are the judicial divisions of (1) and (2) and have competency over departmental or municipal matters.

In general, the evidence indicates that the 1991 constitutional reforms to the system of justice combined both democratic and authoritarian elements. Consequently some institutions became stronger and more independent than before, as in the case of the Constitutional Court, the constitutional jurisdiction with the *tutela* and the Contraloría. In yet other cases, new institutions were given extremely strong powers and granted some functional control of the executive, as was the case with the *Fiscalía*. Similarly, other institutions were strengthened but their independence was curtailed in particular situations, as in the case of the Consejo Superior and the Procuraduría. In addition, important aspects of criminal investigation were limited, in particular the role of the police in the preliminary phase. Since I analyse the semi-accusatorial criminal system and the *Fiscalía* in the section below, I discuss here only the Constitutional Court and the *tutela* in detail, and (more briefly) the Consejo Superior, the Procuraduría, the Contraloría, the extradition ban, the role of the national police in relation to the control of crime, and the implications of these particular reforms in relation to the overall independence of the system of justice. I will devote extra space for the analysis of the Constitutional Court and the *Fiscalía*, since these two institutions play important political roles.

The 1991 Constitution introduced a Constitutional Court for the first time in Colombia. The role of this new court, which forms part of the judiciary, is to be the ultimate interpreter of the Constitution, providing rulings on legal actions filed by any individual or state agency in order to redress violations of the provisions of the Constitution. Such legal actions can be used by any citizen, regardless of their personal stake in a case, to challenge the constitutionality of any law by simply asserting there to be a conflict between the law and the Constitution. The power of judicial review exercised by the newly created Constitutional Court – and before that by the Supreme Court of Justice[158] – is comparable to that of the United States Supreme Court and is a clear indication of judicial independence.[159] Only a few countries in the world have such a controversial and fascinating power structure, something which allows a court to overrule or completely revoke legislative or executive action.[160] According to Abraham, 'Experience has demonstrated that countries which have exhibited stable or moderately stable traditions of judicial review are generally characterised by... a strong tradition of judicial independence, ... '.[161] In fact, as one of the promoters of the 1991 Constitutional reform has claimed, the judicial independence of the system of justice is founded on constitutional justice (which also includes the *tutela*). To paraphrase M.J. Cepeda, constitutional justice will emerge as a giant in front of the other branches of public power. In order to balance the three branches of public power, it was necessary to protect the citizen from abuses. In the Constitutional Assembly there was a patent feeling of distrust which led to a strengthening of the autonomy and independence of the system of justice.[162]

Nevertheless, unlike those of its American counterpart, the powers of judicial review of the Colombian Constitutional Court embodied in the new Constitution are tempered with limitations.[163] According to a number of analysts, these limitations were introduced because some members of the ANC were fearful of the extreme powers of this institution.[164] In addition, the members of the Constitutional Court are elected for a period of eight years only and cannot stand for re-election.[165] According to some the legal limitations represent an attempt to deny this potentially strong court complete independence. Conversely, others argue that the temporal limits to the Constitutional Court's magistrates do not threaten its independence, and that its political origins (see Figure 2.3, above) do not politicise it. The reasons are: first, because the period of eight years is sufficiently long to compromise the magistrates and, second, because experience in other countries such as the United States – where magistrates of the Supreme Court are appointed by the President – have proven that political appointments in the high courts lead in most cases to strict legal commitment.[166]

The evidence so far has proven that in spite of these 'restrictions', some of the more recent decisions of the Constitutional Court – for example, those relating to the military exclusive-jurisdiction, the acceptance of the controversial *Convivir* private civilian security organisations, economic rulings preventing executive regulations, international stipulations, and the maintenance of the *Justicia sin rostro* (faceless judges) until 1999 – have demonstrated the great autonomy of the Constitutional Court in relation to other state institutions, including other high courts of the judiciary, the legislature and the executive. The text of the 1991 Constitution favours a wide constitutional control – however, the Court has allowed itself additional autonomy due to the degree of legitimacy that some of its decisions have enjoyed amongst people who, prior to the existence of the Court, were excluded from the concerns of both the courts and the state institutions. Amongst the progressive decisions it has taken which reflect the benefits of this autonomy and support its legitimacy, are those relating to the legality of voluntary euthanasia for the terminally sick (C-239/1997), the decriminalisation of personal consumption of certain drugs (C-221/1994), the protection of the rights of homosexual school teachers (C-481/1998), the limitations on unquestioning military obedience when serious human rights violations are involved (C-578/1995) and limitations to the exceptional legislating powers of the executive.[167] In contrast, the preservation of the military exclusive jurisdiction and the maintenance of the *Justicia sin rostro* legislation until 1999 have been cited as demonstrating the authoritarian face of the Constitutional Court – yet they have received the support of two important state actors, the military and the criminal judges. Other controversial decisions of the Court, in particular those related to economic issues, have put the economy at risk. Indeed, many sectors of society have begged the Court not to intervene in matters that are outside its knowledge and constitutional power.[168]

A second crucial role for the Constitutional Court is to exercise the constitutional control of exceptional legislation ordered by the executive.[169] This control was enhanced by the 1991 Constitution which added content analysis (material control) to the traditional formal constitutional control that existed under the 1886 Constitution. The evidence overall shows that the new constitutional control has been important, compared with that of the 1886 Constitution. In spite of some controversial decisions by the Court, most analysts have agreed on the importance of the Constitutional Court's power to counterbalance a traditionally overpowered executive – and in this respect they see the Court's extreme independence as a blessing. However, some are concerned about the Court's powers regarding particular issues. For them, a worrying manifestation of this strong independence is the Constitutional Court's assumption of direct responsibility for the direction of public-order policies as a result of its function of controlling the constitutionality of exceptional legislation by the executive. The Constitutional Court's decisions – which have been generally progressive and influential in the reestablishment of social justice – can also lead, according to Orozco, to 'the formation of a strange and excessive criminal constitutional law'.[170] Judicial independence can also produce negative outcomes: 'An independent, active if not activist judiciary may not be a neutral arbiter, but rather another political actor, the functional performance of which becomes less important than its ability to advance certain interests, be they partisan, social or institutional, in the broader political arena'.[171]

In spite of these potential dangers, the power of judicial review assigned to the new Constitutional Court, albeit with some legal restrictions, could be explained as an attempt by the executive or the political elites to legitimate a system in crisis. Legitimation is as much a function of judicial review as is invalidation. As Rosen remarks, 'The Argentine Supreme Court (during the Dictatorship years) developed the practice of issuing accords legitimating *de facto* governments in return for a promise by the leaders of the *golpe* to maintain the supremacy of the Constitution'.[172] It is not a case of dictatorship or *coups* in Colombia, but certainly exceptionality is still the rule and political legitimacy is largely lacking. In a country in the throes of an irregular war, the executive needs the Constitutional Court's institutionalisation of its long states of abnormality. It is in this respect that the Constitutional Court has assumed a political power that is unheard of in the constitutional history of the country – for better or worse, most state institutions and members of society have so far accepted the Court's power.

Arguably, one of the most important decisions of the former Supreme Court of Justice was its decision in 1990 to allow for a constitutional assembly to reform the existing constitution, hence violating the established constitutional procedure. Even when it took such important political decisions, it did so as a response to an executive plea and extreme institutional pressures. Before the 1991 Constitutional Court, Constitutional activism with serious political implications was scarce, in spite of the extreme degree of organic independence of the Supreme Court and an automatic constitutional control of the Court over any exceptional decree of the executive that dated back to 1968.[173] Historically, the poor constitutional control of the former Supreme Court to executive excesses lay mainly in the interpretation of a constitutional expression which ordered that, in times of peace, restrictions to the constitutional rights of the people could not take place. The Supreme Court interpreted *a contrario sensu* that in times of war or state-of-siege, most exceptional restrictions were allowed. This dangerous interpretation, together with the constitutional responsibility of the Colombian President in the maintenance of public order, led to a weak or almost non-existent constitutional control up until the end of the 1970s. By the end of the 1970s, there was an incipient constitutional 'activism' of the Supreme Court. Some politically influential decisions of the former Supreme Court were the declaration of unconstitutionality of the constitutional reform of President Alfonso López in 1977; the annulment of President Julio Cesar Turbay's 1979 constitutional reform two years later for procedural reasons; and the forbidding of military justice for civilians in 1987.[174] The latter decision was strongly criticised by President Virgilio Barco who, in a televised presentation, criticised the Supreme Court arguing that it had notoriously reduced the executive capacity to confront serious public order issues.[175] 'These progressive yet small percentage of important decisions meant that the constitutional control of the Supreme Court started, though shyly, to be taken into account....'[176]

The Constitutional Court presently enjoys great independence, and more importantly, a good degree of legitimacy due to its role as defender and warrantor of the fundamental rights and liberties of the people.[177] This first role is fully legitimate and hardly the subject of debate, as discussed below when analysing the reach of the *tutela*. Consequently, fears that the Court might become a political actor that follows the instructions of the executive, while possible, appear distant. This is because of the incompatibility with the Court's first role of warrantor of rights and liberties, and also because of the incipient, though activist, tradition of the Court in the past against the abuses of the executive. Indeed, having a counter balance in the judiciary, acknowledging that the Constitutional Court can exceed its powers too, is a safeguard in limiting or inhibiting future executive abuses. In a country with an intensive armed conflict, exceptional legislation could always be found to be 'justifiable'. Consequently, checks by the judiciary to balance power and redress arbitrariness are necessary, not only to stop executive and military abuses, but also to legitimise the state of war. In contrast to the political role of the Court in public order matters, limits are necessary for the Court's intervention in economic matters because this topic requires a degree of expertise that is generally absent in the requirements for the appointment of the Court's magistrates. Recent experience has shown that economic rulings of the Court can have disastrous economic effects.

The 1991 Constitution also introduced the *acción de tutela*. The Constitution defines the *tutela* as the prerogative of any individual to file a suit with any judge at any time for the immediate protection of his fundamental and social rights,[178] when these are threatened or have been violated by the actions or omissions of any public authority.[179] The *tutela* originated in Colombia as a mechanism for enforcing the fundamental rights and liberties of the individual, most of which had existed only in the abstract in the text of the former 1886 Constitution, but which were never applied owing to the fact that from 1944 until 1991 there was an almost permanent state-of-siege. The use of state-of-siege legislation allowed the executive to suspend or restrict civil liberties, and also limited the jurisdiction of ordinary judges over certain political crimes which were adjudicated by military courts which almost consistently violated the due process and the rights and liberties of the accused.[180] To paraphrase Barreto, the *tutela* has the capacity to stop or prevent state encroachments of the individual's political rights and human liberties, and also the capacity to guarantee the assertion of social, economic, cultural and collective rights when these are considered or directly connected with a fundamental right. Consequently, the *tutela* has the potential to construct a fairer society.[181] Some even go as far as to argue that many conflicts that could have degenerated into violence are today resolved through a *tutela*; and according to García and Uprimny: 'In many cases, a well adjudicated *tutela* can mean one less homicide'.[182] Most analysts agree that the *tutela* process is at present the most positive instrument of the 1991 reform to the system of justice. The *tutela* is also undoubtedly the maximum expression of judicial independence in a general sense, that is to say, of the independence and autonomy of all judges at any level of their hierarchy and jurisdiction.

The actual scope of the effects of the *tutela* supports this claim of maximum independence. The first and most important role of the *tutela* is the provision of social justice in cases that otherwise would have never reached the system of justice or which would have perished in the court records. In this respect, as some have claimed, the *tutela* is also an instrument of peace.[183] Evidence of the contribution made by the *tutela* to social justice and its role in the first steps of peace making is described in

García's valuable investigation of the social impact of the *tutela*.[184] His investigation shows that 79 per cent of the users of the *tutela* considered it as a useful mechanism for protecting their rights and liberties.[185] This percentage, which is higher than the percentage of *tutelas* which have actually being accepted by the courts, indicates that even amongst those who have their *tutela* turned down, the instrument is still perceived as useful. Concrete examples of the social justice brought by the *tutela* show that in its first five years of operation, 100 000 *tutelas* were filed in the courts.[186] Cases resolved by adjudicated *tutelas* involve the protection of abused or abandoned children (Constitutional Court decisions T-128/1994 and T-205/1994); enforcement of school children's rights (T-420/1992, T-114/1995 and T-015/1994); protection of third-age or other individuals being discriminated against (T-036/1995); the defence of indigenous peoples (ST-082/1994); the protection of AIDS patients (ST-380/1993); the protection of labour rights (ST-483/1993, ST-230/1994, ST-143/1995, SU-342/1995) and others ranging from intra-family violence to abuses perpetrated by prosecutors from the *Fiscalía* or by judges in criminal court cases.[187] The Constitutional Court keeps a systemic record of all the *tutela* cases submitted to it for their revision.[188] This record, which reliably reflects the daily conflicts of the people around the country, demonstrates the unprecedented degree of independence attained by all judges in the vigilance over state violations of the fundamental rights and liberties of the people. The Constitutional Court plays a crucial role in the development of the *tutela* since it is the last judicial instance to revise the *tutelas*, and its jurisprudence defines the way in which all judges should interpret and apply the reach of the fundamental rights and liberties of the people.

A second function performed by the *tutela* has been that of reducing the state authoritarianism which was the product of the almost permanent state-of-siege regime.[189] In this respect, the *tutela* has vindicated some of the 'lost' independence of the judiciary *vis-à-vis* the executive during all those years mainly through the imposition of limits to state actors and agencies when they affect people's fundamental rights. Thirdly, the *tutela* has contributed to reducing the extreme levels of legalism and formalism that had characterised Colombian legal culture. Factors such as the obligation placed on judges to resolve a *tutela* in only 10 working days, the fact that anyone, even children, can present a *tutela* without the need for a lawyer since there is no special procedure entailed (a fax or even a verbal petition is allowed), as well as the possibility of filing one anywhere in the country and at any time since a *tutela* never prescribes, make the *tutela* an exceptionally agile judicial instrument for conflict resolution, offering prompt and effective justice.[190] The Constitutional Court has even ruled that the *tutela* is valid for events which occurred before the 1991 Constitution came into force, provided that the effects of the grievance were still present when the Constitution was proclaimed.[191] This third role of the *tutela* retroactively recovers judicial independence previously lost. Fourthly, the *tutela* has a significant impact on the modernisation of the state and the transformation of cultural patterns. Perhaps the most striking examples of the former concern the transformation in the performance of important state agencies following the impositions of several *tutelas*.[192] With regard to cultural patterns, there have been numerous *tutelas* which have transformed old cultural practices. In particular, there are now new constitutional precedents which have modified the traditionally authoritarian relations between teachers and pupils, parents and sons, and even between the media and private individuals. There is no doubt that these decisions have opened up a transformation in the processes of socialisation of the individual, personality formation, as well as in the democratisation of public opinion.[193] Finally, the *tutela* has served as an instrument of social education on the rights and liberties of the people. In this respect the *tutela* has created citizens who are more aware and active with regard to their rights. This is significant for a country where people, desperate for justice, did nothing to resolve conflicts that often could change the course of their lives, for instance, access to health or education unlawfully denied. Overall, the effects of the *tutela* and its future potential demonstrate the high degree of autonomy enjoyed by the judiciary in relation to the other branches of power, in other words a high degree of judicial independence. In fact, the degree of judicial independence achieved through the *tutela* is such that the former *Fiscal General*, Alfonso Gómez, demanded that it be regulated: 'The *tutela*, which was created as an exceptional mechanism, has ended up replacing judicial power'.[194] The danger of this, according to the *Fiscal General*, is that the *tutela* can also obstruct justice. Instances of this have occurred when drug dealers have used the *tutela* in an attempt to prevent their extradition, and when the *Fiscalía* was forced as a result of a *tutela* to leave an estate belonging to former drug trafficker Pablo Escobar because certain individuals argued that the *Fiscalía*'s presence on the Escobar estate endangered the community. Another criticism of the *tutela* is that it can be used to contest judicial sentences. Aside from the judicial unpredictability that this situation can generate, the *tutela*'s potential as a fast-track appeal system has also increased the large existing judicial backlog. Recent unpublished research suggests that the excessive number of *tutelas* that reach the Court can seriously threaten the Constitutional Court's traditional record of efficiency. The evidence of the predominantly positive effects of the *tutela* is so overwhelming, however, that it is essential that any regulation of this legal instrument be done with great care so as not to endanger the very reasons for its success.

The 1991 Constitution introduced, also for the first time, a Consejo Superior de la Judicatura (High Council of the Judiciary) to administer the judiciary. Since the 1991 Constitution created the Consejo Superior to form part of the judiciary, there is in theory little room for interference by the executive in the Consejo Superior. The Consejo Superior is divided into two courts: the administrative and the disciplinary.[195] The administrative court of the Consejo Superior is mainly in charge of the administration of the judicial civil service, the drawing-up of lists of candidates to enter the judiciary, the control of the performance of the courts and the preparation of the judiciary budget each year.[196] The disciplinary court controls the conduct of public officials in the judiciary and lawyers who litigate in the courts.[197] These are all signs of judicial independence. Moreover, the draft constitutional reform, originally presented to the ANC by the National Government, had proposed the creation of a Consejo Superior comprising of members of the existing courts and tribunals.[198] This proposal, however was rejected by the ANC, which opted for a compromise solution: members of the administrative court would be elected by the three highest courts, but members of the disciplinary court would be elected by Congress for a period of eight years, from lists of three candidates put forward by the National Government.[199] Clearly, the non-judicial origins of some of the members of the Consejo Superior and the direct interference of the executive and Congress in the selection of members of the disciplinary court, together with their lack of tenure, threaten the full autonomy of the judiciary. In fact, the inclusion in the Consejo Superior of non-members of the judiciary has not only caused more problems than it has resolved, as discussed elsewhere, but it also threatens the independence that this type of institution customarily has in countries where it exists.[200]

The ineffectiveness of the Procurador's powers to discipline public officials led the drafters of the new Constitution of 1991, who were concerned with the increasing political and administrative corruption, to increase the number of controls held by the Procuradoría. For instance, the Constitution established control over illegal self-enrichment by public officials,[201] to enable the Procuradoría, after a brief disciplinary hearing, to dismiss immediately any public official found guilty of illegal self-enrichment – in other words without the need to ask the public body in question to carry out the dismissal, as was the case under the 1886 Constitution. Another new function of the Procurador's Office is the control of the legal and constitutional duties of all elected public officials, for example, congressmen.[202] This new power, which appears as another great sign of independence, has been a source of much controversy since the Procurador General is himself elected by the Senate. Doubt has been cast on the independence of the Procurador as a 'judge' of congressmen, especially since 1994 when a former congressman was elected Procurador. In most cases where this Procurador had to discipline a congressman, he declared himself unable to adjudicate owing to a legal impediment.[203] The disciplinary control of congressmen by the *Procuradoría* is likely to be ineffective since the Procurador partly owes his election to the senators, and hence there is a danger that congressmen might put pressure on the Procurador to be lenient with their colleagues. The 1991 Constitution also increased the powers of the Contraloría General. Since 1991 the Contraloría has controlled the fiscal administration of state institutions *a posteriori*, that is to say, after the state institution has used the fiscal resources. Before the 1991 Constitution the Contraloría's control was *a priori*, a situation that obstructed complete fiscal control and also allowed corruption. Fiscal vigilance covers control over finance, management and results.[204] Both the management and result controls were introduced by the 1991 Constitution with the purpose of establishing more thorough control of fiscal resources involving not only numerical control but also control of the management of resources. In addition, since 1991, fiscal control has been carried out via a fiscal proceeding that can result in the imposition of pecuniary sanctions.[205] Furthermore, the initial fiscal proceedings carried out by the Contraloría can be used as evidence in judicial proceedings, as a result of which this Office was also given judicial policing functions.[206] This provision has no precedents in the 1886 Constitution and represents an important gain for the autonomy and power of the Contraloría.

Even though some of the new institutions introduced by the 1991 Constitutional reform enhanced judicial independence, the proliferation of institutions since the 1991 Constitution – three high courts plus a Consejo Superior, the *Fiscalía*, administrative and ordinary tribunals, the 'National Tribunal' and regional higher courts,[207] and two 'control agencies', the Procuraduría and the Contraloría, which are not judicial institutions but perform 'parajudicial' tasks – has resulted in a system that has at least doubled the number of institutions present in any of the three classical models, those of France, England and the United States (see Figure 2.2, above). One of the most common problems caused by this excessive number of high courts is collusion. Since four or five judicial bodies may be entitled to make definitive pronouncements on constitutional and legal issues, 'judge-shopping' has been raised to a dimension which could eventually hinder judicial independence. A recent example of this occurred when the Constitutional Court revoked a sentence of the Supreme Court.[208] Clearly, internal conflicts within the judiciary weaken its overall power and independence and it is an issue that requires to be resolved.

One of the most publicised features of the 1991 Constitution was the ban on extradition of Colombian nationals.[209] Extradition became a very sensitive issue in Colombia at the end of the 1980s. Several acts of violence and terrorism by the drug cartels during the Barco administration, 1986–90, and the murder of the Liberal Presidential candidate Luis Carlos Galán in 1989, forced this administration to declare an open 'war' against the *extraditables* (a group of drug-traffickers whose extradition the United States was entitled to request).[210] Barco had taken the initiative by reviving an existing treaty of extradition between Colombia and the United States, originally negotiated during Turbay's administration, 1978–82.[211] The revival of the treaty was to be considered by the drug cartels as an act of war; they feared that the United States system of justice, unlike its Colombian counterpart, was capable of sentencing them to life imprisonment. Given the perceived inefficiency of the Colombian system of justice, together with the drug cartels' success in intimidating so many judges and in removing legal obstacles – for instance, by the manipulation of laws in Congress, the cartel's widespread resistance to extradition seemed understandable. As a result, the revival of the extradition treaty with the United States launched a period of the worst terrorism that Colombia has ever experienced. Thousands of innocent people were killed by bombs which were placed indiscriminately in shopping centres, streets and state institution buildings.

The main reason for restoring extradition was the Barco administration's conviction that the Colombian system of justice was incapable of convicting drug traffickers, whereas by re-establishing the process of extradition of Colombian nationals to the United States, the Colombian administration sought to shift this particular responsibility to another state.[212] Since the possibilities for constitutional reform had been blocked twice during the Barco administration, he used extraordinary emergency decrees to introduce reforms to the system of justice.[213] Many of these decrees were either to become permanent legislation, or were adopted by the 1991 Constitution. However, the 1991 Constitution prohibited the extradition of Colombian nationals. This Constitutional ban was interpreted, particularly by some in the United States, as a clear sign of the drug traffickers' corruptive influence in the ANC. Recent work by Lee and Thoumi, however, has shown that the influence of drug traffickers in the ANC was only indirect.[214] Most people saw the ban on extradition as a means of ending terrorism. In addition, the political composition of the ANC was such that for the first time in Colombia's history the left held a majority. The left in Colombia has traditionally opposed extradition on ideological grounds, perceiving it as a surrender of the country's sovereignty. Obviously the *extraditables* tried to influence the ANC in other ways and probably 'bought off' some of its members, but the prohibition on extradition reflected a national desire that they did not need to 'buy'.[215] The ban on extradition had two contrasting effects on overall judicial independence. On the one hand, it had a positive impact by freeing the judges involved in such decisions from high levels of intimidation and corruption perpetrated by the *extraditables*. On the other hand, however, the removal of an effective judicial procedural instrument for combating drug trafficking curtailed the incipient success of the *Fiscalía* in the control of this criminal activity. The lack of an effective prison system means that the *Fiscalía*'s strong powers to prosecute drug traffickers could be lost without effective mechanisms such as extradition. In spite of all this controversy, the ban on extradition was short-lived, lasting only six years. In 1997, after pressure from the United States and lengthy and controversial debates, Congress passed a law reviving extradition but only for future cases – that is, the imprisoned members of the Cali Cartel could not be extradited.

In contrast to extradition, one of the issues most disregarded in the 1991 Constitution with regard to the administration of justice, and perhaps also one of the least understood, is the role that the national police should play in crime prevention. The 1991 Constitution decreed that nobody could be searched or preventively detained without a judicial order.[216] This provision, which had no precedent in Colombia, means that no administrative authority, particularly the police, can routinely carry out policing procedures without a court warrant.[217] This new provision seriously undermines the normal operation of the police in the maintenance of public order, which indeed is the main constitutional function of the police. There may be a variety of justifications for this provision. First, it could result from a Colombian habit of trying to resolve all conflicts by means of the intervention of a judge. In the past, this habit made for a great deal of judicialisation of conflicts. Secondly, it could represent a perceived public fear of police arbitrariness.

The national police have traditionally been used as a coercive force rather than as a civil body.[218] This was accentuated during the years of the *Violencia* when the police committed many atrocities against the civil population.[219] It should be noted that it was only in 1991 that the Constitution expressly stated that the police were a civil force.[220] Thirdly, it could be claimed that there was deliberate self-interest on the part of some group or groups in curtailing the police's preventive role in crime prevention in order to maintain the existing levels of impunity. Finally, it could be said that the police's crime prevention role is not recognised in a country where insecurity and crime are usually associated with the military and with the system of justice. Independently of which of these four interpretations is more accurate, or whether they all are to some degree, the constitutional obstruction to the operation of the police is contrary to the philosophy of efficiency that allegedly characterised the 1991 Constitution's reform of the criminal justice system, and does not necessarily prevent police arbitrariness.

The Colombian national police, like most modern police, has two main tasks: to maintain urban and rural public order and to control crime.[221] This latter function, which is directly linked with the administration of justice, entails police intelligence, the traditional judicial police involvement in carrying out the preliminary criminal investigations, and a reactive role which in Colombia is undertaken by police groups specially trained to combat particular crimes and criminal organisations related to drug trafficking, kidnapping and smuggling. However, in practice, the functions of the Colombian police are far removed from those performed by police in modern democracies. Using figures for services carried out by the national police in 1995, which are very similar to the pattern for the 1980s, one can easily conclude that, with the exception of the special police force to deal with drug trafficking (which is trained and partially funded by the United States) general crime control occupies only a small part of police activities.[222] Most police activity (51 per cent) is spent on carrying out searches (*requisas*), followed by surveillance and patrols (14 per cent), with crime control constituting only 8 per cent.[223] In fact, police figures for the homicide rate per department in relation to the numbers of police in that department suggest, disturbingly, that the relationship between police strength (in terms of the number of policemen) in a particular department and the homicide rate is irrelevant. Accordingly, departments with high rates of homicide may have either low police numbers (for example, Antioquia) or high police numbers (Arauca), while departments with low rates of homicide may similarly have high police strengths (Amazonas) or low police strengths (Atlántico).[224]

Furthermore, data from the national police from 1996 show that only 3 per cent of the total number of police personnel are engaged in crime control. Of this 3 per cent, 56 per cent are involved in anti-narcotics activity, 32 per cent are assigned to preliminary criminal investigations (that is, to judicial police functions), and 12 per cent perform intelligence functions.[225] In contrast, countries such as the United Kingdom and Japan, where preliminary criminal investigation is a specialist function of the police, assign between 14 to 20 per cent of their personnel to perform this judicial function.[226] This is a worrisome fact for a country that has such high levels of crime and a traditionally defective preliminary investigation phase. The minimal attention devoted by the police to its role in the preliminary phase of criminal investigations constitutes an indirect threat to the independence of the judiciary, since it leaves the efficiency of judicial prosecution at the mercy of an institution which places the collection of criminal evidence very low down in its order of priorities. Moreover, the deficient crime control role of the police partially explains the great percentage of impunity in the country, an impunity, which as I go on to show, never actually reaches the system of justice.

The solutions which have been adopted to correct police deficiencies in crime control have been as defective as those that have curtailed its powers. Instead of reforming the relevant constitutional provision, two solutions have been adopted to strengthen the limited power of the police. First, the Constitutional Court devised an interpretation of 'administrative preventive detention' whereby the police can detain anyone for up to 36 hours if there are serious motives for their doing so. This new interpretation of the Constitution makes for arbitrariness since one person alone can decide on a detention without following any established procedure to safeguard the rights of the detainee. A second expedient used to solve the constitutional impasse is the traditional recourse to exceptionality (such as state-of-siege presidential decrees) in order to allow the police to operate – that is, a return to the old habits of executive interference in the administration of justice.

Apart from allowing the obvious direct interference of the executive in judicial matters, the constitutional limitations on police powers have affected the efficiency and performance of the system of justice in various ways. Firstly, it has resulted in more cases being judicialised, thus increasing the already large judicial backlogs. For example, Law 228/1995 reversed the positive effects of Law 23/1991 by returning to the municipal criminal judges jurisdiction over misdemeanours such as petty theft and minor personal injuries. Secondly, it leads for police arbitrariness since their actions are not always controlled.[227] Thirdly, it introduces an element of legal uncertainty into crime prevention since the Constitutional Court's interpretation of administrative preventive detention can be over-ruled.

When we come to assess the overall effect of the constitutional reforms in relation to the independence of the system of justice, the evidence shows that the 1991 Constitution established effective judicial instruments and institutions with a good degree of autonomy, such as the Constitutional Court, the *tutela* and the Contraloría. However, some provisions of the 1991 Constitution also hindered judicial efficiency and independence, mainly by curtailing the capacity of the police to control crimes, but also by banning legal procedures such as extradition which can facilitate the course of justice in a country where judges are easily intimidated. Other institutions, such as the Consejo Superior, the Procuraduría and the *Fiscalía* hold effective powers, while still having some degree of dependence from the executive or Congress. The contradictory degrees of judicial independence established by the 1991 Constitution could be interpreted in at least four ways. First, the majority groups of the ANC members did not have a joint project to solve important problems of justice. The records of debates in the ANC, for instance, show that the traditional 'elite's' proposals for reform to the system of justice were adopted almost in their entirety by the ANC.[228] This was made possible by the absolute lack of any proposals for the reform of the system of justice from the left-wing majority that made up the ANC.[229] Second, the ambivalent reforms to the system of justice were the product of the ANC's political agreement. The search for a political agreement is not new in the history of Colombia.[230] However, although such agreements might have been achieved in the past, the ANC represented the most inclusive since it contained representatives from many of the most important social, judicial and political sectors of society, as I show in Table 2.5. Consequently, the ambivalence of the 1991 reforms to the system of justice might be seen to have been the result of a process of negotiation in which some goals were incompatible with others, or in which some interests were irreconcilable and hence had to be sacrificed for others. Third, the traditional coexistence of authoritarian and democratic policies which have informed judicial reform in the last decades could not be overcome in the ANC. The excessive power of the executive in Colombia was immutable even when faced with a democratic assembly such as the ANC. It is no secret that the Gaviria administration's role in the ANC was important and that many of the most far-reaching reforms to the state structure were

Table 2.5 Political composition of the ANC

Political origins	*Number of elected members*
Liberal Party	25
AD M-19 (former left-wing guerrilla)	19
MNS (dissident conservatives)	11
Evangelic, indigenous and former guerrillas	7
Conservative Party	5
Other minority forces	3
EPL (recently demobilised left wing guerrillas)*	2
Total	72

* The two members of the EPL were unilaterally elected by the government. The diversity of the AD M-19 group was however significant: 6 former guerrilla members, 3 Liberals, 3 Conservatives, 3 Trade Union leaders, former members of minority political movements, professionals and even a student.

adopted with the government's consent.[231] In fact, several state-of-siege decrees relating to regional justice enacted prior to the ANC were converted into permanent legislation by means of temporary powers established in the 1991 Constitution. Fourth, powerful and influential private interests managed to manipulate certain crucial aspects of judicial reform to favour their vested interests. This situation has arisen because of the strength and power that the illegal armed actors have acquired, thanks to the state's precariousness. The evidence suggests that these four factors are responsible for the sometimes inconclusive and contradictory results of the 1990s' reforms to the system of justice. In the words of Hammergren, who compares the Colombian 1991 process of judicial reform to those of other countries of Latin America during the 1980s and 1990s,

> Colombia's has been characterized by the most extensive national debate. Here, technical debates and juridic principles were so tightly mixed with institutional and political interests as to make it difficult to determine where one began and the other ended ... the result was a conflict so nuanced and so pervaded by technical detail that observers have difficulties determining who won. It is significant that they, thus, offer surprisingly diverse interpretations as to the implications of the 1991 Constitution and accompanying legal reforms, which represent the culmination of almost three decades of efforts to reshape the nations justice system.[232]

The search for efficiency and the creation of the *Fiscalía*

The search for efficiency has been a constant factor in the reforms of the Colombian system of justice since at least the 1970s. Consequently, most judicial policy in the last three decades has favoured efficiency above all else, with the aim of clearing the judicial backlog of the courts. With this objective in mind, the 1991 Constitution introduced a 'semi-accusatorial' system of justice into Colombia for the first time in the history of the country.[233] To this end, it created the *Fiscalía*, a public body in charge of the investigation and prosecution of all crimes. An understanding of the *Fiscalía*'s role is crucial since this new institution embodies many characteristics of the present-day system of justice, especially the search for efficiency, but also the often conflicting interests and values that informed and characterised the 1991 process of judicial reform.[234]

The creation of the *Fiscalía* as part of the introduction of a 'semi-accusatorial' system of justice represented a great change in the administration of criminal justice.[235] Apart from the investigation and prosecution of all crimes, the *Fiscal General* can prosecute any minister in the cabinet, the Procurador, the Defensor del Pueblo (ombudsman), members of the Ministerio Público and other senior public officials. The investigative powers of the *Fiscalía* are only limited by the fundamental rights and liberties of the defendant.[236] During its short existence, since 1992, several aspects of the *Fiscalía* have been criticised. The two main sources of criticism have concerned the incorporation of the *Fiscalía* into the judiciary,[237] and the amount of power that this institution has been given without any controls.[238] Both aspects are linked and, in order to understand them better, I propose to review the philosophy lying behind accusatorial and inquisitorial systems of justice to examine the type of criminal system that the 1991 Constitution introduced.

Regardless to the claims of some commentators, the creation of the *Fiscalía* in the 1991 Constitution did not represent the beginning of the accusatorial system of justice. Indeed, the evidence suggests that some of the most positive structural characteristics of the accusatorial system of justice were excluded in the Colombian system. In general, accusatorial systems of justice have attempted to resolve the dilemma between ensuring efficiency of investigation and safeguarding the individual rights and liberties of the parties, by drawing a strict functional distinction between investigative bodies, such as the Attorney General's Office, in charge of investigating the facts and prosecuting the defendant, and trial bodies, namely the courts and tribunals, responsible for passing judgment on the culpability of the defendant on the basis of the evidence presented in the case. Commentators on accusatorial systems of justice have argued that an Attorney General's Office should be controlled by the judges in two fundamental respects. Firstly, attorneys should not be able to issue arrest warrants, but should have to request the competent judge to order such warrants. Secondly, any writ or warrant for obtaining evidence that could affect the rights of the defendant must also be ordered by the competent judge. The idea behind accusatorial systems of justice is to articulate the diverse phases of the criminal process involving several bodies. Consequently there should be one body that prosecutes (the Attorney's Office), a representative of the victim (*parte civil*), a defendant (the accused), those who decide whether the defendant is guilty or not (the jury) and finally, the controller of the legality of the trial and hence the protector of the defendant's and the victim's rights (the judge). It has been argued that the interaction of all the above parties in a criminal process guarantees the rights and liberties of the defendant.[239] The main argument proposed by those who support the accusatorial system is that a good investigator is not the ideal person to guarantee a defendant's rights; in other words the idea that the person who is concerned with the efficiency of the investigation shall not be the very one who controls the limits of its investigative power. From this point of view, the accusatorial body should not belong to the judiciary since the judges should control the prosecutor in order to guarantee the rights of the defendant.

To paraphrase ICAC (the Independent Commission Against Corruption in New South Wales, Australia), inquisitorial systems are best understood as a continuous progression from the investigation, through public exposure of the investigation to the determination of punishment at trial.[240] In this process the investigation is the crucial phase as it establishes the dossier which is the basis for the trial and judgment. Hence, unlike the accusatorial system of justice, inquisitorial systems concentrate the prosecution – that is to say the defence of and judgment on the defendant – in one subject or body. For this reason, some critics have claimed that inquisitorial systems can directly threaten the rights and liberties of the defendant, as is considered to have occurred during the Spanish Inquisition. It is also worthy of note that the inquisitorial system has only the one form, irrespective of whether or not the accused admits guilt. 'There should always be the normal full investigation and trial and potential appellate review', states ICAC.[241]

In the case of Colombia, where inquisitorial principles, or at least a combination of inquisitorial principles and others had traditionally characterised criminal investigation, a form of 'mixed' accusatorial system was adopted by the 1991 Constitution. Prior to this the debate was based on the above-mentioned dilemma in the criminal process between efficiency and the individual's rights and liberties. The evidence suggests that the Colombian debate prior to the introduction of the accusatorial system was misdirected. The introduction of the *Fiscalía* in Colombia was aimed above all at improving efficiency, 'to prevent investigative dispersion, thanks to the creation of an apparatus capable of collecting evidence, capturing delinquents and fighting organised criminality and terrorism', rather than providing safeguards for the defendants.[242] This debate over the system of justice led to the introduction of the *Fiscalía* into the judicial system, with the *fiscales* (who approximate to attorneys) were invested with judicial powers, that is to say the power to issue warrants for arrests, searches and other intrusive and coercive measures.[243] Arguments used to support the creation of the *Fiscalía* during the 1991 ANC debates included the view that the previous system of justice lacked a body that was responsible both for overall criminal investigation as well as being able to co-ordinate the various technical investigative bodies such as the judicial police, the DAS, Dijin, Sijin and F-2.[244]

However, the current trend towards accusatorial systems runs directly contrary to these concerns, as other countries seek to guarantee the rights of defendants, even at the expense of efficiency in criminal investigation. This is to say that the essence of the accusatorial system seems to have been undermined in the final text of the Colombian reform. Although the new Colombian criminal procedure bears similarities to accusatorial systems – for instance, in separating the investigation and the judgment so that they are handled by two different bodies – the inclusion of the *Fiscalía* as part of the judiciary, coupled with the judicial powers of the *fiscales*, make the present criminal system of justice a peculiar one.

The justifications for this ambiguous 'accusatorial system of justice' are varied, but they are all tainted by the particular political or judicial interests that were present in the ANC debates. One explanation for the judicial character of the *Fiscalía* concerns the fear that many jurists had of the 'administratisation of the justice system', in other words a fear of the subordination of the administration of justice to the executive. Such a situation would have further enhanced the power of the national administration in a country characterised by a long history of 'presidentialism', as Maurice Duverger calls it, since its independence. A second explanation for the introduction of such a *sui generis* accusatorial system of justice is that the members of the ANC were attempting to introduce a touch of juridical nationalism in a country where most of the laws have been adopted from foreign systems.[245] Thus it could be said that this element of improvisation, combined with the fear of subordination to the executive, led to the creation of a powerful and effective judicial institution with powers that can seriously undermine the rights and liberties of the accused. The main claims that support this belief are firstly, that the *Fiscalía* has no fixed jurisdiction and the guidelines defining their competence are flexible. Judges, in contrast, have a fixed jurisdiction and the norms which determined their competence are strict, thereby guaranteeing their impartiality.[246] Secondly, the *fiscales delegados*, in contrast to the judges, have no stability or independence since they are agents of the *Fiscal General* and, as such, can be named or removed by the incumbent *Fiscal General* at any time.[247] According to Zaffaroni, a hierarchical subordination undermines the independence of the judges, or in this case the *fiscales*, an independence that is required under international doctrine as a minimum safeguard for the protection of the rights and liberties of the defendant.[248] This lack of independence of the *fiscales* is not a problem in the accusatorial systems of the United States or Italy where attorneys are controlled by judges, so that, for instance an attorney requires a court order before issuing an arrest warrant or any writ that might affect the rights of the defendant. Under the Colombian system, the *fiscales* are invested with judicial powers and therefore are not controlled by judges or indeed anybody else, although they ultimately depend on the *Fiscal General*. All these peculiarities of the Colombian semi-accusatorial system leave the way open for arbitrary acts as a result of the enormous powers of the *Fiscalía*.

With regard to the independence of the *Fiscalía*, it is worth remembering that in the original draft of the law, the subordination of the *Fiscalía* to the executive was direct since the Fiscal would be appointed directly by the President as occurs in most accusatorial systems. However, in a typically Colombian paradox, the President's complete control over the *Fiscal* was attenuated in the final version. The *Fiscal General* is elected by the Supreme Court of Justice from a list of three candidates previously selected by the President of the Republic for a fixed period of four years which is not renewable.[249] The *Fiscal* does have some degree of independence, in that once he is elected he cannot be removed for a period of four years – however, the President who elected him also has some leverage in matters that might be of concern to him. This means that there is a risk that the *Fiscal* can become a political actor representing the interests of the President of Colombia. In spite of the latter risk, this partial independence from the executive and the sweeping powers of the *Fiscalía* have led to the investigation and prosecution of unprecedently high impact social crimes and criminals, which the former criminal system of justice would have been powerless to touch. The *Fiscalía,* in what is commonly known as *Proceso 8000,* investigated and prosecuted ministers, congressmen and other senior public officials for their illegal self-enrichment with money from the Cali Cartel, as well as many members of the electoral campaign staff who help bring President Ernesto Samper to power in August 1994. Many of these members of staff, including a Minister from Samper's cabinet, have been convicted and imprisoned.[250] With regard to this particular scandal, there is evidence that the presence of drug money in politics has been widespread since the beginning of the 1980s, yet the system of justice had never even investigated such scandals. Moreover, for the first time ever, the main leaders of the Cali Cartel have been prosecuted, convicted and imprisoned while other leading drug traffickers are also in jail, some having even been extradited to the United States. Corruption scandals in Congress and in public contracts, which have been common in the past, have for the first time led to an investigation of those involved and imprisonment of those found guilty. These types of criminal investigations against well-known public personalities or serious criminals are new in Colombia and the evidence strongly suggests that without the *Fiscalía* they would not have been possible. The *Fiscalía*'s power to control the long-standing impunity of drug traffickers has become so manifest that drug dealers have seen the 'need to assassinate' the *Fiscal.* For instance, in April 1995, the national police discovered a plan to assassinate the *Fiscal* General, Alfonso Valdivieso. According to some, the alleged reason for the assassination attempt on Valdivieso was the fact that he opposed a deal on benefits for convicted drug traffickers, including the possibility of their being released from prison, which had been previously been agreed by a *fiscal sin rostro* (faceless attorney).[251] In fact, the first three *Fiscales Generales* have been the subject of frequent death threats and attempts on their lives.

However, in spite of the fact that the *Fiscalía* has demonstrated the extent of its autonomy, there is already evidence indicating that the *Fiscalía* is not always completely independent of the President of the Republic. In May 1995 a legal row over the retirement date of the first *Fiscal General,* Gustavo de Greiff, which had forced him to retire before the end of his period of office, was stirred up again by a legal action in the Consejo de Estado which demanded that the election of Alfonso Valdivieso, his successor, be declared void. The grounds for this new legal action against the *Fiscal General* were based on a dubious procedural argument, but behind it lay a fairly clear impression that various powerful people, perhaps even supported by President Samper, who was himself involved in *Proceso 8000*, wanted Valdivieso out of the *Fiscalía*. Some suggested that the Cali Cartel was behind this attempt to get Valdivieso out of the way.[252] The final decision of a polarised Consejo de Estado was to allow Valdivieso to stay until his legal period of office ended. The evidence of these episodes involving the first two *Fiscales Generales* indicates that the *Fiscalía* is indeed capable of taking on former untouchables, an achievement that might even be regarded as vindicating its enormous powers. However, it also shows that the *Fiscalía*'s powers are subject to formal restrictions, not by the judges, as in most accusatorial systems, but by the Colombian President. The degree of independence achieved by the first three *Fiscales Generales* so far could also be the product of the personal qualities of the three worthy individuals to have filled the post so far, all of whom have proved to be fiercely independent. Even though there is a danger in the future that the President's three nominated candidates might be politically compromised on account of his political interests – or pressured to use the *Fiscalía*'s powers of crime control against his political enemies or in favour of his friends – the *Fiscalía* has already achieved a level of institutionality and political independence that would be hard to reverse.

Overall, the evidence analysed above reveals that the 1991 constitutional reform to the main institutions and instruments of the system of justice was ambivalent in that, on the one hand, some reforms did strengthen the system and enhance its independence; on the other hand, the very institutions that were created to strengthen the system of justice were in many cases limited in their autonomy, the most relevant example perhaps being the *Fiscalía*. However, even though the independence of many institutions in the system of justice was, from a functional standpoint, relatively weakened as compared with the functional independence of the system of justice before the 1991 ANC (see Figure 2.3, above and Figure 2.5, below), the evidence shows that judges are more powerful and independent today than in the period 1958 to 1991, as is demonstrated by the increasingly prominent role assumed by the judiciary, particularly in the Constitutional Court and the *Fiscalía*. This prominent role of the Colombian judiciary, or the leading role of judges, is similar to that of other Latin American countries in the 1990s. This is perhaps partially the result of transmission from other countries in the

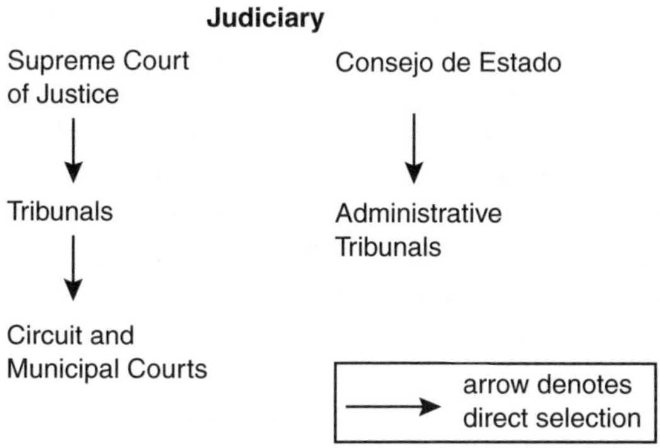

Figure 2.5 Judiciary's functional independence under the 1886 Constitution

NB: The members of the Supreme Court of Justice and the Consejo de Estado were elected for life by direct co-optation (i.e. any vacancy was filled directly by the remaining members of the court).

West, such as Italy or Spain. However, as some analysts have shown, no other country in Latin America has suffered from such sharp protagonism among the constitutional judges as Colombia, nor such a significant administrative independence of the judiciary.[253]

Clearly, the democratic origins of the 1991 constitutional reform did not serve to overcome the traditional problems of judicial reform, in particular executive interference in the judiciary's autonomy. The ambivalent judicial results of the 1991 Constitution originate in two contradictory historical patterns that have informed judicial reform in the past few decades: authoritarianism and democracy. The fragility of a state that is still having problems at the level of basic state building (*pace* Hobbes' *Leviathan*) imposes a need for authoritarian powers, as demonstrated, for instance, in the widespread use of exceptionality, as well as sweeping powers such as those enjoyed by the *Fiscalía*. At the same time, however, a more democratic state, perhaps symbolised by the ANC, is trying to emerge by 'constructing citizenship' with the aid of the *tutela*, the constitutional jurisdiction and a greater use of technical evidence in the field of criminal prosecution.

Consequently, the temporary victories achieved by the post-1991 system of justice in the control of political corruption and organised crime are positive steps; they show that it is possible to control high impact crime in Colombia as well as sowing important seeds for its control in the future. The *Fiscalía* not only changed criminal investigation, it also transformed the relations between criminal law and the political process in Colombia. The independence of the *Fiscalía* from political power showed its first results with the *Proceso 8000*. In this respect, these successes could even be seen as 'legitimating' some of the *Fiscalía*'s authoritarian traits. In addition, the positive results of the *tutela* to some extent safeguard some of the social functions of the rule-of-law, by helping to solve the problem of the large amount of repressed litigation that still characterises the system as well as by removing the traditional monopoly of judges in the resolution of conflicts. However, these victories are not the product of long-term policies. Several decades of low commitment to regularity, exceptionalism and forms of authoritarianism, as well as the absence of a prevalent political culture that is committed to it, probably cannot be reversed by a finite package of constitutional reforms and isolated judicial action – yet they are definitely a step in the right direction.

Part II

Criminal Justice in Crisis

3
The Performance of the System of Justice

> Delay of justice is injustice.
>
> Benham

> At heart the extent of crime is a political as well as a behavioural matter ... The figures for crime ... are not 'hard facts' in the sense that it is true of the height and weight of physical body. They are moral not physical statistics.
>
> Young

> Impunity cannot only be explained by the inefficiency of the administration of justice, but also as a result of the massification of crime and social tolerance.
>
> Salazar and Jaramillo

This chapter discusses the performance of the system of criminal justice. The discussion is based on analyses of the mainstream literature on the subject as well as on statistical and survey data from the three decades preceding the reforms of the 1990s up to 1998. The view of experts and international institutions on the nature of judicial reform in Latin America is that the judiciary in the region suffers from the following problems: (1) a growing level of distrust; (2) functional inefficiency; (3) problems of autonomy *vis-à-vis* the remaining public branches of power; (4) low impact as a bastion for the protection of human rights in societies that still have very vulnerable democratic institutions; (5) lack of predictability in economic relations; and (6) poor results in the efficient and fair resolution of conflicts and controversies.[254] In spite of the fact that academic contributions have been made to the understanding of these issues in the last decade, most analysts do not conceive the judiciary to be an organisational structure that operates in the complex institutional framework where the state, its institutions and the political system, interact. Consequently, the fact that the institutional framework plays a crucial role in the judiciary's failures and successes is frequently ignored. To oversimplify North's theory of institutions and institutional change, he shows that the economic performance of institutions is tied to formal limitations such as the Constitution and the law, and to informal restrictions such as social or cultural conventions. According to North, both formal and informal restrictions play a crucial role in institutional performance and both are equally important in terms of the final institutional outcome.[255] It is therefore important to identify the basic restrictions that have led to the slow change, and continuous judicial crisis, in Colombia – despite substantial reforms to criminal jurisdiction. The following analysis of the criminal justice system's performance suggests that there have been both formal and informal restrictions that have affected this performance. Executive strategies – which have been mainly geared to recovering state autonomy and the incumbent government's own fragile legitimacy, rather than to providing impartial and effective criminal jurisdiction – however, have played a more dramatic role, constantly reforming and destabilising the existing formal conventions and criminal procedures.

Systems of justice play an important role in the legitimation of states. The justification of political authority couples the claim of the right to rule with a broader claim for legitimacy. The legitimacy of state authority rests on its ability to support and uphold just institutions. A state that has a system of justice which impartially administers the law is bound to have a high degree of authority among its citizens. The minimum that citizens should expect if they take their disputes to a court instead of resolving them themselves, is equality of treatment, a neutral and impartial attitude and an objective procedure. Even those who disagree with the particular judicial decision will accept it more favourably, or have no legitimate grounds for complaint, if the rules underlying the legal proceedings are fairly implemented and the decision is impartial. What sustains the authority of a system of justice, therefore, is fairness, equality and impartiality. However, these criteria can only be attained if the system of justice has some degree of both efficiency and predictability.

The literature discussed below suggests that the main problem facing the Colombian system of justice is its extreme degree of inefficiency.[256] This perception comes from the predominant and often uncontested use of numeric data (criminal statistics and criminal surveys) as the main descriptive medium for analysing the system of justice performance.

This type of analysis is by no means exclusive to Colombia. To quote Maguire, 'Indeed, a salient feature of almost all forms of discourse about crime is the emphasis placed upon terms associated with its quantification and measurement. In political and media debates, trends in aggregate crime figures are often put forward as evidence of failure of successes in criminal justice policy, or are treated as a sort of social barometer ...'.[257] However, the evidence shows that the Colombian system of justice not only fails to be efficient (as the high level of impunity shows) but also fails on the grounds of impartiality and equality. This creates distrust in the system. The legitimacy deficit is accentuated by, among other things, a limited access to the system of justice by citizens, and a tradition of class justice – that is, two degrees of inequality.

Following the theoretical framework on state autonomy and legitimacy, and North's theory, I start with the assumption that a significant part of the inefficiency and lack of impartiality of the criminal jurisdiction results from the weak autonomy of the state, the fragile legitimacy of the political system and the informal restrictions to the judiciary introduced by continual executive reformism. I show that much of the inefficiency in the administration of justice has resulted from excessive reformism and exceptionalism, both of which have perverted the course of justice. I also demonstrate that these exceptional decrees have for decades been the source of much of the arbitrariness of the administration of justice. Data are presented which demonstrate the extent of the historical problems in the criminal justice system discussed earlier – in particular the unequal access, the defective preliminary investigations and the unreliability of prisons. I also argue that a significant degree of impunity for high social impact crimes results from actors which are external to the judiciary. In addition to deficient crime detection and recording by the police, there is also a lack of co-operation by the victims and witnesses: such problems are symptomatic of a state lacking in autonomy and legitimacy.

There is no written history of the judiciary in Colombia.[258] Literature concerning the administration of justice in Colombia in any form was relatively scarce until the mid-1980s. Even today, if we compare the existing literature with the daily rhetoric on the topic, and with the importance that the issue of justice should have in a country such as Colombia, empirical research is still lacking.[259] By contrast, there is a well-developed literature on the laws and regulations that govern the actual administration of justice. Empirical research on the problem of the administration of justice in Colombia only got seriously underway in the mid-1970s. It was carried out almost exclusively, at least until the mid-1980s, by the Instituto SER de Investigación (SER Institute for Research).[260] Overall, the evidence suggests that much of the research on the Colombian system of justice until the end of the 1980s is based on the Instituto SER's investigations carried out between 1972 and 1982.[261] The rhetoric[262] around justice in that period is always based on the judicial backlog (*congestión judicial*) or general inefficiency of the system of justice, occasionally focusing on the high level of impunity.[263] Other common claims are the lack of training of judges and public officials of the judiciary the low budget of the judiciary, and the lack of a rational administration of both the courts and the judiciary. The main arguments in the literature relating to the lack of efficiency of the system of justice, and the way in which this preoccupation has shaped criminal laws and policies, are also discussed. In addition, data which supports my claims of partiality, inequality and unpredictability in the criminal system of justice are also analysed.

It is, of course, very difficult to quantitatively measure the actual efficiency of a system of justice. However, statistical data from proceedings and investigations that have passed through the system of justice can serve as indicators of the efficiency of such a system. I use the word 'indicator' since the efficiency of a system of justice depends on diverse factors; the mere number of proceedings that have been decided can have various interpretations. For instance, in repressive systems of justice, the efficiency of the system might inversely depend on the impartiality of the administration of justice. The term 'indicator' also alludes to uncertainty regarding the reliability of the existing statistical data: both extremely poor and incomplete. In Colombia, since 1971, three factors have accounted for this uncertainty. First there are a set of judicial reforms, mainly originated from the executive, which distort the sources of information of DANE.[264] Consequently, many crimes were not counted by DANE; in addition, due to the nature of the reforms, many such crimes have a high human, social or economic impact. The most important statutes that affect the statistical data of DANE are:[265]

(i) Law 75/1975 transfers certain minor crimes to the jurisdiction of Police Inspectorates. The statistical problem here is that the offences that reach the Police Inspectorates are not counted by DANE.
(ii) Law 22/1977 modifies the criteria to identify property crimes. The implications of this statute are that former crimes were de-criminalised.
(iii) Decree 01/1978 transfers crimes such as extortion, kidnapping and other serious offences against the security of the state to the exclusive

military jurisdiction. DANE does not include in their data those crimes which come under the military jurisdiction.

(iv) Decree 050/1987 discards all criminal investigation when the accused is not known. In addition, DANE does not count crimes that the judiciary drops during the preliminary phase of the criminal process.

(v) Decree 2790/1990 introduces the public order jurisdiction (later transformed into the Regional Justice Statute or *Justicia sin rostro*) in charge of crimes such as kidnapping, extortion and terrorism. This jurisdiction stopped reporting their cases with DANE in 1990.

(vi) Law 23/1991 once more transfers certain minor crimes to Police Inspectorates in the hope of decongesting the courts.

(vii) Decree 2699/1991 regulates the newly created *Fiscalía*, affecting DANE statistics during the first months of the transition from an inquisitorial to an accusatorial criminal system. The collection of data from the *Fiscalía* has been progressively restored, though not fully until 1997.

(viii) Decree 2700/1991 introduced conciliation as an alternative form of conflict resolution for certain minor crimes. These crimes are not counted since they do not enter the formal system of justice.

(ix) Finally, Law 81/1993 altered Decree 050/1987, ordering that criminal investigation ought to be carried out even if there is no known defendant.

The second factor that has affected the reliability of data since 1971 is clearly the impact that these reforms have had in the way that criminal justice has been administered. This issue, which plays an essential part in the Colombian crisis of justice, is analysed in conjunction with the indicators of efficiency. The third and last factor to distort statistics is the armed conflict that has characterised Colombia during the period under analysis. Since the 1980s, this armed conflict, which initially involved the left-wing guerrillas and the state, has acquired newly armed protagonists, mainly paramilitary forces and drug traffickers. As a result, many crimes are not even counted because the state authorities cannot operate in or even enter some particularly violent areas of the country where one or more armed actors are in control. In other cases, the state itself can be compromised in dirty crimes such as human rights abuses, kidnappings and so on that it needs to keep hidden. It is in the interests of those on the margins of the law to hide certain crimes, their own or those of areas where they operate, in order to gain 'trust' amongst the population, but also to exaggerate other crimes for strategic reasons; for example, it is in the interest of the guerrillas to inflate numbers of military casualties.

With these warnings in mind I have chosen the following indicators of efficiency, based on an assessment of the available data: judicial backlog, that is, the percentage of initiated proceedings that are not yet decided or sentenced; the length of judicial proceedings; the number of atypical ways (such as writs of filing and prescription) which have been used to conclude a case; the level of impunity and judicial enforcement.

Judicial backlog

The evidence shows that since 1937, when judicial statistics became available in Colombia, there has been a serious pattern of judicial accumulation in the criminal jurisdiction.[266] In fact, between 1940 and 1964, the criminal proceedings that entered the system quintupled, from 30 000 to 150 000 per year. During this same period, the number of criminal investigations that the system could effectively terminate fell to less than 50 per cent, from 10 000 in 1940 to 15 000 in 1964.[267] Data from accumulated criminal proceedings in Colombia during the decade 1958–68, as shown in Table 3.1, reveal the high pattern of accumulation in numbers of proceedings, something which became critical by the end of the 1970s.

In 1971, in view of this excessive and ever-increasingly backlog, the executive, looking above all for efficiency in the administration of criminal justice, introduced a new criminal procedure statute (Decreto 409 de 1971 or 1971 CPP). The 1971 statute introduced judges of criminal instruction whose role was to help the ordinary judge with the prosecution phase, and attempted to divide criminal investigation into two phases: the instruction phase and the judgment phase.[268] Since the

Table 3.1 Flow rate of accumulated criminal proceedings, 1958–68

Year	*Criminal proceedings*
1958	239 561
1960	282 262
1962	310 296
1964	323 597
1966	627 923
1968	832 119

Sources: J. Giraldo *et al.* (1987) and DANE.

purpose of the 1971 statute was to reduce the volume of cases, the new instruction judges, themselves members of the executive, selected cases that were easy to resolve. Statistical evidence shows that, in spite of the fact that they initially helped to contain the criminal backlog in relative terms, they brought about other problems. An increasing number of criminal cases were effectively closed, but justice was not done; that is to say, efficiency replaced but minimised justice.[269] Consequently, since 1971 the criminal backlog has suffered a dramatic decrease due mainly to new procedural norms that minimised justice, rather than from a decrease in crime or a better judicial performance.

In spite of the instruction judges, the criminal backlog remained high throughout the period 1971 to 1977. In 1971 alone, criminal cases had increased by 13.2 per cent of the number of cases in 1968; in 1977 this had risen to 81.6 per cent. Statistical data also reveals that the number of proceedings leading to sentencing each year was well below the number initiated. For example, taking the data from 1976, there is evidence that 278 551 cases were initiated, of which only 63 121 (22.6 per cent) were sentenced in that year. This implies that a total of 215 430 (77.4 per cent) proceedings that were pending had arisen by the end of 1976.[270] In the period between 1965 and 1987, official statistical data shows that, on average, the number of criminal proceedings that were resolved each year was half the number that were initiated in that same year.[271] Studies carried out by the Instituto SER have corroborated this finding (see Table 3.2).

The annual increment of unsolved criminal cases shown in Table 3.2 is consistent with the dramatic judicial backlog that most analysts identify as the main issue of concern in the 1970s and 1980s. However, the 1971 statute managed to contain the numbers and they increased less dramatically than in the period 1964–71. In particular, if we analyse this

Table 3.2 Flow rate of accumulated criminal proceedings, 1972–80

Year	*Initiated criminal proceedings*	*Pending criminal proceedings*	*Percentage of accumulated proceedings*
1972	198 400	156 700	79
1974	264 200	223 800	85
1976	278 600	224 600	81
1978	249 100	188 300	76
1980	**296 800**	**237 500**	**80**

Sources: Instituto SER para la Investigación (1983) and DANE.

Table 3.3 Flow rate of initiated criminal proceedings and sentences, 1980–93

Year	*Initiated proceedings*	*Sentences*	*Percentage of accumulated proceedings*
1980[273]	**296 817**	**14 227**	**95.2**
1982	304 389	13 617	95.5
1984	240 615	21 351	91.1
1986	403 607	22 555	94.4
1988	251 343	42 118	83.2
1990	235 568	42 955	81.7
1991	191 420	41 759	78.2
1992	175 640	31 284	82.2
1993	109 023	31 048	71.6

Source: DANE (1993).

data in conjunction with the raising level of crime during this period.[272] The figures for 1980 to 1993, based on a different methodology, reveal a decreasing pattern of accumulation, one which became clear since 1988 (see Table 3.3).

The statistical reduction at the end of the 1980s and the beginning of the 1990s, however, is also the result of procedural changes rather than a better judicial performance or a decrease in crime. The first procedural change is Decree 050/1987, which discards all criminal investigations when the accused is unknown. This decree is a clear example of the perversity of executive-made law which generates impunity. While the number of homicides rose dramatically in the period 1987–91, the executive – through Decree 050/1987 – limited prosecutions in the case of homicides to cases where the culprit was known. The second procedural change occurred in 1991 when Law 23/1991 decriminalised many minor offences which were under the jurisdiction of the municipal courts, that is, the law converted crimes into misdemeanours and assigned their prosecution and judgment to police inspectorates. This second procedural change becomes clear when one compares the number of initiated proceedings in Table 3.3, above, for the years 1990 and 1991. Third, the initiation of the *Fiscalía*, which has been responsible since 1992 for the prosecution phase of all criminal investigations, relieved the backlog of most criminal courts since for the first time the criminal courts took charge only of the judgment phase. Moreover, Decree 2790/1990, which introduced the public order jurisdiction, excluded kidnapping, extortion and terrorism from DANE's data. It was precisely in 1989 that these three

Table 3.4 Flow rate of accumulated criminal proceedings, 1994–97

Year	*Criminal courts*	*Fiscalía*	*Total*
1994	2 472 951	485 445	2 958 396
1995	2 439 437	662 637	3 102 074
1996	2 642 220	625 514	3 267 734
1997	2 884 662	667 000	3 551 662

Sources: Consejo Superior de la Judicatura (1994–97), DANE (1997) and Corporación Excelencia en la Justicia (1997).

crimes increased dramatically due to the 'war on drugs' against the Medellín Cartel. Consequently, the performance of the criminal system of justice appears to be more efficient when compared with that of the three former decades. In Table 3.4, we can observe that an important part of the criminal backlog between 1994 and 1997 is simply transferred to the *Fiscalía* which since then has been responsible for almost one-fifth of the total accumulated proceedings.

In spite of the fact that the *Fiscalía* began with a huge backlog, some have argued that the pattern of accumulation of proceedings since its initiation in 1992 is partly its own fault. For the first time in the constitutional history of the country the judicial police function was assigned by the Constitution to the national police, the Procuraduría and the Contraloría.[274] In addition, the 1991 Constitution mandates that a law can assign the permanent functions of judicial police to other agencies (such as police inspectorates or mayors). This great constitutional advance is not working, partly because the three agencies in charge of the judicial police are not performing their task, as discussed earlier, and partly because the *Fiscalía* is carrying out most of the preliminary criminal investigations in spite of the fact that the Constitution gave this agency only the direction and co-ordination of the judicial police, and not its full exercise.[275] Even though the *Fiscalía* members I spoke with denied the usurpation of judicial police functions, and though most spoke of a close collaboration with the national police and other state institutions in charge of judicial police functions, the evidence shows that the *Fiscalía* is indeed carrying most preliminary investigations and that there is little co-ordination among the other institutions that act as judicial police. This situation translates into an enormous backlog at the *Fiscalía* level, at least until the end of 1998. The period July 1999 to June 2000, however, shows an important reduction of the backlog according to the internal statistics of the *Fiscalía*, some of which were recently made public.[276] The positive signs of recovery shown in the internal statistics of the *Fiscalía* for the period 1999–2000 are certainly encouraging. After all, it is in the first phases of criminal investigation that the pattern of initial increase in judicial backlog is shaped. However, due to the persistence of the traditional problems of judicial police functioning, it is too soon to tell whether this is a sustained reduction. One optimistic scenario is that the more technical the preliminary phase of the criminal investigation, the less probabilities there are for minimising justice. A more pessimistic scenario is that, in spite of technical improvements, the huge backlog of the *Fiscalía* and the increasing levels of crime resulting from the escalation of the armed conflict will impede a sustained reduction of impunity. Overall, the degree of efficiency in the administration of justice is only important when the system-improved efficiency coincides with an increase in the quality of the justice that it administers, in other words, with its degree of equity and impartiality.

The length of proceedings

A concurrent issue relating to the judicial backlog is the duration of judicial proceedings. Under the subtitle 'The creaking machinery of justice', it has been argued in the case of Italy that: 'The biggest problem in the operation of the Italian judicial system is the extraordinarily slow operation of the courts . . . it is anything but unusual for a trial to drag on for a dozen years or more'.[277] The duration of criminal proceedings in Colombia has traditionally been as long as those in Italy, even though, in accordance with Colombian law, a case cannot in principle last more than 12 years since it would automatically prescribe legally (see note 190, above). In practice, however, an investigation conducted by the Universidad Externado de Colombia[278] (Externado University) demonstrated that the average length of criminal proceedings in Colombia was greater than that stipulated by the statutes or what is the legal term.[279] In this investigation, a sample set showed an average excess in duration of proceedings of 202.9 per cent over and above the legal term, with a range of excess throughout the sample set of between 89 per cent and 86.1 per cent. Interestingly, the Externado investigation also showed that when a criminal case involved a pre-trial detention, a preventative measure, the duration of the proceeding was then considerably shorter than when the defendant was not detained. Another result of this investigation revealed that the longer proceedings corresponded to the jurisdiction of the lower courts. In the case of civil and labour administration of justice, the proceedings lasted an average of 2.5 years in the circuit courts and two years in the municipal courts.[280] The issue of the excessive length of the judicial proceedings is one of the factors contributing to the judicial backlog; however, it also signifies that, even if a case were to go through the system of justice, the length of the proceeding would be such that it would perhaps prove too costly, or even irrelevant, for parties to resort to the system of justice for resolving a conflict. These data help explain the large number of cases of unreported criminality. The abuse in the length of the proceedings, while still a problem in the 1990s, was slowly replaced by atypical ways of deciding criminal cases.

Atypical ways of deciding a case

The judgment in a criminal proceeding may be classed as being final, that is, putting an end to the case, resolving the essence of the conflict, by means of a conviction or of finding not guilty, or as atypical, that is, arising during the progress of a case as a result of some particular procedural matter. Atypical ways of deciding a criminal case arise mainly, although not exclusively, when an initiated proceeding fails because the accused was not identified, or because no evidence was brought to the investigation, or because the case prescribed.[281] Data on the prescription of criminal proceedings for the period 1958 to 1968 is shown in Table 3.5.

In the period 1976 to 1980, the greatest percentage of atypical criminal decisions were writs of filing (meaning that after two years of prosecuting a criminal case without finding possible offenders, the case is temporarily closed until new evidence is brought to it), and writs of prescription, as shown in Table 3.6.

Table 3.5 Prescription of criminal proceedings, 1958–68

	Decisions	*Guilty*	*%*	*Acquittal*	*%*	*Prescription*	*%*
1958	62 202	18 852	17.0	4 552	8.7	38 798	74.3
1960	63 862	11 770	18.6	6 468	10	45 624	71.4
1962	55 029	9 089	16.6	4 571	8.3	41 369	75.1
1964	70 466	14 211	20.2	5 787	8.2	50 468	71.6
1965/66*	58 283	10 386	17.9	3 522	6.0	44 375	76.1
1967/68**	57 942	14 761	25.6	4 255	7.3	38 926	67.1

Notes:
* These data correspond to the period 31 July 1965 to 1 August 1966, since data from the first semester of 1965 is unknown.
** Data from 31 July 1967 to August 1968.

Source: J. Giraldo *et al.* (1987).

Table 3.6 Writs of filing and prescription, 1976–80

Year	*Percentage of writs among the total decisions by the judge (%)*
1976	61
1977	63
1978	66
1979	67
1980	70

Source: Instituto SER para la Investigación (1983).

Table 3.7 Percentage of prescriptions in the total criminal proceedings terminations, 1980–93

Year	*Percentage of prescriptions*	*Others (%)*
1980	68	32
1985	99[282]	1
1990	55	45
1993	51	49

Sources: DANE and H.E. Ortiz (1994).

As shown earlier, the informal trend of filing proceedings where the accused was unknown was accentuated in 1987 when Decree 050/1987 formally prohibited the opening of any criminal investigation in such cases. In statistical terms, Decree 050 considerably diminished the judicial backlog, but in real terms it increased the impunity for crimes where the accused was unknown during the legal term of 60 days.[283] In everyday practice, criminal investigations are generally carried out only when the accused is known, this is in spite of the fact that this provision was annulled in 1993.[284] Decree 050 explains the decrease in the prescriptions during the early 1990s (see Table 3.7).

To see what occurred after the 1991 constitutional reform, I analysed some data from the Instituto SER from 1994, that is, three years after the 1991 constitutional reform.[285] For the period 1998 to the beginning of 1999 I used the official statistics published by the *Fiscalía*.[286] I highlight the fact that, from 1992, most of the judicial backlog is concentrated in the *Fiscalía*, which since then has been in charge of the first two phases of criminal investigation. I also note that the atypical ways of finishing the proceedings that existed before were changed with the 1991

Constitution. This signifies that, instead of prescription and writs of filing, there is now a lack of jurisdiction and the suspension of investigation in the preliminary phase. *Preclusión* and lack of jurisdiction occur in the prosecution phase, and prescription generally happens in the judgment phase. The lack of jurisdiction, which accounts for a high percentage of atypical ways of finishing a process, is simply a procedural way of transferring a case to another judge of higher or lower hierarchy or to another jurisdiction. In many cases, however, it is the perfect excuse to delay adjudication and let the case peter out in the dockets, and it is in this respect that I class it as atypical. *Preclusión*, which signifies the extinction of penal action when the crime was non-existent or the accused did not commit it, can also be a common way of ending proceedings in an atypical way. In spite of the fact that it is legally classed as a regular way of ending a proceeding, *preclusión* allows the judge great discretion, mainly because *preclusión* also occurs when according to the judge 'the proceeding could not be initiated or could not be continued'.[287] This discretionary power, together with the fact that *preclusión* does not always resolve the essence of the case, forces us to class it as atypical in cases where *preclusión* depends only on the judges' discretion; the latter in spite of many *fiscales*' perception of *preclusión* being a legitimate way of extinguishing the criminal action.[288] Finally, it is also worth highlighting that not all atypical ways of evacuating criminal proceedings necessarily generate impunity. For instance, the lack of jurisdiction may delay a proceeding, but a competent court might decide this case at a later stage. The same could be true for *preclusión*. Unfortunately, from a statistical point of view it is difficult to make these subtle distinctions.

The evidence reveals that, in spite of the fact that still in 1994 the majority of criminal cases were atypically resolved – this could result from the fact that criminal laxity is institutionalised – there has been an important reduction in the number of atypical ways of ending a proceeding at the level of the sectional *fiscalías*, as revealed in Tables 3.8 and 3.9.[289]

As Table 3.8, above, reveals, most preliminary investigations terminated by the sectional *fiscalías* (second level of the *Fiscalía*) – more or less corresponding to the District Attorney in the US were for *preclusión* of the investigation for the author of the crime not having been determined in the legal period of 180 days. The pattern of atypical terminations, as compared with the three former decades, is certainly lower at the sectional level. In contrast in the case of the local *fiscalías*, the lower hierarchy of the *Fiscalía*, the percentages of atypical termination are very worrying since these are even higher than those of the three former

Table 3.8 Atypical ways of terminating proceedings in the local and sectional *fiscalías* during the preliminary phase in 1994

Level of the Fiscalía	*Type of atypical terminations*	*Percentage of atypical terminations amongst total causes for termination*
Sectional level	*Preclusión*	37
	Lack of jurisdiction	16
Subtotal of atypical terminations		53
Local level	*Preclusión*	9
	Lack of jurisdiction	78
Subtotal of atypical terminations		87
Total of atypical terminations at local and sectional levels		70

Sources: Instituto SER para la Investigación (1996) and Angel, J. Giraldo (1996).

Table 3.9 Atypical ways of terminating proceedings in the local and sectional *fiscalías* during the prosecution phase in 1994

Level of the Fiscalía	*Type of atypical terminations*	*Percentage of atypical terminations amongst total causes for termination*
Sectional level	*Preclusión*	17
	Lack of jurisdiction	18
	Reassigned cases	11
Subtotal of atypical terminations		53
Local level	*Preclusión*	12
	Lack of jurisdiction	73
Subtotal of atypical terminations		85
Total of atypical terminations at local and sectional levels		69

Source: Instituto SER para la Investigación (1996), Angel, J. Giraldo (1996) and author's calculations.

decades. In the prosecution phase, also in the hands of the *Fiscalía*, the judicial performance of the local and sectional *fiscalías* is similar to what happens at the preliminary level.

Finally, during the judgment phase, in the hands of the courts, the performance of criminal jurisdiction is extremely good. Since 1992, the courts have been in charge only of the judgment of those cases prosecuted by the *Fiscalía* and, due to the latter's enormous backlog as explained above, have had a reduced number of cases coming forward for judgment.[290] The situation where atypical ways of terminating criminal proceedings were in the majority carries on into 1998. However, in that year, the number of atypical terminations, while still high, decreased for the first time at both levels of the *Fiscalía*, in comparison with the past three decades (see Tables 3.10 and 3.11).

Tables 3.10 and 3.11 show a substantial reduction in the percentage of atypical terminations in the years 1998 and 1999 at the local level both in the preliminary and prosecution phases when compared with 1994. In the case of the sectional level, the statistical reduction in the atypical terminations which started in 1994 is sustained at the preliminary phase, while a mild variation occurs in the prosecution phase. I note, however, that according to the *Fiscalía*'s own analysis of its statistics for the period 1998–99, in the prosecution phase, 62.2 per cent of the terminations are counted as standard ways of terminating proceedings whereas only 37.8 are classed as atypical.[291] In contrast, my analysis for this same period and phase is 44.2 per cent of standard decisions and 55.8 per cent of atypical ones. A similar situation occurs at the preliminary

Table 3.10 Atypical ways of terminating proceedings in the local and sectional *fiscalías* during the preliminary phase in 1994 and 1998

Level of the Fiscalía	*Type of atypical terminations*	*Percentage amongst total causes for terminations 1994*	*Percentage amongst total causes for terminations 1998*
Sectional level	Reassigned cases		32.9
	Preclusión	37	13.1
	Lack of jurisdiction	16	4.6
	Prescription		3.7
Subtotal of atypical terminations		53	54.3
Local level	Reassigned cases		22.2
	Preclusión	9	21.1
	Lack of jurisdiction	78	6.3
	Prescription		3.5
Subtotal of atypical terminations		87	53.1
Total of atypical terminations at local and sectional levels		70	53.7

Source: Data based on *Fiscalía* General de la Nación. Informe de Gestión, 1997–98 and author's calculations.

Table 3.11 Atypical ways of terminating cases in the local and sectional *fiscalías* during the prosecution phase in 1994 and the period July 1998 to April 1999

Level of the Fiscalía	*Type of atypical terminations*	*Percentage amongst total causes for terminations 1994*	*Percentage amongst total causes for terminations 1998–99*
Sectional level	Reassigned cases	11	37.1
	Preclusión	17	13.7
	Lack of jurisdiction	18	4
	Prescription		3.9
Subtotal of atypical terminations		53	58.7
Local level	Reassigned cases		23.5
	Preclusión	12	22.1
	Lack of jurisdiction	73	6
	Prescription		1.3
Subtotal of atypical terminations		85	52.9
Total of atypical terminations at local and sectional levels		69	55.8

Source: Data based on *Fiscalía* General de la Nación. Informe de Gestión, 1997–98 and author's calculations.

level. The difference between my analysis (55.8 per cent as atypical) and the *Fiscalía*'s (37.8 per cent as atypical) stems from the *Fiscalía*'s inclusion of *preclusión* for lack of evidence as a form of standard termination. In legal terms, the *Fiscalía* could be right, this procedural instance is indeed a way of terminating proceedings. However, this type of *preclusión* is not entirely standard since it does not resolve the essence of the crime in question and it allows a great degree of discretion on the judge's part.

Overall, the quantitative statistical analysis shows a poor performance on the part of the criminal justice system. However, this poor performance is largely the result of the fact that until at least 1991 judicial performance was limited by executive decrees which it is widely acknowledged perverted the course of Colombian justice. Thus little variation in the performance of the system can be found for almost three decades. Even after the 1991 constitutional reform, the effects of the executive manipulation of the course of justice are still perceptible, as shown in Tables 3.8 and 3.9, above, which measure the *Fiscalía*'s performance for 1994. Consequently, atypical ways of ending proceedings have always been in the majority in terms of criminal administration of justice in the period under consideration. The statistical evidence, however, does show some decrease in the percentage of atypical terminations following the introduction of the *Fiscalía*; that is to say, from percentages of 80 to 65 per cent of atypical terminations during the period 1958 to 1994, it drops from 60 to 50 per cent at the sectional level during the 1994–98 period. The larger variations for the local *fiscalías* from percentages between 70 and 80 per cent during 1994 to 53 and 52 per cent during 1998–99, may result from the Instituto SER's measurement method, which only classifies as 'regular' the criminal proceedings that terminate due to a decision by the judge. Consequently, all other terminations are classed as atypical. This interpretation leads to an overwhelming number of cases that are atypically terminated in the local *fiscalías* for lack of jurisdiction both during the preliminary (78 per cent) and prosecution (85 per cent) phases in 1994. In contrast, four years later the *Fiscalía* classified as 'lack of jurisdiction' only 3.5 per cent of the cases in the preliminary phase and 6 per cent at prosecution level.[292] This wide variation could also be explained as representative of the limitations and problems of statistical data when used as the only measurement of crime. However, the fact that the positive statistical changes occur precisely when the *Fiscalía* is becoming more institutionalised, leads us to suggest that there are positive signs in the struggle against impunity from a quantitative point of view. In qualitative terms (a far more important dimension of impunity), since 1991, the partial liberation from the arbitrary justice imposed for decades (through executive decrees) has the potential to allow a more independent system of justice in the future and one that is less partial and less unequal. In the long term, however, the traditional laxity of criminal jurisdiction and the embedded problems of criminal investigation still need to be solved.

The level of impunity

In spite of the fact that data on judicial backlog, duration and atypical ways of finishing proceedings already shows a high degree of impunity, further analysis is still needed to understand the extent of this phenomenon. For decades, and certainly in the period under review, it has been accepted as fact that the level of impunity in the country oscillates between 95 and 99 per cent. Until very recently, no one either questioned this data or attempted, through rigorous research, to disprove it. With levels of impunity of 95 or 99 per cent, the system of justice becomes irrelevant, and there would not be much purpose in analysing the degree of its performance. New research, however, conducted by

DANE, has challenged for the first time the general assumption, outlined above, of 95 to 99 per cent of impunity. For analytical clarity, before analysing the implications of this research, I introduce here some definitions of the concepts of reported criminality and the so-called dark figure (that is, unreported criminality).[293] Reported criminality constitutes all crimes that are recorded by the administrative or judicial authorities, either as a result of denunciations, direct knowledge of public officials or by other means of communication or perception. The dark figure is made up of the number of crimes that people do not report to the authorities or those that, having been reported, are not officially recorded. The dark figure is usually measured using victims' surveys based on household samples where the interviewer asks if anyone in the house has been the victim of a crime within the previous year. When positive answers are received, the interviewees complete a detailed victim questionnaire for each incident. In relation to the reported criminality, usually in the hands of the police, it has often been argued that police statistics on crime are unreliable. Unreliable police figures are not an exclusively Colombian phenomenon. In Britain, for instance, it is known that official statistics often conceal cover-ups of the true numbers of crimes committed in order to accomplish different goals, such as to show police effectiveness or to send out a particular message to the public. British police, unlike their Colombian counterparts, can caution and prosecute certain crimes. Referring to police abuses in crime recording, in 1999, Her Majesty's Inspectorate of Constabulary (HMIC) deplored British police abuses, arguing that 'There have been many examples where officers have used unethical means to "improve" their figures'.[294] Principal among these were the failure to record crimes where no culprit could be found, wrongly classifying crimes, persuading convicted criminals to admit offences they had not committed and pursuing easy convictions at the expense of more serious cases that might be harder to solve. In the case of Colombia, and to quote Rubio: 'the crucial factor for a criminal incident to be recorded in police statistics is not the seriousness of the offence, but rather, the fact that the victims of the offence have a reasonable knowledge of the identity of the offenders that could make their capture easy for the police authorities'.[295] The Colombian police argue that they do not often capture criminals because the system of justice is unable to prosecute them: 'It's demoralising since then we are forced to release them'.[296] This signifies that even the police acknowledge that they do not actually arrest many offenders. On their side the judges argue that most crimes of high social impact, such as homicides or kidnappings, have no witnesses and without evidence it is impossible to prosecute. It's a vicious circle. Nevertheless, what all these views demonstrate is that a very significant degree of impunity for crimes of high social impact is 'institutionalised' and thus never reaches the system of criminal justice.

The two main sources for analysing crime in general are the victimisation surveys – that is, the dark figure – and the police statistics on crime – that is, reported criminality. In Colombia, as in many other countries such as Britain and the United States, victimisation surveys are carried out to discover the extent of the dark figure. The first victimisation survey carried out in Colombia in 1985 showed that 79.1 per cent of the crimes in the 11 most important cities of Colombia went unreported.[297] The second victimisation survey, carried out in 1991, revealed that in the main cities of the country 73.7 per cent of the crimes went unreported.[298] These two DANE victimisation surveys coincided to a great extent with an analysis of national police statistics, which showed that the percentage of reported crimes for 1990 was 19.6 per cent,[299] and a 1994 Departamento de Planeación Nacional report, which showed that only 20 per cent of crimes were reported.[300] A similar percentage for unreported crime is found in a private survey carried out in 1997.[301] The findings of these surveys and data are interesting. On the one hand, both the national police and the Departmento de Planeación Nacional found similar results to those of the victimisation surveys. In addition, the most recent and comprehensive private survey on values in Colombia, the 1997 survey, revealed the same percentage of unreported criminality. This confirmation, by so many different sources, both institutional and private, allows us to accept as fact that only 20 per cent of offences are reported. If we consider the total number of offences recorded by the police for the same period, 1990–98, there is an average of 218 033 per year. Hence, according to the figures, there should be approximately 1 100 000 crimes committed each year in Colombia (pop. 40 million). However, this seems difficult to believe if one compares this number with the five million offences per year recorded by the police in Britain. Adding in the British dark figure of 46 per cent yields approximately 10 million offences per year. According to Colombia's figures, therefore, there would be almost 90 per cent fewer offences per year in Colombia than in Britain: this leads us to conclude that police criminal statistics in Colombia are quite far from the reality. In Colombia, the institution that receives most crime reports is the national police. According to DANE's 1991 victimisation survey, at least 75 per cent of crimes are reported to the police.[302] If the dark figure is of the order of 80 per cent, this signifies that there is in Colombia a police deficiency in both the recording and the detection of crime. Consequently, the police are curtailing the system of justice's capacity to administer justice, since these police deficiencies are contributing to the institutionalisation of a type of impunity that cannot be judicialised. (This is not surprising considering the small fraction of the national police force which is dedicated to crime control.) However, it is also known that the victimisation surveys in Colombia, as in Britain, fail to register high social impact crimes such as homicides or kidnappings. Sexual crimes, family abuse and business crimes are also generally excluded from these surveys. There are several reasons for this. Some are methodological, others are more profound. For instance, sexual and family crimes are seldom reported in surveys since in some cases victims are ashamed of reporting these to survey interviewers. In the case of kidnappings in Colombia people are afraid to report because kidnappers might kill the victim. In Britain the survey sample may not include the most affected population because sampling frames have limitations in reaching certain minority or transient groups. In addition, homicide in both countries is often not counted in these surveys since obviously there is no available victim. In the case of business crimes people tend to underreport these because again these crimes often have no identifiable victim (see Coleman and Moynihan, 1999 and Mayhew, 2000). Moreover, unlike the British Crime Surveys (BCS), Colombia's victimisation surveys are urban-based, taking place only in the main 11 cities of the country – a situation which, according to some, decreases their value since violence and crime are not problems exclusive to the cities.[303] These deficiencies of victimisation surveys, together with police incompetence in crime control, lead us to conclude that we actually know very little of the quantity and quality of the real criminality in Colombia. Neither the victimisation surveys, nor the police statistics, nor obviously DANE's judicial data, are reliable sources to measure impunity and all that relates to this phenomenon. Maybe there is 95 per cent of impunity; maybe there is only 50 per cent; the truth is that at this stage we do not know for certain. What is undisputed is that the system of justice cannot be totally responsible for a situation where impunity never reaches the courts. Improvements in the collection of statistics and victimisation surveys are crucial, but even more important is the need for enhancing the role of the police in its own methods of detection and recording of crime.

Great efforts are also needed in relation to the perception of impunity. It is irresponsible, to say the least, that, for example, serious analysts, state institutions or the media keep quoting as fact that impunity in Colombia is above 95 per cent. The most recent data on impunity presented by the Departamento de Planeación Nacional in 1998 claimed that there was a 97.5 per cent degree of impunity in Colombia.[304] The calculations for Planeación Nacional report were based on a poll where individuals were asked if they had ever been victims of a crime and if the system of justice had acted promptly. Most people interviewed replied that they had been victims of crime which they had not reported either to the police or to any judicial authority. Consequently, the impunity percentage of this report reflects a type of impunity that is outside the judicial arena.[305] How can the system of justice adjudicate cases that do not even reach the courts?

I turn now to an analysis of judicial impunity, presenting the results of a probabilistic model recently developed by the Universidad Nacional, to quantify the levels of judicial impunity. In this model, judicial impunity defines those crimes that enter the system of justice but which the system fails to adjudicate. The Universidad Nacional model can help to reconsider some of the unfounded assumptions on those levels of impunity which are directly caused by the system of justice.[306] The model also measures social impunity, a phenomenon which is essentially equivalent to the unreported crime. In the case of Bogotá, this model has proved that there is a high degree of social impunity, represented by the fact that 63.7 out of 100 offences were not reported. This percentage is lower than that of the figures for unreported crime revealed by previous national victimisation surveys and other official and private research data at the national level.[307]

In the case of judicial impunity, the Universidad Nacional model makes important revelations. It divides judicial impunity at the three levels of criminal investigation, that is: preliminary, prosecution and judgment phases; and also, according to the jurisdiction of the two main courts: that is, local and sectional *fiscalías* and circuit and municipal courts.[308] At the level of the circuit courts' jurisdiction, the model shows that the probability of a crime going unpunished in the prosecution and judgment phases is very low (approximately 2.5 per cent on average for all causes for impunity). In the preliminary phase, the probability of impunity is higher, 25.5 per cent, mainly because of the great number of cases where there is no identification of the culprit.[309] An additional reason is because the preliminary phase, being the first door to the judicial process, is the procedural phase with a greater number of cases. Some of the cases where the culprit is unknown, however, can later be reactivated. According to the model, there is a 14 per cent probability of reactivation against an 11.5 per cent probability of the case becoming definitively suspended: that is, generating judicial impunity. Adding up all the probabilities of the three phases at the circuit (or sectional) jurisdiction, the model shows that with 26 out of 100 proceedings, the culprits are left unpunished. Accordingly, the Universidad Nacional concludes that the level of impunity at the circuit jurisdiction level is not as high as has always been thought.[310] This is significant since the circuit courts are in charge of some of the offences that have the greatest human and social impact such as homicide, kidnapping, sexual offences and fraud.[311] In contrast, in the preliminary phase at the municipal (or local) level, there is a worrying degree of impunity. In this phase, 92 out of 100 cases are suspended due to lack of identification of the culprit. There is, however, a 55 per cent probability for these suspended proceedings to be reactivated. In the prosecution and judgment phases of the municipal courts, the probabilities of impunity are generally low, even though at judgment level the performance of the municipal courts is not as good as that of the circuit courts. Accumulating all three phases, the probability in the municipal jurisdiction is that 43.9 out of 100 cases will remain in a state of total impunity. This is a very high figure if one considers that it is in the municipal jurisdiction where the largest number of criminal cases are initiated. Moreover, since the type of offences that fall under the municipal courts' jurisdiction usually relate to repressed litigation, this judicial impunity seriously undermines equality of access to the system for the less well-to-do sectors of society. At the level of misdemeanours such as theft of value property, something that is also under the jurisdiction of the municipal courts, impunity is even higher: 66 out of 100 cases are left in total impunity. These misdemeanours, however, were only transferred to the municipal courts in 1995 as part of a process of re-judicialisation of some offences that had been previously transferred to police inspectorates.[312] In the case of misdemeanours, the evidence suggests that the impunity was caused at the level of the police inspectorates, since most of these proceedings came from those inspectorates without known culprit, and also very near to their legal terms of prescription (i.e. when the legal set period to decide these misdemeanours has expired). In summary, according to this model, judicial impunity in Bogotá is in the order of 43.9 per cent for offences under the jurisdiction of the municipal courts, 26 per cent for circuit jurisdiction and 65.7 per cent for special misdemeanours.

The Universidad Nacional model also analyses judicial impunity that occurs when an offence is reported versus judicial impunity when the offence is identified by the action or perception of the state. The model shows that, when the offence is reported, the probability of judicial impunity is substantially lower than when the offence is identified by actions of the state, that is, without the support of the victim or his representative. This revelation has interesting implications for the analysis of impunity since it signifies that judicial impunity can be substantially reduced when the victim of the crime cooperates with the system of justice.[313] Overall, the Universidad Nacional model demonstrates that at least at the level of Bogotá, judicial impunity for all crimes is not as high as has always been claimed at the national level. The model also reveals the importance of distinguishing between social and judicial impunity. Moreover, it demonstrates that judicial impunity in Bogotá is lower for crimes of high social impact, such as homicides, which are under the jurisdiction of the sectional *fiscalías* and circuit courts, and that the probability of impunity is generally reduced for crimes that are reported by the victims.

The empirical evidence of the model could, however, be contested on two grounds. First, the fact that the evidence comes from Bogotá which, as the capital city, is an atypical part of the country thus throws doubt on the reach of the probabilistic model results for the rest of the country. One could argue that in the capital city impunity should be lower, since there are more police, more courts, usually some of the best-qualified *fiscales*, judges and lawyers, as well as the fact that judges are generally more protected and there are more resources. However, it is a city of approximately 8 million people and also serves as a microcosm of the country's problems. Moreover, Bogotá is the country's second most violent city in terms of homicides per capita. A second, and perhaps more significant limitation of the Universidad Nacional model, is the fact that judicial impunity is based on the number of crimes that the system of justice decides to prosecute. This signifies that not all offences known by the system of justice are necessarily included. The latter type of impunity, which for reasons of clarity I shall call procedural impunity, is usually understood as the quantity of judgments produced in a year in relation to the percentage of crimes reported or known by the system of justice. According to recent studies, procedural impunity is in the order of 90 per cent. Analysts such as García and Uprimny show that, 'What is really worrying in the Colombian case is that practically 9 out of 10 cases that arrive at the *Fiscalía* don't even reach the prosecution phase'.[314] The Universidad Nacional model reaches a similar conclusion at the level of Bogotá. It shows that in 1997, at municipal and circuit levels, 128 040 cases entered the system of justice at the preliminary phase, of which only 17 023, that is to say 13.29 per cent, passed to the prosecution phase.[315]

There are however, some objections to the figure of 90 per cent procedural impunity. Firstly, one could claim that not all conduct that is reported as a crime necessarily is so. Some could be classified as examples of deviant conduct that are not crimes, others never existed, and some could no doubt be constituted as perjury. It could also be the case where some of the reported deviance do indeed constitute crimes, but these require neither judicial proceedings nor punishment: that is, offences where there are causes of justifiability and *inimputabilidad*.[316] Secondly, if one accepts the qualitative limits of comparing a country like Colombia with, say, Britain, it is worth stressing the fact that in Britain every year since 1995 there have been over 5 million offences recorded by the police, of which only 10 per cent actually lead to caution (police jurisdiction) or sentence (courts' jurisdiction). For instance, in 1995, out of more than 5 million offences recorded by the police, 203 000 (approximately 4 per cent) were cautioned by the police and 301 000 (6 per cent) were sentenced by the courts.[317] This certainly does not mean that in Britain there is 90 per cent impunity. In fact, in Bogotá, according to the Universidad Nacional model data, 4.7 per cent of the people whose cases enter the preliminary phase at the local and sectional levels of the *Fiscalía* end up with a sentence.[318] Thirdly, the model also shows that the main cause of judicial impunity is the lack of identification of the culprit. It could consequently be argued that a great part of this procedural impunity is caused by the lack of support, either voluntarily or not, of the victims of the offences. In fact, the model shows that when the crime is reported the level of impunity is lower. This signifies that the victim's or the witness's indifference affects the performance of the system of justice. One could argue that people do not perceive the system of justice as efficient or sufficiently legitimate, and consequently, they do not rely on it to resolve their conflicts. This would constitute a vicious circle where impunity is fed by impunity; that is to say, the less the system is trusted by people the less well it performs and the more impunity it generates. However, as analysed in more detail in the following chapter, fear to accuse and fear to provide evidence form a great part of the problem of judicial impunity.

Judicial enforcement

Having discussed the most important variables of judicial performance, I turn finally to the degree of effectiveness of judicial enforcement, understood as the capacity of the system to enforce the convictions that the courts adjudicate. The matter of enforcement, which is not the direct responsibility of the system of justice but rather of the executive through INPEC and the Ministry of Justice, as a subject, allows us to analyse in greater depth the issue of equity and impartiality in the adjudication process.

An analysis of the statistical data on prisoners in Colombia shows that the prison population remained constant over the period 1973 to 1992, as an average of 30 000 prisoners, representing 0.085 per cent of the total population.[319] This constancy trend would only change in 1997,[320] when the number of prisoners reached 40 617: that is to say, one prisoner for every 100 000 inhabitants.[321] By contrast, a country like the United States has 426 prisoners per 100 000 inhabitants. The number of Colombian prisoners is surprisingly low for a country that has had one of the highest rates of violence in the world during the past three decades, and the highest, excluding countries at war, in the period 1987–91.[322] The state has, furthermore, shown a very low capacity for apprehending former defendants when they are finally convicted. Not all criminals can legally be preventatively detained; in fact, many actually manage to escape this preventative measure. For example, in 1990, the state only managed to imprison 49 per cent of convicted criminals who were given jail sentences.[323] Finally, not all punishments necessarily impose imprisonment as a sanction. Alternative methods of punishment such as fines or conditional freedom exist – statistical data showed that at least 50 per cent of the convicted criminals received such alternative forms of punishment. In summary, according to the evidence, an average of 20 per cent of crimes are reported of which a high percentage have unknown defendants, and only 49 per cent of all those convicted are imprisoned. These data do not suggest that the system's judicial enforcement is efficient: the 49 per cent corresponds to half of all those who are convicted and, as shown earlier, the level of impunity appears very high. Seen this way, there is less reason to expect a close correlation between the prison population and the real criminality of the country.

Another reason why the prison population in Colombia can be a somewhat misleading tool for measuring the efficiency of judicial enforcement is that a large percentage of prisoners have been jailed preventatively: that is, they have not yet been judged and convicted. For example, in 1986, 62 per cent of those incarcerated were not yet convicted. In 1987, this percentage was 63 per cent and, according to the statistics, this figure remained fairly constant throughout the 1980s.[324] At the beginning of the 1990s the value was around 50 per cent, while from the mid-1990s until the time of writing there has been a slow decrease in this percentage, yielding a value in 2000 of 43 per cent.[325]

Another issue relating to the prison population worthy of mention, is the fact that of the prison population that exists, the majority was convicted or preventatively detained for homicides, personal injuries and robberies. In 1991 for instance, 29 per cent of the total percentage of prisoners was convicted for homicide and injuries, 35 per cent for robbery, and 15 per cent for crimes related to the possession or traffic of drugs (these were mainly petty traffickers). According to Ministry of Justice data, this statistical pattern remained much the same between 1977 and the end of 1991.[326] White-collar criminals – such as those convicted for corruption, sophisticated criminality such as computer theft and paramilitary, guerrilla and drug-trafficking associated criminals – only began to appear in the prison statistics from 1992 which suggests that jail has generally been used for marginal criminals from the less well-to-do sectors of society.[327] As early as 1979 a well-known Colombian writer criticised the system of justice using the famous adage: 'In Colombia justice is a dog that only bites those wearing a *poncho*'.[328] This all led me to explore whether there has been a tradition of class justice and if so, whether it has been purposely implemented or if it is the result of the state's own weakness. One of the most important studies of the profile of the prison population in Colombia, carried out in 1989, corroborates the claim that there has indeed been a tradition of class justice.[329] The Universidad Nacional data revealed that while 86 per cent of prisoners (an average of 95 per cent of the prisoners were male) knew how to read and write, 55 per cent had only had a few years of primary school, 38 per cent had received some high-school education and only 7 per cent had been through university education. DANE's data on the characteristics of the accused or convicted population for the years 1971 to 1993 corroborates the Universidad Nacional evidence, showing, however, a mild increase in the number of prisoners who had some secondary and university education since the 1990s.[330] Moreover, the Universidad Nacional research also demonstrated that 85 per cent of the prisoners were working when imprisoned; of these 44 per cent were independent workers, 32 per cent employees, 17 per cent manual workers, with only 6 per cent being owners or managers of a company. Most prisoners had started work at the age of 14 and had been working for at least two years before their detention – a typical characteristic of less well-to-do people. The average wage of prisoners before detention was the legal minimum salary. The characteristics of the prison population described above suggest that there has been a high percentage of individuals coming from the working class – that is from the poorer sectors of society – and a conspicuous absence of affluent or powerful criminals; the latter in spite of the existing widespread drug trafficking, political corruption-related scandals and the crimes of atrocity associated with the armed conflict. This apparent tradition of class justice minimises equality and impartiality, two of the most important principles that should underlie any system of justice. This class justice situation is, however, not exclusive to Colombia. The 1991 National Prison Survey in Britain showed that a disproportionate number of prisoners came from ethnic minorities (15 per cent of male prisoners and 23 per cent of female prisoners described themselves as black or Asian). As far as social class was concerned, 41 per cent of males had unskilled or partly skilled jobs compared with 18 per cent of the general population. Other striking findings included the fact that over a quarter of prisoners had at some time been in local care (compared with 2 per cent of the general population), and 40 per cent of male prisoners had left school before the age of 16 (compared with 11 per cent of all British males).[331] However, the case of Colombia cannot be blindly compared to that of Britain, not only because the British system of justice is perceived as efficient, but because the less well-to-do percentage of population in Colombia is substantially higher than that of Britain.

Evidence of class justice in Colombia is also highlighted in surveys. Polls taken in 1981 showed that 81 per cent of the population thought judges did not apply the law equally for all citizens.[332] In a 1992 survey where people were asked 'Which term best describes the administration of justice?', 65 per cent pointed to a lack of equal application of the law to all citizens.[333] Other surveys on justice corroborate these findings.[334] In relation to this alleged unequal application of the law, even judges have confirmed the findings of the public-opinion surveys. According to some judges, the groups of citizens who have been favoured by the administration of justice tend to be those in high economic positions (42 per cent), followed by the upper classes (24 per cent), the political class (17.5 per cent), and finally those who can manage to pay for a lawyer (3.3 per cent); that is to say that in the past even judges have accepted that 'conviction is for the less well-to-do sectors of society'.[335] Chapters 4 and 5 analyse still more surveys (mainly those from 1994 and 1997) which show the same type of inequality. This inequality is accentuated by the cost of legal proceedings. Since lawyers' fees and the costs of the legal process are high and state provision of legal aid or counsel is still deficient, most of the accused who come from the less well-to-do sectors of society are immediately put at a disadvantage. When compared with the rich or powerful defendant, who can afford a good defence lawyer or to buy his way out of the system through forms of corruption or intimidation, there is good reason to believe that the state is greatly responsible for this class justice, since it does not provide general legal aid for those who need it – and when it does, the legal aid is usually 'mediocre' since lawyers for the defendant are extremely poorly paid and hence are generally uninterested in the outcome of their defence.[336] This signifies that in most cases where they are present, public defenders do the minimum to satisfy the formal requirements. Even more distressing is the fact that in many regions of the country where the system of justice operates, legal aid still does not exist, and defendants are convicted and imprisoned without legal defence.[337] This partially explains why an overwhelming number of prisoners come from the less well-to-do sectors of society. It is worth noting that since 1992 the characteristics of the Colombian prison population have started to change, with more rich and powerful delinquents being convicted and put in jail. However, this slow change is still not perceptible at the level of general statistical data to allow for deeper analysis on its impact on the efficiency of judicial enforcement or on the equality of treatment.

In summary, I reiterate that fairness, impartiality, equality and some degree of efficiency are important qualities for a system of justice to have in order to be deemed legitimate among the population and to command sufficient authority as part of the political system. From data analysed in this chapter, it is clear that the system of justice, in the period under review, has not been efficient. For decades the 'efforts' of the state and its policies to reduce judicial backlog were misguided – both purposely and due to the state's own weaknesses – because they sought efficiency at the expense of justice and got neither. From the existing statistics, lack of fairness and impartiality are more difficult to prove. However, both can be inferred from the survey data and also from the trend towards the minimising of justice that also characterises the period under review. In relation to the issue of equality, some data on the prison population and also the survey results (which include the judge's opinions) seem to corroborate the notion that equality both in access to the system and in judicial treatment is generally lacking. The net result is that there is a high level of impunity, something which is fuelled by the inefficiency and inequality of the political system. I have shown here that impunity is not just the fault of the criminal system – it also feeds off the precariousness of the state as well as the lack of commitment and strategy shown by certain institutions external to the judiciary such as the executive and the police. In spite of this observation, it can be stated that the poor performance of the judiciary does indeed account for the lack of trust which is placed in it.

4
Fear to Accuse and Fear to Prosecute

> I urged the informants to denounce him, but they refused, saying that if they did so, they would be assassinated along with their wives and children.
>
> Guzmán Campos

> If the capacity and willingness of the Colombian judicial institutions to uphold and interpret the law were eroded, the willingness of individual members of Colombian's judiciary to do so was not. The roll-call of those killed because of their commitment to the rule of law in the face of almost certain death and rapidly decaying institutions is humbling.
>
> MacRae

In this chapter, I make use of surveys to analyse the general perception on the administration of justice as well as of the judges. Particular attention is paid to the issue of people's fear to report either crimes committed against them or crimes for which they have been witnesses. I also discuss the judges' own perception of the administration of justice, placing particular emphasis on their feelings of insecurity and how fear affects their ability to prosecute crime. These surveys disclose the little trust that people have in the administration of justice and the main causes for this distrust. Such distrust, which often results from the poor performance of the criminal jurisdiction, implies that people tend not to use the system of justice to resolve their conflicts. There are two important consequences of this: either they prefer not to do anything, implying that crime then pays, or they take justice into their own hands, implying that crime generates more crime. Fear has an even more perverse effect since it inhibits the victim from making any accusation; that is, it annuls the judicial existence of a crime. In the 'better case' scenario, the crime is reported or discovered but there are no witnesses to testify and hence the case is dropped for lack of evidence. As for the judges, fear destroys the possibility of prosecuting crimes – it either forces them to absolve those responsible, or in the 'best' of cases they condemn the culprit yet pay with their own lives or with fears for their family's safety. It is hard to see how justice can operate in such a climate of fear and distrust – there is therefore a danger that justice then becomes an irrelevant institution. This takes us back to the main claims of this book that the crisis of the system of justice cannot be divorced from the crisis of the state and of the political system, and without the latter's resolution there is little that justice can actually do in the long run.

In Chapter 3, I showed that the system of justice is not entirely responsible for its inefficiency and high level of impunity, yet its poor performance is the source of its elusive legitimacy. In this chapter, I also demonstrate that a high degree of impunity results from fear: the fear of the victims to accuse, the fear of the witnesses to testify, and the fear of the judges to prosecute. These fears originate from the precariousness of a state that lacks control over its territory – a state that has allowed the existence of powerful armed actors that are able easily to subvert it. There are areas of the country where people are forced to follow alternative orders to those of the state, provided by the guerrillas or the paramilitary – this following is essentially fear-driven. Such 'alternative order' does not provide any lasting guarantee for either the citizens or the judges since the ongoing conflict periodically renews the set of armed actors which enjoys local control. Occasionally the state, via military action, manages to recover a particular area from the guerrillas – however, this shift of power is usually temporary. The remainder of the country, where the state is present, is divided into three types of region. First, there are regions that are remote geographically, where the state's presence is minimal – often there are few (if any) courts of justice in such regions. The problem in these parts of the country is that judges are isolated and hence unprotected. Many judges and *fiscales* dealing with high impact crimes in such areas have been threatened, or even murdered – invariably they are forced to decide in favour of the most powerful local actor. In this no-man's land, decisions tend to be taken in response to the interests of the most powerful local actors, either because of direct threats or because of fear of such threats. Second, there are marginal or 'frontier' regions where there is constant fear of armed intervention, either by the state military or by other armed actors in neighbouring areas. Here the reign of silence rules; fear is the main cause for failing to recognise or report certain crimes and for failing to testify and prosecute. The third type of region is where the state is fully present and where there is a degree of autonomy. In these areas, however, the state is often unable to remove the causes of fear by ensuring sufficient protection for witnesses or judges – this is particularly the case for crimes related to drug traffickers. In these regions there is some degree of autonomy for the judges – however, witnesses remain at risk in spite of recent efforts, in particular the Witnesses Protection Programme of the *Fiscalía*, to protect them. The implications of this fear for the administration of criminal justice are dramatic. It subverts the capacity of the state to administer justice, helping instead to institutionalise private justice as a more efficient alternative. Fear – like distrust – corrupts the pillars of democracy and threatens criminal jurisdiction.

General perception of the administration of justice

The politicians' and bureaucrats' perception of justice was much the same from the 1960s until the beginning of the 1980s. For instance, previous to the judicial reform of 1964, the incumbent President of Colombia tried to justify the projects of judicial reform in his message to Congress in August 1961: '… to satisfy the national wish to reform substantially the Judicial branch… given the existence of a general complaint about the inefficiency of the system of justice… and considering as a grave thing that nobody can deny this public understanding with sufficient authority. A country that does not believe in its judges or in its system of justice is always on the verge of great disasters'.[338] The former concern is similar to that articulated by the Colombian President almost two decades later when he sought to justify the failed 1979 constitutional reform to the system of justice: 'Among public opinion there is great scepticism concerning the criminal administration of justice.… There is a growing insensibility towards law violations reported by the press, and people presume beforehand that the justice system will not punish most crimes. I can sense from the people the feeling that this continual breakdown of the Colombian institutions at all levels and hierarchies has to end'.[339]

The general perception on the crisis in criminal jurisdiction became even more blatant when the phenomenon of drug trafficking became an issue in Colombia at the beginning of the 1980s. The latter situation made more apparent the existing weaknesses in the Colombian system of justice to the point that some even blamed drug trafficking for the failures of the system. 'The collapse of the system of justice – as a product of the emergency of drug-trafficking and, to a lesser extent, the guerrillas and the weakness of the system of justice – allowed the upsurge of all types of delinquency or, what is effectively the same, great levels of impunity between 1978 and 1984'.[340] However, the evidence also suggests that one of the reasons for the Colombian boom of drug trafficking was precisely the inefficiency and the fragile political legitimacy of most state institutions, in particular those of the system of justice; in other words, the problems of the system of justice preceded drug trafficking.

In order to locate the general perception on the administration of justice in a wider context, I begin by quoting the results of a survey that relates to the Colombian state in general. In 1992, a survey in which people were asked three questions relating to their trust in the government and the rule of law, revealed some interesting opinions. To the questions 'do you accept the law and the present form of government?', 'do you find lots of failures in the system but feel a positive gradual change?' and 'do you reject the present system and believe that the only solution is a total social change?', 10 per cent, 34 per cent and 48 per cent answered yes respectively.[341] This latter view is surprising for a country that just one year earlier had undergone complete constitutional and structural reform. It also reflected a distressing fact: that the majority of Colombians rejected the existing legal and political system. In contrast, when an international survey asked the same three questions in a number of countries the results are as shown in Table 4.1.[342]

To the second question, 'do you find lots of failures in the system but believe in a positive gradual change?',[343] the percentage of positive replies ranged from 84 per cent in the case of Japan to 30 per cent in Singapore (34 per cent in Colombia and 59 per cent in the case of England). Five years later, in 1997, a general survey on values, institutions and social capital in Colombia provided some relevant perceptions that could widen the significance of the opinions registered in the 1992 survey.[344]

Table 4.1 Comparative percentage of rejection of the existing system (%)

	Colombia	*India*	*France*	*England*	*Brazil*	*Italy*
Do you reject the present system and the only solution is total social change?	48	40	26	24	22	20

Sources: International Public Opinion (1980–81) and Lemoine, C. (1993).

In 1997 the vast majority of Colombians (80 per cent) supported democracy over any other system. This suggests that the 1992 majority rejection of the rule of law and the system, and the wish for total change (10 and 48 per cent respectively) was more related to lack of satisfaction with the performance of the institutions, such as Congress, the system of justice and the administration, than with democracy as a form of government. The degree of dissatisfaction with the institutions is enormous. In this respect the 1997 survey shows that with the exception of Argentina amongst the 25 countries included, Colombians are the individuals who most openly distrust their institutions. Moreover, the 1997 survey shows that politicians and political parties are the most distrusted institutional actors, a perception that justifies the 1992 findings. Furthermore, 34 per cent of the population interviewed considered that on certain occasions political violence was justified. In spite of the fact that the questions included in of the two surveys are not comparable, both reveal a general degree of dissatisfaction with the existing regime and the performance of its institutions, something which poses serious questions for the consolidation of democracy in Colombia. Notwithstanding this comment, one should also highlight the fact that the majority of Colombian people (80 per cent) prefer democracy to other alternatives.

In relation to the administration of justice, there are two main surveys worthy of discussion. The first is the 1994 survey, which is analysed in detail in Chapter 5. The second is the 1997 survey mentioned above, which is the most recent general survey to date, and includes a detailed analysis on justice.[345] In general terms, the 1997 survey demonstrates that there is a great need for both civil and criminal justice among the general population and also a great degree of dissatisfaction with the system. This survey reveals that the degree of satisfaction with criminal jurisdiction is very low, though not as low as that of civil jurisdiction. Even though this book focuses mainly on criminal jurisdiction, this new evidence reveals that crime and violence can often result from frustrated civil disputes. In fact, 2 per cent of those interviewed admitted threatening a person in order to settle civil accounts against only 1 per cent in the case of criminal offences. In this respect, the huge discontent that exists on the performance of civil justice is a potential source of violence that should not be underestimated. In the case of the criminal justice system, the survey revealed that one out of three Colombians has been affected by a crime in the previous year (1996). This proportion is one in two in the case of civil conflicts. On average, each of the affected persons has been the victim of two crimes. In the case of judges and the armed forces, the proportion of crimes per victim reached almost three.

The most common crimes were those against property, representing 24 per cent, but those against life and personal integrity amounted to 12 per cent. Consequently, there is obviously a great necessity for criminal justice here.[346] Yet the 1997 survey reveals that 40 per cent of the victims of a crime did nothing either to resolve it or make any 'amicable arrangement'. This submissive attitude is more prevalent in the less well-to-do sectors of society. Interestingly enough, it is also the less well-to-do sectors of society as a group who are the greater users of the criminal system of justice – perhaps because there is no preferable alternative. In terms of dissatisfaction with the system of justice, it is even more distressing to note that judges are as incredulous of the criminal system of justice as the rest of the population; consequently, they are the ones who use more informal mechanisms, such as conciliation, to resolve their own conflicts.[347] However, according to this survey, in percentage terms, judges are also the sector of society most likely to use more violent ways to resolve conflicts (2 per cent in contrast with 1 per cent from the general population and the armed forces). This fact, which is very worrying, ought to be contrasted with data that reveals that 9 per cent of judges claimed to be the victims of life threats, as compared with 7 per cent for the armed forces and the general population. Two distressing observations from these data emerge in relation to the judges: firstly, that a system where not even the judges trust the justice that they administer is permeated by external pressures or forces that from the point of view of the judges, appear insurmountable. Secondly, the use of 'private justice' by 2 per cent of judges suggests that they too are involved in the murky arrangements that usually characterise the most violent actors of society. Does this mean that Colombian judges are either victims or victimisers? I deal with both issues later.

The main reasons for the general low degree of satisfaction with the criminal system of justice, according to the 1997 survey data, are lack of efficiency in the criminal justice system and the perceived degree of effectivity of 'private justice'.[348] Accordingly, the 1997 survey shows that only 48 per cent of the general population use the criminal system of justice, whereas 15 per cent seeks 'private justice' alternatives. (The greater proportion of users of 'private justice' are the young and the most wealthy.) Equally worrying is the evidence that 30 per cent of those interviewed did not use the system of justice for fear of reprisals. This evidence is corroborated by the former *Fiscal General*, Alfonso Gómez Mendez, who argues that one of the great problems of the administration of justice is that witnesses do not speak up out of fear.[349] In the case of offences where organised criminality is involved, fear is increased and, even when hardened publicly known criminals are captured, there is often no evidence to prosecute them. This happened in January 1990 in the case of one of the largest military operations against a drug trafficker's criminal band in Medellín, where more than 300 alleged *sicarios* (paid gunmen) were preventatively detained and put in the hands of the criminal judges. Not long after their successful detention, the criminal judges had to release them due to lack of evidence and absence of witnesses.[350] In the words of the Commander in Chief of the Military at the time, General Harold Bedoya: 'The potential witness knows that he is not confronted with a particular *sicario* or drug dealer, but rather with a whole criminal organisation. No witness dares to go to a judge when his testimony can imply his own death'.[351] The 1997 survey also shows that the perception of impunity is higher in the case of homicides. To the question 'Do you know someone who has been assassinated in the last five years?', 44 per cent said yes (68 per cent in the case of judges), and 78 per cent of that 44 claimed that justice had not been done.[352]

Even more catastrophic is the proportion of interviewed people who claimed to know who was responsible for a homicide, but still preferred to do nothing about it. The latter percentage is one out of three for the general population and the judges, and one out of two among members of the armed forces. This reveals that impunity is fed by fear: the fear to accuse. Fear is greater in areas of the country where there are armed actors, such as guerrillas, the paramilitary or drug traffickers, as the perceived performance of the criminal system reveals. In fact, the 1997 survey reveals that, in the areas of the country where there are no armed actors, 16 per cent of the homicide cases are resolved by the administration of justice. By contrast, in those areas where four or more armed groups operate, only 6 per cent of the homicides are judicially adjudicated.

So far, the 1997 survey confirms our earlier statistical findings on the low degree of performance of the criminal system of justice; however, it also reveals the low level of general satisfaction with the administration of justice. Moreover, the 1997 survey demonstrates two additional factors: first, that 'private justice' competes with the formal administration of justice and even more worrying that 'private justice' is not only efficient, but has reached a good degree of credibility among a not-so-insignificant percentage of the population, including a percentage of judges. Second, and equally grave, the 1997 survey reveals that many homicides are not reported in spite of the victim's knowledge of the assassin's identity. The latter, while clearly a sign of the lack of trust in the system of justice, is also and perhaps more importantly a sign of a fear of reprisal.

The 1997 survey poses another question which reveals fear of reprisal to be one of the main reasons behind judges' fear to prosecute. 'Which of the following crimes do you fear the most: crimes against property, interpersonal conflicts,[353] "private justice",[354] crimes by state authorities or none?' The results of this question show that judges and members of the armed forces mostly fear 'private justice' (52 per cent and 51 per cent respectively), as compared with the general population (33 per cent) which fears equally crimes against property (31 per cent) and interpersonal conflicts (23 per cent). By contrast, judges and the armed forces perceive crimes against property as less worrying, at 25 and 27 per cent respectively, and interpersonal conflicts as only 6 and 7 per cent. The fear of 'private justice' is understandable in a country that has an ongoing irregular war in which, in theory, the armed forces are the main target. What is more worrying for the overall performance of the administration of justice are the implications of this fear amongst judges. As discussed in Chapter 6, during the mid-1980s and the beginning of the 1990s 'private justice' against judges managed to semi-paralyse the operation of the system of justice.

Since perception of the system of justice is so low, I have analysed the public perception of judges themselves. Only a few studies concerning judges and public officials of the judiciary in Colombia exist. One of the first of its kind was carried out in 1987.[355] Despite this lack of research, as part of the common rhetoric that has characterised the administration of justice in the past three decades, judges have been blamed as inefficient and corrupt. The following quote sums up this feeling clearly:

> In this country judges have been chastised, there is a general image of judges as corrupt, their education and training has been criticised. There is a general rhetoric on clientelism in the election of judges and while most countries have a respectable and prestigious image of the judges' profession, in Colombia by contrast being a judge is not perceived by people as a mark of distinction. Recently, due to drug trafficking the image of judges has deteriorated even more.[356]

Moreover, the image that people actually have of judges is quite the opposite of how the judges see themselves.[357] As early as 1968 a national survey revealed that 68 per cent of those interviewed thought judges could be bribed. The image of judges grew worse, as a more recent poll confirmed.[358] In 1986, 88 per cent of the adult population claimed that judges in Colombia could be bribed, while 85 per cent thought that judges did not apply the law equally to all citizens. These surveys led some scholars to the worrying conclusion that the majority of citizens did not trust judges nor, by extension, the administration of justice, and thus felt justified in either taking justice into their own hands or offering bribes to obtain the desired results.[359] Furthermore, two recent surveys on people's perception of the administration of justice carried out in 1991 before the 1991 constitutional reform and in 1994, three years after this reform, corroborate the low esteem in which Colombians hold their judges.[360] In 1991, those interviewed were convinced that lawsuits were never investigated fully due to a lack of efficiency of the judges, and also that suing usually implied a prejudice toward the suer. In 1994 there was some optimism among those interviewed with regard to the new system of justice and the efforts made to unveil the major scandals of political corruption that led to *Proceso 8000*. However, most showed disillusionment concerning the moralising role of some institutions of the system of justice, arguing that there had been more scandals than convictions. In 1997 – that is, after it appeared as though *Proceso 8000* was on the brink of being buried – a survey (different from that which I have called the 1997 survey) revealed public disillusion and disbelief in judges. To the question 'how much trust do you have in judges?', 42 per cent said 'little' and 15 per cent 'none', while only 20 per cent claimed they had a significant amount of trust.[361] This suggests that changes of public perception can also be affected by specific events. Yet the reality is that, in the period under review, people did not trust judges and by extension have a very low perception of the administration of justice. In summary, the polls' evidence clearly shows that there is a general distrust and rejection of judges, who are generally perceived as inefficient, partial or corrupt.

In spite of the disastrous performance of the criminal system of justice, the low degree of satisfaction with the system, and the low esteem for judges that the data from the surveys analysed above reveals, the 1997 survey shows that when compared with other institutions, that of the judiciary is among the least distrusted. To the question, 'how much trust do you have in the following institutions: the press, television, Congress, public administration, political parties, justice, the military, and the police', the only trusted institution was that of the military with a degree of acceptance of 21 per cent. The remaining institutions all had negative percentages ranging from −75 per cent in the case of political parties to −3 per cent in the case of the police, with the judiciary at −18 per cent, a percentage very similar to that of the press and television. When analysed in conjunction with further data, this lack of trust in most of the country's institutions is obviously symptomatic of a country in crisis. The comparatively 'not-so-low' ranking of justice therefore simply results from the even more critical state of most other institutions. Such improvement in its ranking could also be a result of the recent achievements of the *Fiscalía* against former untouchable criminals, such as the heads of the Medellín and Cali Cartels, and high-ranking corrupt politicians or bureaucrats. As a result of *Proceso 8000*, corrupt congressmen were preventatively imprisoned as well as public officials involved in state contracts and high level corruption. One should also take into account the small but significant achievements of the *tutela*, and the extremely independent role played by the Constitutional Court.

The stance taken by judges and the issue of intimidation

Having described the public perception of the system of justice and its judges, it seems only fair to analyse what judges themselves actually thought about the administration of justice before the reforms of the 1990s and what they think about their present position. A judge's pre-1990s feelings are summed up in the following phrase:[362] 'the sensation of abandonment from the government is alarming. 87.7 per cent of the judges believe that in general the national administrations have not taken any care of Colombian judges'.[363] Evidence of this sensation of abandonment showed itself from 1980 in an upsurge of violence against judges in the country's main cities. In some cities 'the main cause of violence in the last few weeks has been a running battle between the drugs Mafia (sic) and the local judiciary. So far, two judges have been murdered, apparently because they refused to drop cases against local Mafia (sic) bosses'.[364] Consequently, in 1980, several judges and magistrates took to the streets in demonstrations, shouting slogans such as 'the mafia kills us; the Minister of Justice insults us'.[365] In fact, following this protest, more than 150 judges resigned, and the Supreme Court of Justice indirectly supported their concerns claiming that judges had been put in the front line of the battle against drug traffickers. The situation of a judge's security was to worsen by the end of the 1980s, when judges were also threatened by many other actors, including the paramilitary, the guerrillas and other agents not exclusively related to drug trafficking.

In 1987 some judges stated quite openly what they thought were the main problems of the administration of justice.[366] I shall quote a specific set of complaints since these seem representative of the judges' general opinions on the problems of the administration of justice:

> [These are] ... the poor resources of the Judiciary and the lack of autonomy of the judges in the administration of their budget; the

> poor physical resources (the buildings and the working instruments) as a direct consequence of the scarce resources; the lack of training of both judges and public officials of the judiciary, the absence of good salaries and systems of promotion, clientelism in their election and the lack of stability in their posts; the necessity to modernise the courts administratively and technologically, the lack of security for the members of the judiciary, the insufficiency of the national administration's support, and the little respect for the judges by the public; defaults in the laws and bad promotion of the existing statutes; and finally, a deficit of judges and judicial personnel, judicial backlog, ... dishonesty of some of the members of the judiciary, clientelism and political pressures ... .[367]

When asked how the problems of the administration of justice could be solved, most judges demanded the following: (1) the creation of more courts; (2) the rationalisation of court work; and (3) a decrease in the number of judicial investigations by the use of alternative methods of conflict resolution such as conciliation, dejudicialisation and decriminalisation.[368] Clearly, judges agree with the main issues (mainly the inefficiency of the system) and solutions that have made Colombia's system of justice a system in crisis. However, many judges recognised more worrying facts: the dishonesty of a number of judges, clientelism and political pressures – three issues that could indicate their preoccupation with deeper problems, particularly corruption both in the law and policy making, and in the adjudication process. Unfortunately, judges have not directly rejected corruption by external actors; perhaps because some may benefit from this situation.[369] I will come back to this issue later. However, the reason judges do not speak up could also be out of fear. There is plenty of evidence to support this claim, beginning with their concern for the lack of security for members of the judiciary expressed in the 1997 survey. Clearly, a major issue for the Colombian judges was, and still is, their personal security.[370] Not many commentators have actually mentioned this issue, nor have they referred to it as a serious threat to the impartiality of the administration of justice; yet some of the judges I interviewed felt seriously intimidated. In addition, the few that could had left the country. I had to use a written questionnaire because I was unable to interview personally a *fiscal sin rostro* dealing with the infamous *Proceso 8000*, because of threats made against her.[371] The number of victims among the judiciary suffering at the hands of drug traffickers and other criminals is extremely high and from 1979, violence against judges and lawyers began to have important connotations. For instance, in the period 1979–91, there were 515 cases of violence against judges and lawyers of which 329 were homicides or life threats.[372] This signifies that during this period, 40 judges or lawyers annually were the victims of some type of violence and, of those 40, 25 suffered life threats or were assassinated.[373] These numbers include a large proportion of the members of the Supreme Court of Justice, 11 out of 12 magistrates, and the Consejo de Estado assassinated in the Toma del Palacio de Justicia in 1985.[374] Between 1994 and 1998 there were 132 cases of violence against judges, *fiscales* and clerks (including members of the Procuraduría). These 132 cases of violence included 82 assassinations, 28 threats and 22 kidnappings.[375] Further victims related to the system of justice included a Procurador General and two Ministers of Justice.[376] Probably the closest similar case is that of Italy at the beginning of the 1980s, where several judges were threatened and assassinated for investigating drugs-related activities.[377] Moreover, at least 25.4 per cent of judges experienced a threat against their own personal safety or that of their families. This explains why in August 1989, after the charismatic presidential candidate Luis Carlos Galán was murdered (allegedly by the Medellín Cartel), 20000 members of ASONAL staged a three-day strike protesting against the government's lack of judicial protection.[378]

A more recent example of the judges' generalised fear is the resignation of many of the 38 former *jueces sin rostro* who, since July 1999, have become ordinary judges.[379] The extreme degree of vulnerability of the judges is also shown in the 1997 survey that demonstrates that 68 per cent of the judges have been affected by a homicide of someone close to them in the last five-year period.[380] This percentage is higher than that of the population of the most violent regions (60 per cent), and higher than the national average (44 per cent). Consequently, judges as a social group carry more guns than the rest of the population: 29 per cent of judges are armed, as against 11 per cent of the general population.[381]

Up until 1989 the only response of the state to counteract the risk of administering justice was life insurance for every member of the judiciary and the Procuraduría. Suffice it to say that this insurance was not geared to protect the life of judges, but rather to provide their relatives with a monetary and symbolic compensation in the event of their death or handicap. In addition, in 1989, a state-of-siege decree created the National Security Trust of the judiciary for the construction and acquisition of buildings and elements geared to the protection of judges and members of the judiciary.[382] Not much is known of the structure and functioning of the Trust due to its secret character. However, most judges and clerks interviewed coincide in their claim that security conditions for justice personnel are still precarious, particularly outside the big cities. So far, the only beneficiaries of the Trust have been the magistrates of the high courts, a few magistrates of the district tribunals of Bogotá and the capital cities of each department as well as members of the recently abolished *Justicia sin rostro*.

The evidence reveals that in Colombia the controversial *Justicia sin rostro* mechanism offered significant protection for some judges. According to Ministry of Justice statistics, from the introduction of the Regional Justice Statute in 1991 and until December 1996, only two faceless judges were actually assassinated. Consequently, those who defended the mechanism argued that, since the introduction of the *Justicia sin rostro*, it had become more difficult to kill or bribe judges and that this implied that the general conditions for administering justice had improved. Those who opposed the *Justicia sin rostro* demonstrated that on the contrary it violated the rights and liberties of the accused and showed, after a careful analysis of its performance, that this type of justice was in fact as inefficient as that of the traditional courts.[383] Others argued, with some cynicism, that there was no such as thing as a faceless judge, since most names could be found out fairly easily. In spite of these claims and data, there is also evidence – backed by an intelligence report in December 1995 – which demonstrates that a group of congressmen tried – on three occasions and without success – to abolish the *Justicia sin rostro* through clandestine legislative 'micos'.[384] This suggests that this type of justice could be inefficient in terms of numbers, but precisely effective against some of those who had managed to remain on the margins of the law through various forms of intimidation and corruption. Some examples are the 7 leaders of the Cali Cartel who are in jail and several other important drug traffickers who have been extradited to the United States or are in the process of being so.

Due to the controversies of the *Justicia sin rostro*, in particular the violations to the rights of the accused caused by the secrecy of the judges and the witnesses, and the shorter legal terms, in June 1999 a law (Ley 504/1999) abolished it and most of its controversial procedures (in particular the anonymity of the judges) and replaced it by a Special Justice Statute. For a while, some of the special procedures of the abolished *Justicia sin rostro* remained, such as some sort of exceptional reserve regarding the names of certain judges who were particularly vulnerable. Important changes also took place, however, in particular the crime of rebellion, a conduct that usually involves members of the fighting guerrillas, was transferred to the competency of ordinary judges, putting these judges in turn in a particularly vulnerable position.

Controversy over the Special Justice Statute began shortly after it was enacted because many argued that this type of justice was only a 'disguised form of *Justicia sin rostro*'. After 5 citizens' petitions of unconstitutionality in April 2000, the constitutional court held that the most relevant parts of the Special Justice Statute were indeed unconstitutional.[385] Its abolition could be interpreted in different ways. In practical terms it implies one more victory for the powerful criminals, those who have no interest in a system of justice that can challenge their traditional impunity.[386] In fact, the unconstitutionality of the Special Justice Statute forced a massive release of extremely dangerous criminals for procedural reasons (such as shorter terms of prosecution) while leaving in jail prisoners who were guilty of petty offences. These latter prisoners were the cause of overcrowding and were precisely the ones who should have been released from prison since they posed little threat to society. In Antioquia, since the abolition of the *Justicia sin rostro*, one former *fiscal sin rostro* and two *fiscales seccionales* belonging to it have been assassinated and seven *fiscales* have been forced into exile, while a non-specified number of the *Seccional Fiscalía* of Medellín were forced to resign under threats. In addition, 12 members of the CTI have been murdered and there was an attack on the *Fiscalía Delegada ante el Gaula* (the Anti-kidnapping Unit) where another *fiscal* was assassinated.[387]

Another related issue is the motive behind the threats made to the judges and their families as well as the high number of assassinations of judges. Data from the Comisión Andina de Juristas, Bogotá, suggests that the violence against judges is mainly caused by the paramilitary, drug traffickers, guerrillas, agents of the state, common criminals and private individuals.[388] According to the Comisión Andina, this violence is mainly related to the adjudication process in cases where corruption, fraud and extortion are involved or in cases involving human rights' violations, extradition and homicides.[389] In spite of the fact that it has been suggested that guerrilla violence against judges has been less pervasive than that of the drug traffickers, it is also a phenomenon that has received less attention and is less well documented.[390] The motives behind guerrilla violence against judges appear to be those of replacing state justice with their own. This situation became clearer after 1999 in the demilitarised zone or *despeje* where judges and *fiscales* were forced to abandon the area.[391] The FARC guerrillas made it more than clear that they were 'the authority' in the *despeje*.[392] Such a situation suggests that guerrilla violence against judges occurs mainly in those areas of Colombia where these groups have a military and territorial presence. The latter represent considerable areas of the country (see Map 4.1).

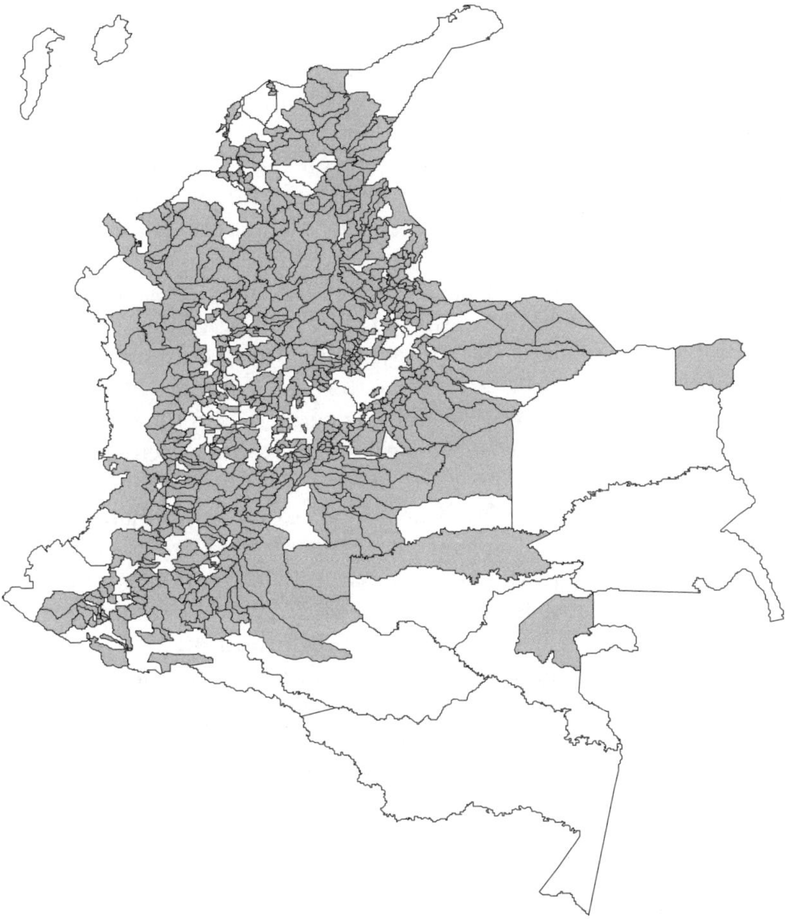

Map 4.1 Guerrilla locations in Colombia

There are perhaps many other motives behind the violence against judges, but there is still a kind of *omerta* around this topic. Extraordinary events such as that of the *Toma del Palacio de Justicia* in 1985 – where most of the magistrates of the Supreme Court of Justice and some from the Consejo de Estado were killed in an attempt to eradicate extradition, one of the main motives – also account for some of the assassinations. The judges whom I asked preferred to remain silent; some were too anxious to talk. Suffice it to say that judges cannot continue to be lonely heroes in a political system that is incapable of giving them physical and moral protection. As Brecht once claimed: 'Unhappy is the land that needs heroes'.[393]

To summarise, the low perception of the system of justice and its judges is clearly the result of the system's poor performance and the lack of impartiality and inequality of the adjudication process. However, all these issues should be discussed in the context of fear: the fear to accuse and the fear to prosecute. In the former case, surveys and testimonial evidence reveal that the fear of reprisal by victims and witnesses of certain crimes is strong and responds to powerful forces. The fear to prosecute is revealed by statistical data on the number of assassinated or threatened judges, and is also suggested by analysis of the surveys. Fear among judges threatens their impartiality. The precariousness of the Colombian state has failed to remove the causes of fear – in many areas of the country where alternative orders operate, fear is the rule that governs societal exchanges. However, fear also pervades the cities and areas of the country where the state is present. This fear among people is demonstrated via the surveys. However, its extent is still hard to determine. Unlike the case of judges, where there is statistical data concerning judges' deaths and kidnappings that fully justify the fear registered in the survey data, it is very difficult to carry out a similar analysis for ordinary citizens. Fear also generates distrust in the state – a lack of legitimacy – since it makes people aware of the state's incapacity to protect them, and in particular its lack of autonomy. Fear-to-accuse and fear-to-prosecute are relatively new issues in the Colombian criminal jurisdiction. Only in the 1980s, as analysed in Chapter 6, does fear become a weapon of the armed actors (including some state agents) in order to silence judges and witnesses. Yet fear is so pervasive that it impedes the consolidation of democracy as well as the efficiency and legitimacy of the system of justice.

5
Judicial Corruption: Heroes and Villains

This chapter analyses the issue of judicial corruption. First there is an attempt to measure the level of corruption in the judiciary to identify the extent of the phenomenon and some of its causes. Then the difficulties of controlling a specific case of judicial corruption are discussed. The chapter demonstrates that, despite the existence of the legal possibility for controlling judicial corruption, the system of justice is subverted by overwhelming forces that impede impartial control – the state is either too embattled to secure the protection of its judges or too instrumental in the process to provide for impartial judicial control of corruption. Hence corruption, which in the Colombian context is critically linked to fear, is symptomatic of the state's weaknesses and the political system's own corruption.

The extent of judicial corruption

It is in fact very difficult to prove the existence of corruption since its immediate effects are often invisible and in most cases the victims of corruption are rarely aware of it. In addition, since both the corrupter and the corrupted usually benefit from corruption, it is unlikely that they will confess their corrupt conduct – especially as there is only rarely a direct witness or someone to 'whistle-blow'. In most cases, therefore, the evidence needed to prove the existence of corruption is secondhand. With these difficulties in mind we are faced with the issue of whether it is possible to measure the level of corruption in the Colombian system of justice. The evidence suggests that one way of measuring the corruption of judges is to use the existing judicial and disciplinary statistics in those cases of corruption that have gone through the system of justice. Since in the case of Colombia such statistical data is poor and incomplete,

I have used other complementary sources to measure judges' corruption, such as surveys, cases and personal interviews. The evidence shows that, although the results of such measurement are far from exact, they represent a useful way to analyse the incidence of corruption in the Colombian judiciary and also, in some cases, a way of identifying the causes of judges' corruption.

With regard to the statistical data in cases of judges' corruption, I reviewed the existing judicial statistics. However, it is very difficult to assess the general level of corruption in the Colombian judiciary from the judicial statistics that exist. Apart from the statistical deficiencies themselves, the recording of corruption is perhaps the most deficient in the whole field of Colombian statistics. Moreover, the few existing judicial statistics on corruption fail to distinguish whether the plaintiff is a private individual or a public official. In other words, it is impossible to determine from the existing statistics whether the corruption cases involve judges at all. Hence from a criminal perspective, at least up to 1998, it is hard to establish how many judges or members of the judiciary, such as clerks or assistants to the courts, have committed crimes that can be classified as corruption. From a disciplinary point of view, data exist which indicate what the Procuraduría interpreted as cases of 'corruption' of judges and members of the judiciary for the period 1991–93. Before analysing the data of the Procuraduría's report, therefore, I discuss some characteristics of 30 cases of 'corruption' on which the Procuraduría ruled between 1990 and 1996 in order to understand the type of control that this body exercised over judges and clerks, and what it defined as corruption.[394] In most of the cases to which I was allowed access, the Procuraduría defined inefficiency as corruption. This inefficiency mainly took the form of unjustified delay[395] in the administration of justice by the competent judge or a clerk of the judge's office.[396] A typical case of delay challenged by the Procuraduría is when a judge investigating a particular case leaves it inactive for a period of a year or more without any legal justification. From the cases reviewed, I could only trace one straightforward case of delay caused by corruption in that sense.[397] The Procuraduría, inexplicably, also defines inefficiency in the administration of justice as cases where judges or clerks violate the law or the Constitution. Among the cases of law violation that I reviewed only one could be interpreted as corrupt.[398]

With the aim of finding out more about the level of corruption of judges and clerks from a disciplinary perspective, I carried out two personal interviews with members of the Procuraduría.[399] I was told by both that there had been some complaints of bribes and intimidation of judges, but that these cases were very difficult to prove and, therefore, most never even got as far as preliminary investigation. According to the two clerks interviewed, those who engage in corruption in the system of justice are mostly lawyers.[400] Another clerk of the Procuraduría made the following claim (using an extremely ironic tone) when I asked about the presence of corruption in the system of justice: 'the system of justice has always been immoral. The difference is that today you need to convince [bribe, or threaten?] six clerks who deal with a case, whereas before you only needed to influence the judge'.[401]

In a more informal conversation with another member of the Procuraduría, I asked whether corruption at the level of the judge was common, and what the members of his office understood as corruption.[402] The first answer clearly revealed that he, and consequently many other members of the Procuraduría, were well aware of what judges' corruption meant – mainly a public office definition approach – and that they clearly distinguished it from inefficiency resulting from excessive backlog.[403] During the course of the conversation, it also became clear that the control of judges, whether from corruption or other disciplinary offences, was as inefficient as the 'inefficiency' of the judges they were trying to control. Overall, the evidence suggests that the lack of control of judges stems from several factors: firstly, judges are perceived as generally less corrupt than other public officials.[404] Secondly, procedural deficiencies of the system – for instance the fact that the Procuraduría lacked the hierarchical power to take the final decision on whether to penalise the judge or clerk – were also considered as limitations to the investigation of the full extent of the corruption of judges. As happens often in Colombia, many controls exist, yet these are more formal than actual.[405] The 1991 Constitution tried to resolve the Procuraduría's problem by giving it full power to discipline judges and sanction them directly. Yet the 1991 Constitution also assigned the disciplinary function of judges to two different bodies of the system of justice, namely the Procuraduría and the Consejo Superior de la Judicatura. As a result, the 1991 Constitution, whether intentionally or not, recreated similar problems to those which existed before, since both the Procuraduría and the Consejo Superior now claim exclusive jurisdiction over the disciplinary control of judges. Since the competence over the control of judges was not clearly defined, this tension has meant, at least until 1998, that the Consejo Superior decided internally that they would discipline judges and that the Procuraduría would control judicial clerks.[406] Thirdly, the Procuraduría clerk spoke of a general 'unwillingness' by the members of the institution to discipline certain corrupt judges because of a feeling of solidarity.[407] Overall, the problems of judges' corruption did not appear to worry the members of the Procuraduría and most cases investigated by this agency appeared to be isolated ones. Indeed, the mere absence of a disciplinary definition of corruption, contrary to what happens in criminal law, shows how little commitment there is in the Procuraduría to control judges' corruption.

Accordingly, the data supplied in the 'Corruption Report' by the Procuraduría reveals the marginality of the judges' control. Indeed, from 1991 until the end of 1993, the Procuraduría investigated 84 members of the judiciary for inefficiency in the administration of justice, of whom 20 were judges.[408] The Procuraduría's 'corruption' data also showed that 25 members of the judiciary were penalised in the period 1991–93 – a total that does not distinguish between judges and clerks. Finally, the Procuraduría's report showed that only 1 of the 25 penalties actually ended in the sacking of a judge, while the remainder involved fines and temporary suspensions from duties.[409] Most of this statistical evidence corroborates my empirical finding: most corruption cases that are subject to disciplinary proceedings are really cases of petty inefficiency and, consequently, only a few judges are disciplined for corruption.

The Consejo Superior created by the 1991 Constitution began its disciplinary functions in 1992. In its report[410] for the period 1992–96 it stated that 7 judges were disciplined in 1992, 62 in 1993 and 74 in 1994.[411] The most common disciplinary faults throughout the 1992–96 period were related to delay or omission in judicial duties (25.8 per cent) and violations of the law and the Constitution (37 per cent). In contrast with the Procuraduría, the Consejo Superior did not refer to these activities as corruption. According to a magistrate of the Consejo Superior, the number of complaints against judges has had a tendency to increase since the creation of the Consejo Superior, probably due to subsequent publicity and the knowledge that the public has recently acquired concerning the possibilities for controlling judges. In 1996, for instance, there were 635 complaints (mainly from the public) in the form of letters, telephone calls or even anonymous communications. I was told that all of these complaints were actually investigated.[412] The Consejo Superior's data, like the Procuraduría's, do not seem to include disciplinary control over activities that could be considered as corruption. In June 1999 I asked to see the statistics on disciplined judges to date. After several weeks and some formalities, I was given general information about the numbers (not the conduct) of disciplined lawyers and judges; this did not reveal much other than lawyers are still punished six times more than judges.[413] In fact, when asked specifically about the way in which the Consejo Superior could discipline a corrupt judge (the legal approach), the magistrate interviewed answered in an ambiguous way and evaded the question. From my experience in interviewing members of the judiciary, the topic of corruption, with few exceptions, is still taboo and even more so when it involves corruption of judges. As in the case of the Procuraduría, it is likely that most cases of judicial corruption do not even reach the system. Hence, as with the Procuraduría's data, it is hard to infer from the Consejo Superior's data the level of judges' corruption: firstly, because the Consejo Superior's report presents the same definitional problems as the Procuraduría's report, not even mentioning the word corruption; secondly, because I did not have access to specific cases that have been subject to disciplinary proceedings by the Consejo Superior; thirdly, because since 1993 a decision of the Consejo Superior held that cases of law violation could only be disciplined if they were the result of deceit.[414] In other words, the Consejo Superior does not consider violation of the law from mere negligence by public officials of the judiciary to be a disciplinary fault.[415] This qualification will only lessen the already deficient control of judges' conduct since it is difficult to provide evidence of subjective behaviour such as that which implies a distinction between negligence and deceit. Finally, the level of corruption is hard to infer because the disciplinary jurisdiction of the Consejo Superior is even more congested and less efficient than that of ordinary jurisdiction.[416] Data from October 1993 show that the Consejo Superior started with an inventory of 5575 disciplinary investigations, and that 13 191 new investigations entered the system of which only 5266 were resolved definitively: that is, 13 500 investigations (more than the ones that entered the system) were left unsolved.[417] According to a Contraloría audit of 1997, the index of accumulation of the disciplinary jurisdiction in charge of the Consejo Superior since its creation is of approximately 60 per cent, as compared with the ordinary jurisdiction which adds up to 16 per cent. Overall, the disciplinary data tell us little either about the level of judicial corruption or its causes. What the Consejo Superior data does tell is that there is an absence of awareness of corruption precisely from the one entity in charge of the control of the judges' conduct and clearly this is a matter of concern.

In spite of the fact that there are no official judicial statistics giving the percentage of corruption cases[418] involving judges in Colombia, an investigation by the Universidad Externado de Colombia offers some relevant data in this respect.[419] From the Externado's investigation we can tentatively infer a general view of the incidence of corrupt conduct by judges from 1980 until 1991.[420] This investigation analysed 1000 cases that reached the Supreme Court of Justice. The evidence showed that many legal proceedings took up to eight years in the judge's office.[421] Independently of whether or not these delays are cases of corruption, the scarcity of cases in which the Procuraduría had disciplined judges for this 'delay' corroborates the view that the disciplinary control over judges has been weak and, in most cases, almost non-existent. In addition, many of the cases analysed by the Externado investigation revealed that lawyers are accomplices or major agents of judicial corruption: lawyers force their cases in the direction of a particular judge; they are often the initiators of extortion; they falsify documents, carry out procedural frauds and initiate reckless lawsuits.[422] In some cases lawyers accuse judges without good cause in order to intimidate them into following their 'instructions'. In others, lawyers make 'arrangements' with the judge to share the profits of the contested goods, something which occurs mainly in civil and labour cases.[423] The level of corruption of the lawyers identified in this research is corroborated by some statistical data for the years 1992–96 from the Consejo Superior de la Judicatura. These statistics reveal that, in this period, 1989 lawyers were penalised, of which 28.1 per cent were penalised for corruption-related causes.[424] For a country where the levels of impunity, particularly at the disciplinary level, are so high, these statistics suggest that the actual number of corrupt activities by lawyers (there were more than 80 000 registered lawyers in 1996) could be significantly higher. The Externado investigation concludes that there is a high and worrying level of judicial corruption. However, a detailed analysis of the 108 documented cases of the study reveals several factors that need to be taken into account before reaching any conclusion. First, only 42 of the 108 cases are of judicial corruption, that is 38.8 per cent. Only 15 of these 42 cases were corruption by criminal judges or their clerks, whereas the rest were by civil judges or their clerks.[425] If the pattern is similar for the remaining 892 cases which were not documented, there will have been less than 400 cases of judicial corruption in the criminal jurisdiction in the period 1980–91. This could imply that judicial corruption is not so generalised as has been thought, and that it is definitely not systemic. Second, among these 42 cases, nine were cases of clerks' corruption. Clerks were also accomplices of corruption in some of the 33 judges' cases. This could support Procuraduría evidence where clerks are found to be more corrupt than judges. Third, many cases of unjustified delay are cases were there is usually a lawyer as an accomplice of corruption. This data reiterates former evidence, which shows that lawyers are often the initial perpetrators of judicial corruption. Fourth, between the lines of the

Externado main conclusions, it is suggested that judicial corruption often results from improvisation, ignorance, negligence and the lack of a good legal education in the case of both clerks and judges. These are not excuses for corrupt behaviour, but it certainly helps to qualify some of the motives behind judicial corruption. Fifth and more importantly, most of the 42 cases of judicial corruption were cases of petty corruption. By this, I am not discrediting the Supreme Court judgment or the criteria of the Externado investigators, but only pointing out that cases of intimidating judges to change the course of justice or systematic corrupt practices by judges are but seldom present in the Externado data. These five factors could imply several things: first, that although there is some level of judicial corruption it is not systemic. It could also mean that there is a fair amount of corruption that is not reported or investigated, precisely because the system itself is inefficient and impunity is so high. It could also indicate that those judicial corruption cases that reach the system are the petty cases since the most serious ones actually manage to escape and hence 'corrupt' the capacity of the system to investigate them. The latter reinforces an earlier claim on the triviality of the offences that usually reach the system of justice (the minimising of justice trend).

Surveys are another source for the measurement of corruption, serving at least as indicators and sources to corroborate the scarce statistical data that actually exists. In 1968, a national survey revealed that 68 per cent of those interviewed thought that judges could be bribed. Two decades later, in 1986, another survey showed that 88 per cent of the adult population thought that judges could be bribed.[426] Even though these results did not coincide entirely with the opinion of judges (only 26.7 per cent of the judges interviewed acknowledged that they had indeed been bribed), they suggest that as early as 1968 bribes to judges were already an issue of concern among the public.[427] It is worth stressing that, in spite of these two surveys' reference to bribes, the issue of corruption among judges is not discussed in the mainstream literature on the subject (or in any other survey) until the mid-1990s.[428] In this decade, corruption becomes a main concern in Colombia, mainly as a result of the anti-corruption campaigns around the world in the 1980s and 1990s. This global anti-corruption movement hit Colombia largely as a result of a process of contagion. In Colombia, corruption became an issue at the beginning of the 1990s mainly because the Gaviria administration, 1990–94, felt the need to be recognised internationally after a severe and visible penetration of drug traffic money into the political sphere and also because the administration's economic model was incompatible with the costs of corruption. Amongst the effects of the Gaviria moralisation campaign was an unprecedented boom of surveys related to corruption. In general, these surveys initially excluded corruption in justice as a specific topic of concern, with the exception of two: the 1994 and 1997 surveys. It could also be that justice was deliberately excluded from most corruption interviews because it did not appear to be a major problem.[429] It could also be due to the generalised conviction that the problem of justice was its inefficiency and that this distracted the courts from corruption-related surveys until the mid-1990s.

The evidence from the 1994 public-perception survey of the administration of justice reveals that both the general public and users of the system of justice perceived a relatively high incidence of corruption of judges. The 1994 survey, which is arguably one of the most comprehensive and technical surveys on the perception of the administration of justice,[430] revealed some important data on the level of corruption of the judiciary.[431] I divide the results of the 1994 survey into three parts. First, the general perception of judges' honesty and the type of corruption that seems to prevail; second, discrimination in the administration of justice; and third, the influence of the media on the administration of justice. All three issues relate to corruption and can serve as indicators of the level of corruption in the judiciary. With regard to the level of judges' honesty, the results of the interviews suggest that users of the system thought that 87.7 per cent of judges accepted bribes, whereas the general population perceived this possibility as even higher (96.8 per cent).[432] Another result relating to corruption which appears to confirm this opinion was the following: when asked how many judges in every 10 they thought accepted bribes, users said 5.2 and the general public 6.[433] The assistants or clerks in the judges' office were perceived as more corrupt than the judges – this opinion coincided with statistical data from the Procuraduría and Consejo Superior. It is interesting to note that most of those interviewed said that they had heard of cases of corruption in the judiciary but most denied direct knowledge of specific cases, perhaps to avoid acknowledging any participation or complicity on their part. Most interviewed also recognised the corruptive power of organised crime in the administration of justice in the last two decades: 'Yes, undoubtedly there are pressures … in the first place there are all sorts of criminal organisations; secondly, since people have lost their trust in the system of justice, they have taken justice with their own hands … it is the world of threats and *sicarios* that is growing in this country …'.[434]

In fact, one of the experts consulted in the 1994 survey claimed that in cases where drug trafficking was involved, corruption was very common. In his opinion, other types of crimes such as homicide or robbery involved a lower incidence of corruption, mainly, he argued, because the level of impunity was so high in these cases that it overrode any possible interest in corruption. Other experts' opinions in relation to corruption suggest that the level of corruption in the judiciary is due not to a high number of dishonest judges but rather to a minority of audacious judges who compromise the prestige of the whole system of justice. This seems to be an opinion shared by the judges. The 1994 survey's data also reveal that when talking about corruption it is crucial to differentiate between pressures, threats and offers (bribes). What these have in common is that they are all ways of getting people to do things. However, the mechanism to persuade the recipient to comply in each of these cases differs and so does the level of its usefulness.[435] In the case of offers, there is no coercion. Moreover, offers presuppose and cannot be effective without, some minimum shared values or expectations on the part of the recipient. In the case of pressures, some form of coercion may be present. In addition, in the cases of both offers and pressures there is no penalty if the recipient does not comply, and in the case of offers there is an actual benefit in complying. On the contrary, threats and what have become known in the literature as throffers (threats with offers) are cases were the recipient is forced (or coerced) to do something, since his non-compliance entails a penalty: '... a rational individual would prefer not to be the recipient of a threat (whether or not he thinks he would comply) whereas he would generally be willing to have offers made to him and would not regret their having been made ...'.[436]

Corruption can occur as a result of pressures, offers, threats and throffers. The evidence from the 1994 survey shows that in Colombia pressures and threats are more common than offers (bribes). There is no particular reference to throffers. For instance, many testimonies from the interviewees acknowledged that judges who had been menaced had often been assassinated or had to flee the country. In addition, many testimonies by retired judges claimed that they had heard or had had direct knowledge of threats or pressures: 'One speaks and hears of pressures. In my personal case I have never had offers or threats fortunately. But I do know that for many judges and clerks these have cost them their life or posts. ... Each court is another world'.[437] 'It happened to me when I was a local *fiscal*, I was threatened. I also know that another judicial clerk has received threats related to a particular case that is being prosecuted.

There have been extremes in which the judge has had to ask for bodyguards or a license to go abroad ...'.[438]

Clearly, organised crime in Colombia, in particular drug trafficking, has used its intimidating power of violence to discourage lawsuits from being brought before the judiciary, as shown earlier when analysing the issue of judges' security. It is publicly known that at the end of the 1980s the members of the judiciary were subjected to what has been called the option of the two metals: '*plata o plomo*' (silver or lead). The booming drug trafficking 'industry' has allowed those involved enough power and money to buy or target any judge or policemen. The power of drug traffickers is overwhelming as the following episodes show. During my brief fieldwork in Cali, the director of *Fiscalía Regional*, Felipe López, was dealing with the preliminary investigation and prosecution of the now-imprisoned and convicted bosses of the Cali Cartel. Although he gave me little information on these cases, he did acknowledge that he had received several calls from Cali Cartel members. My perception was that López was scared. He continually changed cars, did not stop at red lights, and had never spent a weekend in Cali during his two years in the *Fiscalía*. A year after leaving the *Fiscalía*, López was murdered in Bogotá. All the evidence suggests that his assassination was ordered by the Cali Cartel. His case is under investigation. Also, in a personal interview with a former *fiscal sin rostro*, I was told that she was sacked from the *Fiscalía* after having been in the judiciary for more than 17 years (six as a *fiscal sin rostro*) because she was handling a drug-trafficking case and had complained about being subjected to pressures to handle the case in a partial way. In her words: 'a rich, corrupt delinquent has more power over the *cúpula* (meaning the "powerful ones"), than a poor honest *fiscal* who has served for almost two decades with an impeccable curriculum vitae'.[439]

The 1994 survey also indicates that the type of threats and pressures applied often depend on the socio-economic level of the defendant involved in the judicial proceeding. There is general agreement among those interviewed that pressures or threats are not applied by plaintiffs or accused belonging to lower socio-economic levels of society, who tend rather to use bribes (offers). On the other hand, people of higher social, economic or political status often apply direct pressures in preference to bribes. A testimony of a former *fiscal sin rostro* is very revealing in this respect, '... when you deal with white-collar criminality there are no threats, the demands are clear and direct. That excess of power can be intimidating ...'.[440] Moreover, people with economic means who are accused of serious crimes tend to employ threats, as various testimonies from the 1994 survey revealed, although this type of conduct has not as yet been quantified.[441] Some even mention the existence of pressures applied to the judiciary from other state institutions. The following testimony exemplifies this situation. 'Undoubtedly there are more pressures and threats than bribes. There are lots of threats from criminal organisations to the members of the judiciary. Something really worrying is that amongst what I call qualified criminal organisations, in many cases we have detected the participation of members of the armed forces against the *fiscales*. This has not been measured or quantified'.[442]

A second issue relating to dishonesty of judges was analysed in the 1994 survey; this is the issue of discrimination in the administration of justice. The majority of those interviewed agreed that discrimination in the treatment of the parties involved was common in the administration of justice. For instance, amongst users of the system, 76.2 per cent claimed that there was preferential treatment for some parties in the following order: first, those plaintiffs and accused that had higher economic positions or resources; second, those having influential positions; and third, friends of the judges. In addition, the survey (39 per cent of the users of the system believed this) showed that judicial cases involving large sums of money were also treated preferentially – the survey data does not specify whether preferential treatment was within the case or between cases but I suspect that both are common.[443] When asked about the objectivity of the procedures, 85.9 per cent claimed that equity only prevailed when the 'value' of the dispute was considerable. This evidence supports earlier claims of what I have called class justice.

A third issue, which could be related to the dishonesty of judges, is the influence of the media in the administration of justice. Some experts claimed that the importance given by judges to cases involving prominent political or economic figures was more the result of media attention, hence public opinion 'interest' in the particular case.[444] The most influential media in Colombia are owned by large economic or political conglomerates, as in most parts of the world. Understandably, most of the users who were interviewed (89 per cent) claimed that the system of justice was, in some cases, subject to the pressures of the media. With regard to the question of how the media influenced the system of justice, the general public responded as follows: first, that it accelerated procedures (44.2 per cent); second, that the media reported only certain types of cases (32.9 per cent); and third, that it only revealed irregularities in a subset of these cases (20.3 per cent).[445] According to the experts, how the media reports can either generate or diminish credibility in the system of justice. In Colombia, both a democratic and a 'show' media coexist; both seem to exert pressure on the administration of justice and its results. This situation is by no means exclusive to Colombia; for instance, in the case of France during the de Gaulle and Pompidou administrations, the television media were under the control of the President. During Giscard d'Estaing's administration, this control was replaced by patronage: associates of the President were put in charge of television and radio organisations.[446]

According to the experts interviewed in the 1994 survey, in Colombia the pressure of the media on the administration of justice is enormous. In their view, the influence of the media often distorts the image of the system of justice since it lacks objectivity, veracity, impartiality and propriety.[447] Some journalists share this opinion concerning the lack of veracity and objectivity of the information transmitted by the Colombian media. Antonio Caballero, for instance, claims that before *Proceso 8000* it was perceived as almost subversive to report truthfully about violence, corruption or drug trafficking.[448] With similar arguments to those of Caballero's, some of those interviewed excused the judges for many of their questionable decisions, blaming their lack of impartiality on the media – itself a representative of 'the powerful groups' – which they felt manipulated the administration of justice. The following testimony of a judge is very revealing: 'It is a vicious circle: once the opinion is formed on a case it is very difficult for the judge to change it ... I have had many experiences where the media stated its opinion on a particular case and then did everything possible to maintain it ...'.[449]

There is an additional factor to take into account in the Colombian case: the media are very powerful compared with the public opinion. Hence the media can affect the system of justice's performance since, in some cases, it can make it difficult for the judge to remain impartial. This is revealed by the following testimony of one particular *fiscal*: 'When the media pressures too much a particular proceeding, it is a case where the member of the judiciary, consciously or unconsciously, will pay more attention and sometimes these pressures could threaten his impartiality. Consciously because he reaches the expected decision to avoid responsibility in front of the public opinion or the press. Unconsciously sometimes for the sake of protagonism or even for opportunities to be quoted in the press'.[450] Since the media are generally more concerned with commercial interests, they want the best and newest story; therefore their capacity as impartial reporters is often very limited. In Colombia, however, it is possible for the media, as well as other institutional and non-institutional actors, to influence the administration of justice: it appears that the whole system of justice has become porous to the influence of other forces. Yet in most cases it is hard to prove that this influence can become a case of corruption: contrary to what the 1994 survey suggests.

One of the most recent surveys on corruption corroborates some of the data of the 1994 survey while also introducing new variables for the interpretation of judicial corruption. The 1997 survey shows that among the different sectors of society the proportion of judges (30 per cent) who think that the first priority for the country in the next 10 years is to fight corruption almost doubles compared to that of the rest of society who are equally concerned with unemployment, the guerrillas and the ongoing violence.[451] More than 60 per cent of the population think that most or the majority of public officials are involved with corruption. By contrast, only 26 per cent of the judges think this way. However, all sectors agree, judges included, that corruption only benefits a few. The 1997 survey also shows that judges and teachers are the two social groups who most often visit the elected members of local councils and members of Congress. In the case of the judges, visits to members of Congress for 'personal reasons' are the most common. However, the percentage of judges who visit members of Congress is not particularly high in relative terms.[452] The evidence of the 1997 survey suggests that, although there is a generalised perception of a judge's corruption, judges too are victims of this corruption, and there is little they can do about it. The generalised view is that the beneficiaries of corruption are but few and the high percentages of judges who rank corruption as the most pressing problem for the country support the latter claim. From the 1997 survey it can also be inferred that judges' visits to members of Congress, visits which could question their independence and thus indicate possible corrupt exchanges between politicians and judges, is not generalised. Hence in accordance with other 1997 survey results, the percentage of judges that benefit from a politician's corruption are only a few – this if we assume that corrupt exchanges arise from these visits.

Clearly, the measurement of corruption analysed above is useful in attempting to gauge the incidence of corruption in the judiciary. The statistical data is inadequate and reveals only a small incidence of corruption of judges. However, in the case of Colombia, the levels of corruption may not actually be reflected in such statistical evidence, particularly if we analyse this data in conjunction with two proven facts: the levels of impunity are high and corruption in Colombia, already inherently difficult to prove, leaves few traces since it seems to prevail in the form of threats and pressures, both of which are almost invisible actions. This would suggest that there might be a high incidence of corruption among judges. Judging these factors in conjunction with personal interviews, case studies and the surveys, there appear to be two opposing conclusions. On the one hand, the Externado case study and the 1997 survey suggest that judicial corruption is not systemic. The existing criminal and disciplinary statistics of corruption support this claim. By contrast, the 1994 survey, analysed in conjunction with most of the personal interviews and with the data on judges' intimidation, appears to suggest otherwise. The latter reveal that the level of judicial corruption is very high and that the corruption that exists, most of which is obviously not reported, is extremely threatening, and usually comes from outside the judiciary.

Two preliminary conclusions can be drawn from the existing evidence. A first conclusion is that, in spite of the fact that there appears to be a high level of judicial corruption, it is not systemic. The problem with judicial corruption, however, is that it is highly pervasive because the judiciary is supposed to provide an essential check on other public institutions. 'A fair and efficient judiciary is the key to an anticorruption plan, and corruption in the judiciary should therefore dealt with from the start'.[453] Consequently, in spite of the fact that judicial corruption is less widespread, its effects can be more devastating for society than corruption from other political actors, not only in terms of the state legitimacy, but also as a deterrent for organised crime. 'Official corruption is an essential precondition for the growth of organized criminal groups with the capacity to pose a significant international security threat.... Where deterrence is weak, there is an opportunity for organized crime to develop. In extreme cases, as in Colombia, the response to this can be the emergence of vigilantism and paramilitarism'.[454]

A second preliminary conclusion is that much of the corruption amongst judges can be the product of pressures and threats coming from actors who are not part of the judiciary, such as members of Congress, lawyers, drug traffickers, the paramilitary, guerrillas or even members of the armed forces and state security agencies. This leads to a concern as to whether many judges, through the corrupted, are in fact coerced into corruption – that is, whether judges are themselves also victims of corruption. This interpretation arises from the following factors. The high level of corruption among lawyers as compared with that of judges suggests that powerful and often intimidating agents outside the system lead judges into corruption. In addition, the predominance of threats and pressures over bribes suggests that in many cases judges receive no direct gain from their 'corrupt' conduct – in many cases they lose, as in the *fiscal sin rostro* case, where the *fiscal* ignored the pressure being applied and ended up being sacked or, in the worst cases, when they are assassinated. In addition, the interpretation of judges as victims rather than perpetrators, comes from their own preoccupation with corruption, something that leads the majority of them (and twice the percentage of the general population) to rank the fight against corruption as a number one priority for the country in the next decade. Finally, and perhaps more importantly, the high degree of judges' intimidation reveals that judges as a group are directly threatened by corruption. Clearly, the results of corruption arising from offers and pressures or through threats or throffers are the same: corruption allows agencies other than the judges to make decisions, and consequently the system of justice fails to deliver effective and impartial decisions. However, the case of intimidation of judges poses a more serious problem: is it possible for the judges to administer justice at all? Even though there are several publicly known examples of heroic judges who openly defy these types of intimidation, it is perhaps unreasonable to expect that judges should put their families and personal security at risk when, in fact, the state is unable to protect them adequately and when, moreover, the political system is itself extremely corrupt.[455]

A perverted judicial control

The weak control of judges is another factor that helps to explain the perversity of judicial corruption. I discussed the general problem earlier while analysing the Procuraduría's deficient procedure of control of judges before the 1991 Constitution and the new problems that arose with the 1991 Constitution, mainly jurisdiction collusion between the Procuraduría and the Consejo Superior. I shall now briefly explain why the system of justice failed to exercise control in a particular case and why, in spite of the Consejo Superior's legal possibility of controlling the corruption of judges, the system seems to have failed in most cases.

The system of justice's lack of ability and will to sack or discipline a 'corrupt' judge became evident during a press scandal that developed in January 1997, after a *juez sin rostro* from Cali gave a sentence of 6 years' imprisonment to the two ex-bosses of the infamous Cali Cartel, Miguel and Gilberto Rodríguez Orejuela. The Cali judge allegedly selected and applied the most favourable laws from the existing criminal legislation, thereby managing to translate 20 years of criminal activities, related mainly to the trafficking of cocaine, into an extremely lenient sentence of six years. The incumbent Minister of Justice, Carlos Medellín, blamed the leniency of the sentence on the existing criminal legislation.

He argued that the lax sentence was the result of the PSJ, which was made law during the Gaviria administration.[456] The PSJ Statute was indeed the result of a commitment by the Gaviria administration to lower the penalties of the leaders of the Cali Cartel who were still free at the time, and other drug traffickers, in return for their surrender and further cooperation with the system of justice. The negotiation of the PSJ – understood by many as the surrender of the executive to drug interests and the usurpation of the Congress's original law-making power – went so far that American-style plea-bargaining and additional benefits, such as reduction of penalties for confession, were enacted by extraordinary decree (executive-made law) and became part of the criminal statutes. Neither the Rodríguez brothers nor other drug dealers surrendered, in spite of the soft laws passed during the Gaviria administration. The Samper administration, 1994–98, began its term of office faced with the scandal of the alleged use of drug-money in their campaign. In an effort to show the world, in particular the United States – which had threatened to decertify the country – that his administration was determined to fight the drug issue, Samper ordered the Elite Police Force (*Cuerpo Élite de la Policía*) to capture the Rodríguez brothers and other leaders of the Cartel.[457] Decertification involves not only the severing of diplomatic relations but also the imposition of (usually) economic sanctions. In spite of the Rodríguez' detention, however, the country was decertified for the first time in March 1996. Although it did not change the PSJ legislation, the Samper administration, fearing a second decertification, rushed approval of a 'package of laws' to confiscate the properties and goods of the drug bosses and increase some of the existing sanctions for crimes related to drug trafficking through Congress. Both laws were rapidly approved by Congress in this last, somewhat desperate, attempt to stop the imminent second decertification by the United States. On 1 March 1997, Colombia, together with countries such as Libya and Iraq, was decertified for only the second time in its history. The way in which the issue of the PSJ was handled exemplifies three characteristics of the Colombian system of justice which make control of the judges so difficult. First, it suggests that state autonomy is hostage to both external pressures, the drug traffickers' interests and international ones, mainly those of the United States. Hence, the system produces rules and legislation that are often incompatible with existing laws. For example, the bland PSJ legislation, favouring drug traffickers' interests, coexists with stronger legislation, 'imposed' by the United States. Secondly, a system of justice that has *carte blanche* to apply hard or soft laws breeds corruption since judicial control depends only on the personal criteria of each judge.

In the case of the Rodríguez brothers, the evidence shows that the system of justice could not discipline this judge since he had not acted illegally. In other words, in this case it was the political system that was corrupt and not the conduct of the judge. First, the judge could not be prosecuted because he had applied the existing law which, since the advent of the PSJ, allowed for the reduction of penalties. Secondly, the judge committed no crime in applying the lowest possible penalty since judges are autonomous in their decisions – a principle upheld in the constitutional court's jurisprudence on various occasions – and also because of the criminal principle of favourability of the laws.[458] Third, the judge was a faceless one – a device introduced to protect judges' security and impartiality, that is, to protect them against threats and bribes – the system would thus have been failing to protect this judge's impartiality if he was bribed or threatened, something for which there is no evidence as yet. To sum up, the judge's shortcomings were the result both of the existing rules and policies – that is, they were part of the existing legal political arrangements – and also, it seems, the incapacity of the system to enforce its own laws, in this case to protect the judge. Moreover, even though the judiciary in Colombia has shown signs of independence, it is a part of a state that is often compromised by particular interests and consequently has become less autonomous and legitimate. The danger is that this lack of autonomy and legitimacy of the political system can compromise the system of justice's own autonomy and legitimacy, as happened in the Rodríguez brothers' case.

The remaining control mechanism for the judge in the Rodríguez case was the disciplinary control exercised by the newly created Consejo Superior. I interviewed a magistrate of the Consejo Superior, asking her what they could do about this judge. She answered that they had no legal mechanisms with which to punish such an 'obviously' corrupt judge. The magistrate argued that, since 1995, when a new disciplinary statute was enacted to regulate the conduct of all public officials, all previous legal instruments which would have permitted the disbarring of the judge in question had been reformed.[459] In her opinion, the widening in the new 1995 disciplinary statute of activities that could be typified as disciplinary misdemeanours had led to the practical impossibility of sacking a corrupt judge.[460] I carefully reviewed the 1995 disciplinary statute and found that this law does not include specific causes for the disbarment of corrupt judges[461] – but it does contain general precepts which allow this, as happened in 1998 when the Consejo Superior disbarred a magistrate who bribed a judge to be partial in another case involving one of the Rodríguez brothers.[462] Even if the sentence by the

Rodríguez' judge had been motivated by fear (as a result of a threat or a throffer) of taking a decision that could affect the interests of the two bosses of the Cali Cartel, in other words 'corruption' in the form of intimidation by the power of the Cartel – or if in fact the judge was actually bribed by the Rodríguez brothers – it is clear that the political system failed to provide adequate laws, directives and safeguards for the impartiality of this judge's important decision.

Despite this rather murky panorama, the magistrate I interviewed was optimistic about the result of the four years of control that the Consejo Superior had exercised over judges. In her opinion, the fact that in 1997 there were fewer complaints against judges meant that the Consejo's 'exemplary' control up to 1995 had reduced common violations of the law by judges.[463] In her view, the implications of the Rodríguez judge's case were both a reaffirmation of the independence of the judges and consequently a sign of democracy, but also the fault of the existing laws. From the interview, I sensed that although the magistrate regretted the Rodríguez judge's decision, she thought the system of justice was not responsible for the control of a judge's decision, and strictly speaking, she was right. At its height, this case generated strong complaints from some sectors of the press – one of the leading national newspapers, under the heading 'Judges and Drugs Trafficking: more than one obscure connection', claimed the presence of drug-related corruption in the Colombian judiciary. 'Attempts to change proceedings location, omissions to alter the proceedings regular allotment, concealment of drug traffickers public proceedings by some Notary Public, bribes to obtain favourable *tutelas* and the imposition of derisory penalties for years of drug trafficking are only the reflex of the peculiar relation between the Mafia (sic) and the judges'.[464]

The case of the Rodríguez judge seems to suggest that the system of justice is partially responsible for some of the corruption that it attracts, yet there is no clear incentive for the judges to act differently. The judges are part of the political system; most judges of the lower courts are elected through forms of patronage and owe their positions to their political bosses. The common dream of most low-ranking judges is to become a member of the highest courts of the state; this motivation seems to keep them in the judgeship.[465] Aside from those rather heroic examples who decide openly to confront corruption cases and big crimes – a significant percentage judging from the statistics for the assassinations of judges – most judges have no incentive to act against the powerful interests that prevail in Colombian politics, nor do they have any form of protection of their own lives, as the López case showed.

The case of the judges in the highest courts is however different. These judges do have some incentives to reject corruption in the judiciary. First, in most sectors of society, they generally enjoy prestige and credibility. Second, they are 'protected' (not always successfully) against possible attempts on their lives, being accompanied by bodyguards and being driven around in bullet-proof cars are signs of status in Colombia. Third, they are well paid. Finally, they deal with issues that can in turn regulate and control the activities of the Executive and the members of Congress. In fact these high-ranking judges have had an significant amount of power over the Executive since the 1991 constitutional reform; the magistrates of the Constitutional Court, for example, check the constitutionality of extraordinary legislation or, over Congress, for instance, they control members of Congress' criminal, political and disciplinary responsibility.

When faced with the question of whether it is possible to control corrupt judges, the answer that seems to emerge is that, in theory it is, although in practice there seems to be little political incentive for doing so. The political possibility of exercising control over corrupt judges exists – the institutions and the legal framework are there – yet the political system is subverted by the particular private interests of many of the actors (here, the drug cartels' interests) and thus produces rules and legislation where the principal source of exchange is not a political one. Clearly, the system of justice is porous to all types of influences. In the present situation of irregular war and intimidation most judges are caught between two equally bad options: heroes who sacrifice their lives or their personal tranquillity in the name of justice, or villains as accomplices or instigators of corruption. The judge has been left on his own, particularly at the lowest hierarchies of the judiciary. This signifies that at present only magistrates in the highest courts and some members of the *Fiscalía*, particularly those who manage to work anonymously in the main cities, can administer justice with a minimum, though still insufficient, degree of security and independence.

To summarise, the awareness of judicial corruption is relatively new in Colombia. The commonly-held belief that the main problem of criminal justice was its inefficiency, may have prevented judicial corruption from becoming an issue of concern until the 1990s. Surveys from 1994 and 1997 showed that judicial corruption originated from actors external to the judiciary such as drug traffickers, and from other economically and politically powerful agents – in some cases even state agents. These surveys also show that the corruption that seems to prevail comes via threats and pressures. This is a form of corruption which not only confirms the overwhelmingly powerful origins of the corruptors, but also demonstrates the obvious difficulty judges have in opposing it. Such a situation often renders judges 'victims' of their 'own' corruption. While the surveys suggest that corruption is not systemic, they do suggest that judicial corruption is extremely common. So far the evidence shows that in spite of the fact that the criminal jurisdiction has shown signs of independence since 1991, the state is compromised as for as particular interests are concerned and is hostage to pressures from all sorts of legal and illegal actors. This lack of autonomy of the state compromises the system of justice's own autonomy. Linking this claim to one of the main arguments of this book, I argue that judicial corruption is to a large extent caused by a political system that fails to provide adequate laws, directives and safeguards for the impartiality of judges – this is a crucial failure given that the system of justice is continually being subjected to such overwhelmingly strong pressures from powerful external agents.

Part III
Fear and Distrust

Do you want to prevent crimes: ... See to it that men fear the laws and only the laws. The fear of the law is salutary, but the fear of one man for another is a fertile source of crime.

Beccaria

Can anybody divorce the situation of insecurity and violence characteristic of Colombia from the crisis in the administration of justice?

Cepeda Ulloa

6
Impact of Drug Trafficking on Judicial Institutions

The political and judicial crises of Colombia have been associated with decades of endogenous and decentralised forms of violence, in particular those of armed conflict, organised crime and drug trafficking. These in turn have fuelled the growth of different forms of illegal 'private justice'. The main forms of 'private justice' that exist in modern Colombia are the paramilitary, urban militias, *sicarios* [hired assassins], armed bands and the guerrillas' own revolutionary 'justice'. These violent actors have used fear against both the state and the people in order to strengthen their own positions as well as to administer forms of 'justice' and provide some sort of 'security'. However, none has used fear against the judges in a more successful way than have drug traffickers, relegating the system of justice to a state of semi-paralysis for almost a decade.

The traffic of illegal drugs has been one of the factors that have had the most dramatic influence on the evolution of the Colombian system of criminal justice. Throughout this book I have shown examples of the perversity of the drug trafficker's influence in the administration of justice. Analysis of the impact of drug trafficking in judicial institutions shows the extent of the power of fear instigated by the most pervasive actor that exists in Colombia. It reveals that, in contrast to other illegal forms of 'private justice', which simply ignore and seek to supplant the formal system of justice, drug traffickers also subvert and corrupt the formal adjudication process, often with a good degree of success. In fact, as Merrill argues 'The *narcos* want to incorporate themselves into the establishment, not destroy it'.[466]

The influence of drug trafficking on the formal system of justice can be divided into four different phases, which extend from the beginning of drug trafficking in the late 1970s to the present day.[467] The first phase, from its beginning in the late 1970s to the beginning of the

1980s, presents no major threats to the system as a whole or to the system of justice in particular. It is a period characterised by an emerging phenomenon, still disorganised and experimental. 'Violence or enforcement activity engaged in by different traffickers was limited to their private bodyguards. The dispersed and poorly co-ordinated decision-making of individual traffickers meant that bribery was limited to those individuals best known to the separate traffickers who possessed specialised and protected knowledge of transportation routes'.[468] As McRae shows, at the beginning of drug trafficking, anti-narcotics' enforcement was not so much a priority for the Colombian government as the United States would have preferred. This is mainly evidenced by the two-year delay in the ratification of the extradition treaty signed between Colombia and the United States in 1979 – and, also, by the absence during this period of any special statutes geared to control drug traffickers and their activities. A second phase extends from 1980 to 1988.[469] In this period two different events were to surface, showing the beginning of a dark and threatening alliance that has flourished to the present day, that of the drug traffickers and the paramilitary as well as the drug traffickers' direct involvement in politics and the administration of justice.[470] In relation to the administration of justice, the drugs traffickers' main agenda in this second phase was the intimidation and assassination of judges and high officials connected to the judiciary. The first most symbolic assassination was that of the Minister of Justice, Rodrigo Lara Bonilla in April 1984, a crime perpetrated by the Medellín Cartel under the leadership of Pablo Escobar.[471] One year later, magistrate Tulio Castro Gil, who was in charge of Lara Bonilla's criminal investigation, was gunned down, and so was Judge Carmen Londoño who had also initiated an investigation of Pablo Escobar. These mark only the beginning of a long list of assassinations of and threats made to judges, public officials, politicians and journalists who dared to challenge the interests of the powerful drug traffickers.[472] Amongst the most notorious victims related to the system of justice were three magistrates of the Supreme Court – Alvaro Medina in 1985 and Hernando Baquero and Gustavo Zuluaga in 1986; the former Director of Anti-Narcotics Police, Colonel Jaime Ramirez Gómez in 1986; the attempt against former Minister of Justice, Enrique Parejo in Budapest in 1987; the killing of former magistrate and presidential candidate of the UP,[473] Jaime Pardo Leal, in 1987; and the assassination of the Procurador General, Carlos Mauro Hoyos, in 1988. All these notables had, in one way or another, influenced policies against drug traffickers, either prosecuting them or denouncing their presence in the state. These assassinations, together with those of a high number of judges and court clerks discussed in Chapter 4, and those in the Toma del Palacio de Justicia (see note 374) in 1985 are the catalysts for an even more activist Supreme Court of Justice which, driven by fear, declared the unconstitutionality of the United States/Colombian Treaty of Extradition signed in 1981.[474] The limited ability of the state to protect its citizens and judges, together with the judicial system's incapacity to uphold the law, significantly eroded the state autonomy in this phase. The decline of the state was such that the Minister of Defence, General Alvaro Camacho Leyva, and the Minister of Justice, Felio Andrade,[475] even suggested that judges should arm themselves.[476] But the efforts of drug traffickers in this second phase did not stop at the level of the intimidation of judges. The power of the drug traffickers' corruption was such that their former enemies ended up working for them. An example is the M-19 left-wing guerrillas' alliance with the drug traffickers in the Toma del Palacio de Justicia, where the latter paid the guerrillas to destroy the archives of the Supreme Court, which contained the files of extradition. The level of intimidation and corruption of the system by drug traffickers proved very successful during this phase: judges were unable to sentence drug leaders in any meaningful way. This situation reinforced both a growing distrust among Colombians of the system of justice's inability to prosecute and punish criminals and a decreasing confidence in the government and the state. This second phase was characterised by the semi-paralysis of the system of justice caused mainly by the assassinations of and death threats to judges by the drug traffickers. The third phase extends from 1988 until 1991. In this relatively short phase the MAS and the paramilitary based on the Magdalena Medio region imposed their own 'private justice' to defend and enforce the interests of the drug traffickers. Initially, drug traffickers did not worry too much about the system of justice, which was sufficiently intimidated so as not to affect them. However, the shadow of extradition was still there. Consequently, the *extraditables*, paramilitary was born out of the drug traffickers' fear of extradition to the United States. After the assassination of presidential candidate Luis Carlos Galán, in August 1989, the Barco administration restored extradition by decree.[477] In October of that same year a fearful and intimidated Supreme Court of Justice declared extradition unconstitutional for the second time.[478] One hundred judicial resignations followed the assassination of Galán.[479] The debate over extradition at the national level would be put on hold after the main two political parties failed to support Barco's idea of putting the issue of extradition to a public referendum. In spite of the judicial and political lack of support, Barco ordered a few extraditions by decree.

He also issued state-of-siege decrees geared to empower the national police with discretionary powers of search, seizure, arrest and suspension of the *habeas corpus*. Clearly, these extraordinary measures of the Barco administration against the Medellín Cartel were intended to empower, by any means, an intimidated and semi-paralysed system of justice. Barco's inability to reform the system of justice[480] and the abuses and violence of the Medellín Cartel forced his administration to adopt by decree justice of war mechanisms,[481] where justice for the drug traffickers was partially 'adjudicated' by the national police and, to a smaller degree but yet a very symbolic one, by the system of justice of the United States in the cases where extradition took place.[482] This third short phase marks the return to exceptional legislation – an old trend in the administration of justice formerly used to control left-wing guerrillas and some forms of social protest. Hence the jurisdiction related to drug trafficker's offences was removed from the ordinary courts and replaced by special justice for war measures imposed by exceptional decree. The effects of this harsh policy and external law enforcement against the cartel interests would not only increase violence but also introduce terrorism for the first time in the history of the country. However, it was also Barco's empowering of the state which allowed a mild recovery of the very weakened state autonomy and legitimacy that characterised phase two. The fourth phase extends from 1991 until 2000. This phase covers the last three years of the Gaviria administration, 1991–94, the Samper administration, 1994–98, and the beginning of the Andrés Pastrana administration. This last phase initially adopted a 'stick and carrot' approach, in other words a mix of justice-for-war mechanisms and negotiation. The year 1991 marks the introduction by the 1991 Constitution of two crucial institutions to deal with drug trafficking: the *Fiscalía* and its special anti-narcotics unit, and the regional justice statute commonly known as *Justicia sin rostro*.[483] The degree of arbitrariness that both these institutions could legally infer was 'justified' by the inability of the system of justice to deal with drug trafficking and other forms of organised crime in phases two and three. In contrast, 'carrot' policies were also adopted in phase four. Extradition of Colombian nationals was banned in the 1991 Constitution in a successful effort to end terrorism, as discussed later in this chapter in more detail. The Gaviria administration also introduced the soft PSJ statute – this allowed drug traffickers to turn themselves in, plead guilty to one relatively minor crime, and receive a short sentence – and a new criminal procedural statute, the 1991 CPP, was enacted by decree.[484] This 1991 CPP, which contains obvious precepts that favour the interests of the drug traffickers, supports claims that Cali Cartel lawyers participated in its drafting. Even though Gaviria's overall policy against drug traffickers appeared contradictory, the evidence showed that the co-existence of hard and soft policies or the stick and carrot approach against drug traffickers resulted from the distinction in the Gaviria administration between 'narcotrafficking', that is illegal drug trafficking, and 'narcoterrorism' or terrorism perpetrated by drug traffickers throughout the country. Gaviria supported the former administrations' long-sustained statement that narcotrafficking was a global problem that Colombia could not solve alone. By contrast, narcoterrorism, a new issue in the country, was an internal problem that needed to be immediately controlled internally. Hence the main three 'carrot' criminal policies against drug traffickers were the ban of extradition, the soft PSJ (Policy of Compliance with Justice), and some precepts of the 1991 CPP. Whereas the issue of extradition was the result of a national desire to stop drug traffickers' terrorism (narcoterrorism),[485] the flexible and soft judicial PSJ for those drug traffickers who voluntarily surrendered and collaborated with the system and the soft precepts in the 1991 CPP were the result of the direct influence of drug traffickers in the Congresito and in the commission that drafted the 1991 CPP: that is, the result of political corruption.[486] It is likely that this influence of drug traffickers in judicial policy making was accepted by the Gaviria administration as part of the price that the state had to pay to stop narcoterrorism. By contrast, 'stick policies' resulted from the need to empower some institutions of the system of justice legislated in the 1991 Constitution, mainly the *Fiscalía* and the *Justicia sin rostro*.

The results of the stick and carrot approach were ambiguous. During the Gaviria administration some traffickers, the most important being Pablo Escobar, agreed to the PSJ. The Ochoas clan and other minor traffickers also harboured the PSJ. All this suggested that soft policy was a good option to control drug traffickers. However, a year later Escobar escaped from his tailor-made 'velvet prison', defying the PSJ and the credibility of the state powers to control drug traffickers. It was only during the following administration of Samper that the ANC and Gaviria's hard policies would determine the first judicial success in the fight against drug traffickers. The Samper administration, itself the first administration ever to be directly tainted by a scandal of illegal drugs-money in the presidential campaign finances, had to prove hard on drug traffickers. From a judicial point of view, this led to pushing for tougher legislation against drug traffickers, mainly strengthening the existing weak statutes of money laundering, the judicial co-operation of the United States, and the seizing of property and goods belonging to the drug traffickers.[487] In addition, pressured by the United States, Samper established an elite force which in 1995 captured the Rodríguez Orejuela brothers, leaders of the Cali Cartel as well as other drug traffickers; they were convicted by a faceless judge and, to date, remain in jail. Once again justice-for-war mechanisms, such as police empowerment and the *Justicia sin rostro*, will prove the only way to 'control' drug traffickers. By 1997, under pressure by the United States, the extradition of Colombian nationals was re-established by Congress, though only for future crimes. The approval of extradition, however, was not totally unconditional. Firstly, the future effects of this mechanism exonerated the extradition of the powerful leaders of the Cali Cartel, showing the degree of their power even behind bars. Secondly, the Colombian administration has shown an ambiguous position as to the applicability of the 1979 existing Treaty of Extradition between Colombia and the United States which was declared unconstitutional by the Supreme Court of Justice in 1989. In fact, only recently have the Ministers of Justice, Rómulo Gónzalez and Foreign Relations, Guillermo Fernández de Soto, claimed publicly that 'the extradition treaty between Colombia and the United States is valid, but it cannot be applied in Colombia because it lacks a requirement that inhibits its incorporation into the internal legislation via Congress'.[488] The absence of an 'operating treaty' between Colombia and the United States shows the Colombian government's ambivalence towards the illegal drugs industry, an ambivalence which has been exploited by the *extraditables*. The lack of a treaty has also inhibited many cases of extradition to the United States, and the few that have taken place have been ordered by unusual procedures: that is, extradition by decree during the Barco administration and, most recently, by request of the *Fiscalía* using the precepts of the 1991 CPP. However, in spite of these complications, the re-establishment of extradition endangers drug traffickers prosecuted and captured since 1997. In 1999, a car bomb, attributed to the *extraditables*, exploded in Bogotá killing several innocent people. In retaliation, the administration of Andrés Pastrana, 1998–2002, who had successfully captured a good number of hard drug traffickers in the 'Millennium Operation', extradited one to the United States and threatened the others, using for the first time the restored possibility of extradition of Colombian nationals.[489] By contrast, in this fourth phase, the Special Justice Statute (which replaced the *Justicia sin rostro*) was declared unconstitutional by the Constitutional Court in April 1999, yet another victory for the drug traffickers who are still free. Whether this victory was the result of the drug traffickers' direct influence remains unclear, mainly because serious academic research by UNIJUS, the Centre for Socio Judicial Studies of the Universidad Nacional – carried out well before the abolition of the *Justicia sin rostro* – showed that this statute violated the rights and liberties of the accused and was extremely inefficient, in spite of not having to follow the complex proceedings of the formal administration of justice.[490] However, and while acknowledging that the *Justicia sin rostro* statute did indeed contain authoritarian elements – mainly lax terms for prosecution, anonymous judges and *fiscales* and secret witnesses – there is evidence that suggests some degree of influence by the drug traffickers in its abolition. On the one hand, only since the *Justicia sin rostro* was created were the Cali Cartel leaders and other big-time drug traffickers finally prosecuted, convicted and imprisoned. On the other hand, there is evidence to show that, at least since 1995, drug traffickers have tried to abolish the *Justicia sin rostro* by different means. Indeed, the *Justicia sin rostro*, which originated in an executive exceptional decree in 1990 and thus was meant to be temporary, was given permanence by the Congresito until the year 2002. Moreover the Constitutional Court had held in 1993 that the statute did not violate the rights and liberties of the accused and did not violate the fundamental right of equality, since the crimes under this special jurisdiction comprised exceptionally high social-impact crimes, such as terrorism, kidnapping, and extortion. In June 1995, Congress shortened the life of the *Justicia sin rostro* until December 1999. However, the initial proposal, originated in the House of Representatives, was to abolish it. At the time, both the *Fiscal* and the administration had to intervene to stop the House of Representatives' abolition initiative.[491] In September 1996, the Constitutional Court impeded another attempt to limit the statute by rejecting an impeachment, which sought to reduce the jurisdiction of the *Justicia sin rostro* by removing the judges' secrecy during trials.[492] Then, as analysed elsewhere, the *Justicia sin rostro* was replaced by the Special Justice Statute, a milder statute yet still with some of the former *Justicia sin rostro* mechanisms. On 3 April 2000, the Special *Fiscal*, Margarita M. Pulgarín, responsible for the prosecution of drug trafficking and paramilitary cases, was assassinated. Following Pulgarín's murder, most specialised *fiscales* threaten to resign or seek exile.[493] On 6 April 2000 the Constitutional Court, contradicting its formal arguments that favoured the *Justicia sin rostro* and Special Justice Statute, declared the latter unconstitutional. Overall, these two arguments reveal that drug traffickers used the system, represented by the House of Representatives and the Constitutional Court, to achieve the abolition of the *Justicia sin rostro*'s statute. Whether progressive or legal aspects determined the decision of the Constitutional Court to annul the Special Justice Statute, its abolition served the interests of the drug traffickers. The immediate effects of the abolition of Special Justice by the Constitutional Court is unfortunate from the judges' point of view since it puts them once again in a very vulnerable position. However, it is a sign that checks and balances are in place and hence it represents an important step for the legitimation of the justice administration and, more importantly, for the legitimation of the state. The abuse of justice-of-war mechanisms, such as the *Justicia sin rostro*, has generated more violence – as was briefly shown in phases three and four – and it has neither stopped nor even diminished the growth of drug trafficking. However, the judges and *fiscales* responsible for prosecuting and convicting drug traffickers together with the witnesses for these cases, need to be protected 24 hours, seven days a week. Unless this is done, it would be impossible to make any progress in fighting drug traffickers. Nevertheless, it is very difficult for the Colombian system of justice to successfully fight drug trafficking, this global criminal multinational, on its own.

From a judicial point of view, what this fourth phase shows is that drug traffickers can only be controlled in a limited and temporary way and only through mechanisms of justice for war or extradition. The re-establishment of extradition in 1997 forces the reappearance of the *extraditables* group in their long-standing battle against extradition to the United States. Recent events, mainly marked by their latest proposals, suggests their willingness to have a more institutional and political approach to the state, which, as in the case of the *Justicia sin rostro*, proved successful. Hence the search for solutions which for the first time are not necessarily violent or directly corrupt. The decreased use of violence against judges by drug traffickers comes mainly from their new organisation, that is to say from the disintegration of the former powerful (vertical) cartels.[494] The diminished use of corruption in the *extraditables'* new 'judicial' strategy results mainly from institutional weakness and legal loopholes – many of which exist thanks to their past influence in the drafting of some of these same laws. However, the drug traffickers' ultimate objective remains to impede their extradition to the United States, this time using existing procedural technicalities that could inhibit the extradition procedure. A first technique consists of initiating judicial proceedings in Colombia for exactly the same *litis* contested in the United States, so that as a result they need to be judged in Colombia and hence cannot be extradited.[495] This provision, recently used by the leader of the Cartel de la Costa, Alberto Orlandez Gamboa alias el Caracol, who was captured in 1999 to be extradited to the United States, failed, thanks to a favourable ruling of the Supreme Court of Justice after the *Fiscalía* asked for his extradition.[496] A second technique that is used in order not to be extradited is grounded on a provision of the 1980 criminal code (1980 CP) which establishes that extradition of Colombian nationals can only proceed when there is an applicable Extradition Treaty between the two countries involved. It is up to the Constitutional Court to decide on this matter, but there is a consensus amongst the magistrates of the Court that the procedures of the 1991 CPP are applicable when there is no treaty between the two countries involved.[497] In fact the criminal code provision under discussion allows for alternative forms of extradition.[498] Finally, a third judicial strategy used to escape extradition is based on a decision of a federal judge from Pennsylvania who held that he did not have enough substantial evidence to judge a Colombian drug trafficker, Manuel Tafur, in the United States.[499] The argument used by Tafur in his defence was grounded in a constitutional decision that widened the nature of the evidence that the Supreme Court of Justice needs to provide in order to extradite a Colombian national.[500] This signifies that the Colombian Supreme Court would have to judge the potential *extraditable* before a foreign country could ask for his extradition. In this case, paradoxically, it was the Constitutional Court's interpretation of a legal provision which impeded the extradition of a drug trafficker.[501] As the *Fiscal General* warned publicly at the time, this decision set a dangerous precedent that could inhibit future extraditions.[502] Finally, the *extraditables* created their own web site where they establish essentially that drug trafficking is as unethical as most parties involved, mainly the left-wing guerrillas in Colombia and United States agents and institutions that deal with the issue. They accuse the FARC and ELN guerrillas of monopolising coca paste in their areas of control, whereas the United States is blamed for carrying on secret negotiations with some traffickers in exchange for judicial and tax benefits. They offer to reactivate the depressed Colombian economy using their capitals.[503] The ultimate purpose of the drug traffickers is, of course, to fend off extradition yet again.

The end of this fourth phase demonstrates that threats and violence to judges from drug traffickers have lessened. Clearly, the disappearance of monolithic and vertically organised cartels and their replacement by more horizontal organisations or cells around the world, signifies that drug traffickers have lost the power to intimidate the system as a whole or to make demands such as those of the former *extraditables*. This obviously does not imply that corruption of and violence towards judges by drug traffickers is going to disappear, but it at least means that this situation will occur more from individual bases. The new threats of violence and corruption to the system of justice will come mainly from the armed actors, among which there is obviously still a lot of direct involvement of drug traffickers, mainly within the paramilitary, but also among the guerrillas.

Overall, one could conclude that drug trafficking has had devastating results at the level of state autonomy and legitimacy. The judiciary's semi-paralysis in phases two and three had tremendous implications for the rule of law, particularly if we take into account that it is in this period that 'private justice' becomes 'institutionalised'. In this regard, the drug traffickers' impact in the already inefficient system of justice exacerbated all the system of justice's problems. However, it is also drug trafficking which forced the beginning of a much-needed and still inconclusive process of judicial reform and revision. The inconclusive and sometimes contradictory state policy on drug trafficking has been determined by two opposite interests: repression and negotiation. Judicial and police repression of drug trafficking usually results in retaliation by the state on the drug traffickers when these latter perpetrate assassinations, terrorism or corruption scandals that provoke public outrage. As Thoumi argues, 'The Colombian government has been able to obtain widespread support for anti-drug activities and to implement strong anti-drug policies only when illegal drug entrepreneurs have used terrorist tactics against key social figures and have been seen as a social threat to all other consequential social groups'.[504] Negotiation, both public and secret, with drug traffickers usually takes place as a result of particular interests of the state. From a judicial point of the view, the PSJ is a very representative result of these negotiations. Moreover, the continually changing status of extradition illustrates the power of drug traffickers, but also their weakness, since it is the one mechanism that they really fear. The enforcement of extradition usually responds to the pressure of the United States, whereas its ban is usually a concession to the drug traffickers, either as a result of negotiation or of state weakness. However, the recent developments of extradition are pointing in the right direction. In fact, they are mainly the result of an activist Constitutional Court which, unlike the Supreme Court of Justice of phases two and three, is more independent and less fearful. Whether these efforts can be sustained depend both on the incoming administrations' public policies and on the complex variables that rule the relations between Colombia and the United States.

Linking this chapter to Part II of the book, it appears that inefficiency is partially caused by drug trafficking, which has been the driving force behind much of the executive exceptional legislation since the 1980s. Drug trafficking has also increased judicial corruption. The evidence suggests that corruption is almost always present in judicialised cases of drug trafficking, and it is widely used in the drafting of criminal statutes – for example, the CPP of 1991. Fear itself has become a way of subverting criminal jurisdiction since the advent of drug trafficking, and is presently used by many additional actors who profit from its perverse results and from the state's precariousness. While many of the problems affecting criminal jurisdiction preceded drug trafficking, drug trafficking notoriously diminished the autonomy of the state. This situation arose either because drug trafficking managed to paralyse the state's capacity to realise its goals (the embattled state), as in the case of phases two and three described in this chapter, or because the state was used by drug dealers to fulfil their own interests (the instrumental state), as demonstrated by the PSJ and the abolition of the *Justicia sin rostro*. I have also shown that the state has recovered part of its autonomy with the use of justice-for-war mechanisms such as the confiscating of the property and goods of drug traffickers as well as the *Fiscalía*'s powers. However, these justice-for-war mechanisms can create more arbitrariness, as discussed in the chapter that follows. In addition, its success is usually short lived – either because of the judicial activism of a progressive constitutional court or because the mechanisms only provide temporary and limited controls on drug trafficking. Since the end of the 1990s, the diminished use of violence by drug traffickers appears to be more an effect of their change in organisation. There is also a perception that drug traffickers are making less use of open forms of corruption – this is mainly due to the wealth of current legal loopholes (many of which are of their own creation) and the obvious institutional weakness. This, together with the 'new' state priorities in the armed conflict, has 'relegated' justice-for-war against drug traffickers to a less visible place and, consequently, their threats to the system of justice have also lessened.

To summarise, this chapter has demonstrated the success of the drug trafficker's influence on the formal system of justice and its capacity to corrupt the state or paralyse the system of justice. However, the survival of the system of justice – in spite of drug trafficking's severe subversion in phases two and three – gives signs of hope. Most systems of justice would have succumbed under these circumstances. In the long term, however, the judiciary and the state cannot fight this global criminal multinational industry alone. Sooner rather than later, this issue will have to be resolved with international co-operation in all fields – possibly leading to the legalisation of 'illegal drugs' and their traffic.

7
Justice in a Country with an Irregular War

> Looking at the issue of law and order in global Italy throughout the nineteenth century one observes that 'the consistent abuse of power and repeated attempts to violate the law in Liberal Italy should be seen not as indication of the strength of the State, but rather of its administrative and political weaknesses'.
>
> Davis

> [In Northern Ireland] the special courts, interrogation centres, exclusion orders, plastic and real bullets and wide operational powers conferred on the army and the police have not succeeded in eliminating it [the violence]. More importantly, they have not managed to defeat the organisations orchestrating it. On the contrary, it can be argued that they are actually fuelling the violence and increasing support for the organisations involved. This stems from the impact that the persistent malpractices and abuse have on sections of the community.
>
> Walsh

In modern Colombia there are many forms of violence. No civil war exists in the sense of a bipolar conflict between two parties that polarises the population at two extremes, but rather a generalised and fragmented violence where numerous armed actors interact, and where most of the victims are unarmed and innocent civilians. Some refer to this as a process of politico-military feudalisation which has occurred since the 1980s when drug traffickers entered into this arena.[505] In terms of a theoretical definition, Colombia's war resembles Kaldor's 'New Wars'. According to Kaldor, the term war is used to emphasise the political nature of this new type of violence, even though new wars involve a blurring of the distinctions between war, organised crime and large-scale violation of human rights.[506] In general, the circumstances surrounding new wars have allowed many governments to justify a degree of state arbitrariness. In the case of Colombia, however, state arbitrariness has increased violence, as shown earlier when discussing the effects of exceptionality, as well as multiplied the causes for war, as discussed in this chapter.

The relationship between the system of justice and this 'new war' is very complex. In some cases, the state has used the system of justice to consolidate its military efforts. Elsewhere, the system of justice has tried to limit state abuses – however, often with little success. Attempts to explain in detail the roots and nature of the relationship between justice and Colombia's new war, would necessarily be lengthy and complex. I shall therefore only analyse the issue in a very general way. Initially this chapter explores the role that justice has played as an instrument of war, before turning to the role and prospects of justice in the construction of the much-needed lasting peace.

Justice as an instrument of war

During the nineteenth century, 'In the face of mounting social unrest and political opposition, successive Italian governments exploited real and imaginary threats to public order as a pretext for an unprecedented experiment in arbitrary government'.[507] In Italy, banditry and brigandage served, in the eighteenth, nineteenth and twentieth centuries, to justify the expansion of state authority and for the adoption of arbitrary and emergency measures. Martial laws in 1894 and 1898, emergency legislation to detain political suspects and the banning of all forms of political association are some of the examples. In the 1890s, the outcome of the crisis demonstrated that support for the rule of law outweighed the recourse to authoritarian forms of government. Historians have considered the 1890s' crisis in the light of what came after World War I, and many argue that remarkably illiberal measures employed by subversive governments after the unification reveal the continuities that linked liberal Italy with its fascist successors. Similarly, in the case of twentieth-century Colombia, successive governments have exploited real but also imaginary threats of social movements, guerrillas and drug traffickers as an excuse to expand exceptional or state-of-siege legislation. A state such as Colombia, which is faced with armed subversion and powerful organised crime, needs some sort of extraordinary justice in order to control these phenomena. The recourse to exceptionality in the period under review, while not always arbitrary, has allowed the executive to legislate most of the crucial aspects of the criminal jurisdiction. This exceptionality has restricted due process of law and limited the fundamental rights and liberties of the people with serious repercussions for the legitimacy of the administration of justice, while not always differentiating the ordinary from the extraordinary. The excessive recourse of the executive to exceptionality in the drafting of criminal law for the purposes of consolidating the state's military efforts is what I call the use of justice as an instrument of war.

As early as during the years of *La Violencia* period (approximately 1945–65), the administration of justice had a minor role since it was used as an instrument of the sectarian politics that characterised this period, that is to say, justice was at the service of the incumbent Liberal or Conservative government.[508] The role of justice as an instrument of war, however, has empowered the military jurisdiction since the mid-1960s, when the Executive established the application of military justice to civilians. Initially, the executive assigned to the military courts jurisdiction over crimes committed by civilians who threatened the existence and security of the state, that is political crimes.[509] The fact that the law gave too much power and discretion to the military courts, combined with the rather blurry dividing line between civilians who threatened the security of the state and those who committed ordinary crimes that could be perceived as threatening, led to military justice rapidly entering the social arena – it subsequently interfered in many other conflicts that were not political, mainly common crimes but also social protests that had no criminal connotations. The use of exceptional legislation in Colombia was so extended that in the 16-year period of the National Front, 1958–74, and during the following administration of Alfonso López Michelsen, 1974–78, they were 14 years and 11 months under a state-of-siege legislation, which was enforced by approximately 300 exceptional decrees.[510] Ironically, as mentioned elsewhere, the beginning of the National Front in 1958 marks the end of the last dictatorship in Colombia. Another Colombian paradox lies in the fact that in spite of the lengthy usage of exceptionality, the degree of arbitrariness that it generated was never as generalised or repressive as that of Pinochet's Chile, for example. As in the case of Northern Ireland during the 1970s and 1980s, large sections of the community across Colombia rarely experienced any abuses. Colombia had no media censorship or restriction of movement during the state-of-siege periods. However, during the 14 years and 11 months of exceptionality of the National Front period, there was repression of students' movements, workers' unions, the indigenous movement and other civic associations, protests, illegal strikes and civic standstills – and such repression was often brutal.[511]

Part of the reason why exceptionality was so widely used was the fact that under the 1886 former Constitution, and until 1968, a degree of state arbitrariness was constitutionally allowed. During this period the executive could, through state-of-siege decrees, legislate in 'times of external or internal war', annul most rights and liberties of the people, retain any suspects attempting to subvert public peace without judicial warrant, expropriate without indemnity, and implement military justice and military administrative authority.[512] Moreover, state-of-siege decrees, although limited to specific periods by the 1886 Constitution, had in practice an indefinite duration since the temporal limit established by the law allowed for this interpretation.[513] Consequently, the four presidents who governed Colombia during the National Front period and the administration that followed, that of Alfonso López M., did so mainly by decree. State-of-siege legislation was always justified to the public by threats of violence or subversion from different actors. However, as Gallón shows, the objective of state-of-siege legislation throughout the period was not always the repression of violent actors.[514] In fact, state-of-siege legislation was also used as a mechanism of power to sustain the legitimacy of the incumbent administration. The evidence shows that when legislative or presidential elections approached, state-of-siege repressive mechanisms were eased in order to increase the electorate.[515] The recourse to state-of-siege legislation also served to enhance the 'governability' of particular administrations, allowing these to bypass the slow and complex congressional proceedings which delayed executive projects. During this first period, 1958–78, state-of-siege legislation allowed great interference by the armed forces in a function alien to their goals and natural tasks: the administration of justice. Martial courts or Consejos de Guerra judged civilian crimes, using speedy procedures and limiting the rights and liberties of the accused. Judges, attorneys and the jury, themselves members of the military, were obviously tied to a vertical and hierarchical organisation that allowed little or no independence. Some commentators even argue that martial courts almost invariably condemned the accused.[516] However, the overall impact of the arbitrariness of court martial trials was lessened as a result of the military jurisdiction's large degree of inefficiency.

The first president of the National Front, Alberto Lleras Camargo, 1958–62, used exceptional legislation only modestly compared with the other three administrations of this period. Nevertheless, ordinary judges were forced to admit as sufficient evidence to condemn the accused of certain crimes, reports under oath provided by the secret agents of the state (SIC) or by the military. During the following administration, that of Guillermo León Valencia, 1962–66, the crimes of rebellion, criminal association, kidnapping and extortion were passed over to military jurisdiction. This was in spite of the fact that the system of justice had been fully reformed in that same year.[517] With the excuse of a general 'state of war', state-of-siege legislation allowed the judgment of civilians by military courts in 1964. In addition to the military administration of justice for civilians, some areas of the country under state-of-siege were subject to the authority of the military mayors.[518] During the Valencia administration, state-of-siege legislation was also used to repress poorly paid workers' protests, the most repressive being the military campaign, supported by the United States, to exterminate a popular movement that participated in an oil strike.[519] The recourse to exceptionality and suppression of some rights and liberties continues in the following administration, which was that of Carlos Lleras Restrepo, 1966–70. Under the Lleras administration, however, the public justification for the state-of-siege legislation was the guerrilla threat. The most criticised operation of the Lleras administration was the detention without judicial order of 300 individuals in March 1967 – these were mainly members of the MRL, workers' associations and communist leaders. Shortly afterwards, the state-of-siege was suspended. In 1968, a constitutional reform will further strengthen the power of the executive. The return to normality is compensated, however, by an increase in the salaries and other privileges for the military. However, normality does not last and in 1970, Misael Pastrana Borrero, a Conservative, was elected as President to succeed Lleras by an alleged electoral fraud which impeded the ANAPO, a political party outside the National Front pact from reaching the presidency. In view of possible upheavals the president of the time, Lleras Restrepo, imposed state-of-siege legislation once more, this time to maintain the Conservative candidate in power and with this to sustain the National Front arrangements between the Liberal and the Conservative Parties. The state-of-siege decree also gives more power to military justice, introducing into their jurisdiction offences totally unrelated to the political crisis of the moment.[520] According to Gallón, these decrees in the short term maintained Pastrana Borrero in power, while in the long term, they progressively extended military control over civilian matters. During the Pastrana Borrero administration, 1970–74, the state-of-siege was generalised throughout the country, in contrast to the other three administrations of the National Front. In addition, some collective liberties such as public meetings, demonstrations and alcohol consumption, were partially restricted. Military jurisdiction was widened once more, this time not only to include all crimes that were part of it in the former administration, but also (and weirdly) to incorporate common theft. According to Silva, this signified that at least 30 per cent of the crimes codified in the existing criminal code came under military jurisdiction.[521] Consequently, the military judicial backlog increased dramatically, a situation that was 'resolved' with another reform of military justice which allowed, this time specifically, the usage of speedy proceedings with few procedural guarantees. There is no evidence as to the effects of these new procedures in the overall efficiency of military jurisdiction. However, this reform allowed for an increase in the penalties of offences under military jurisdiction. Furthermore, the ordinary judges of criminal instruction were forced to collaborate with the military judges. The police, on their side, could detain those carrying weapons for up to 60 days, while DAS was entitled to follow any other 'suspect'. Repressive measures were extended to workers' associations and strikes were banned for all public officials.

The first administration after the constitutional end of the National Front, that of Alfonso López Michelsen, 1974–78, was elected with the highest percentage of votes ever. In spite of his legitimacy, he re-established the state of siege with the justification that the guerrillas had infiltrated state bureaucracy. Once more some civil liberties were restricted, and homicides and injuries against the armed forces were passed to military jurisdiction. More extreme measures, such as decree 2195/1976 for instance, established the possibility of the arrest of any 'suspects'. Suspects were amply defined as those who organise public meetings without following legal proceedings, those who obstructed the traffic of cars or people and, more extreme, those who produced (or drew) offensive writings. The most criticised extraordinary decree of the López administration is decree 70/1978, also known as the 'James Bond decree'. This decree exonerated the armed forces from crimes committed while controlling or carrying out operations against kidnappers, extortionists and drug traffickers.[522]

During the 16 years of the National Front period, and the four years of the López M. administration, the Supreme Court of Justice was relatively passive, in spite of the fact that since 1968 a constitutional reform to the 1886 Constitution had introduced the constitutional control of exceptional decrees by this agency. As analysed in Chapter 2, most arbitrary decrees were not contested by the Supreme Court of Justice. Other courts of the judiciary, however, managed to impose torts on the state for abuses and excesses of the armed forces throughout this period, as shown by the evidence of condemnations related to unjustified deaths of detained persons, torture of prisoners, manslaughter during military operations, and illegal detentions. Numerous judicial decisions also annulled military proceedings on political prisoners for the violation of due process.[523] However, most of the penalties for the excesses of the military were not enforced, many condemned military personnel continued their careers with no internal consequences, and those penalties that were indeed enforced, mainly fines, were all costs that were subsumed by the state. Also, in theory, there was disciplinary control of the military by the Procuraduría. However, by law, the public official of the Procuraduría, Procurador for the military forces, in charge of this control was always an active military official which signified that disciplinary control could not operate during this period.

A second period of state-of-siege legislation extends from 1978 to 1982. This relatively short four-year period coincides with the administration of Julio Cesar Turbay Ayala. Exceptionally, Turbay regulated decree 1923/1978, commonly known as the Estatuto de Seguridad (the security statute). The evidence shows that the Estatuto de Seguridad emerged as the crystallisation of the first period of exceptional decrees during the National Front, amalgamated with the fear of an escalation of the guerrillas' armed conflict and a new emerging phenomenon of political terrorism. The Estatuto de Seguridad basically created new categories of criminal offence, increased the punishment of existing crimes, widened military jurisdiction and established a censure mechanism for both radio and television.[524] According to Orozco, the main victims of the Estatuto de Seguridad were the political and social movements.[525] Indeed, in spite of the fact that since the mid-1960s military jurisdiction had competency over crimes against the security and existence of the state (decree 1290/1965), it was only during the Turbay administration that the Estatuto de Seguridad assimilated civil disobedience with political crime, common crime and terrorism. In 1982 a new short stage – the peace process with the left-wing guerrillas – was inaugurated by the administration of Belisario Betancur, 1982–86. Betancur sought to replace the Turbay administration's repressive treatment of the guerrillas for political measures. The process started with an amnesty in 1982 for all organised guerrillas and a set of dialogues with the fighting guerrillas. Following this trend, in 1983, the Supreme Court of Justice declared as unconstitutional the law that had ordered the procurador for the military forces to be a serving military officer – a first step, at the time only symbolic, in the establishment of accountability for the military. This brief process of non-executive intervention was however interrupted in 1985, when the negotiation between the guerrillas and government was broken by the Toma del Palacio de Justicia. This Toma hurt the military's image. The military obviously did not agree with Betancur's soft policies, but ended up being perceived as the aggressors as a result of this tragedy.[526]

Military justice for civilians was abolished in 1987 by a decision of the Supreme Court of Justice.[527] A new period of exceptional legislation began in the mid-1980s, empowering the common judges with special judicial powers to fight the 'new' enemy of the state: the drug traffickers. The Virgilio Barco administration, 1986–90, exceptionally legislated a set of decrees known as the Public Order Jurisdiction which regulated the prosecution and judgment of drug trafficking and terrorism. The following administration, that of Cesar Gaviria, 1990–94, exceptionally legislated the *Justicia sin rostro* statute. This 'special justice', gradually introduced during the Barco and the Gaviria administrations, constituted a third stage in the justice-for-war mechanisms. It sought to establish special procedures for the adjudication of certain crimes considered as dangerous, initially crimes committed by drug traffickers against well-known public figures such as journalists, civic leaders or politicians. As part of the Public Order Jurisdiction, Barco introduced the antiterrorist statute, decree 180/1988, which indirectly included in the category of terrorism crimes related to armed conflict and social protest, a situation resembling that introduced by the short-lived Estatuto de Seguridad of the Turbay administration.[528] The Supreme Court's inability to redress the ambiguities and repressive measures of the antiterrorist statute show the still fragile degree of independence of the judiciary from the executive.[529] During the Gaviria administration, special justice took a further step. This time the new Constitution of 1991 converted the exceptional statutes for the defence of democracy (decree 3664/1986; decrees 180, 181, and 182/1988 and decree 1857/1989) and for the defence of justice (decrees 2790, 99, 390 and 1676/1990), grounds for the controversial *Justicia sin rostro*, into ordinary legislation.[530] The special justice statutes of the Barco and the Gaviria administrations, as well as being the products of exceptional legislation, are, in contrast to the former military justice, in the hands of the common judges. Originally designed to fight drug traffickers, the Gaviria *Justicia sin rostro* statute was also a powerful weapon against social and political movements. Like the Barco antiterrorist statute, it included a set of open and diffused criminal conducts (*tipos penales abiertos y difusos*) that as well as giving protection to judges from powerful criminals, also allowed for arbitrariness against civilians. Orozco even argues that the statute for the defence of justice was in reality a lenient statute for the acts of the military and police security forces and, as such, 'a state weapon for the repression of the civil population'.[531] Whether or not Orozco's opinion could be exaggerated, it is true that civilians could still be repressed, this time by the ordinary judges. Originally, the grounds of the *Justicia sin rostro* were condensed and enacted by decree by the executive during the 1980s to tackle crimes against the security of the state and public order such as terrorism, rebellion and drug trafficking. Then other offences against the individual liberties of the people, mainly kidnapping and other high-social impact crimes, were included. While the revocation of the *Justicia sin rostro* in 1999 was publicly deplored by some sectors of the judiciary, the abolition of faceless judges, faceless witnesses and restrictions to the due process contained in this statute represented, at least from a symbolic point of view, the Constitutional Court's rejection of justice-for-war mechanisms.

Exceptionality was also limited by the 1991 Constitution. In fact, the 1991 Constitution, unlike the former 1886 Constitution, differentiates the types of abnormalities that can give origin to exceptional decrees, that is external and internal war, social or economic emergency, and so on. It also qualifies the motives to legislate in cases of internal conflict (former state of siege), that is to say, only when very serious disturbances aimed directly against institutional stability, state security or citizens' coexistence occur. Furthermore, the 1991 Constitution establishes a temporal restriction to the use of exceptionality. Finally, a set of additional precepts introduce the political accountability of the president and his ministers for the abuse of exceptionality, ban the suspension of the fundamental rights and liberties of individuals by decree, and establish a more extensive constitutional control over all exceptional decrees – a control also extended by the Constitutional Court, as analysed in Chapter 2.[532] Following this trend, the Gaviria administration also reduced military power. The creation of a presidential councillor for defence and security, and the justice and security division of the national planning department – both part of the executive – together with the nomination of a civil Minister of Defence, removed the traditional 'tactical monopoly' of the military in the operation of public order policies. For the first time in decades, civil authorities took control and responsibility for military operations. In addition, the 1991 Constitution expressly forbids military justice over civilians in order to erase the possibility of this formerly established practice. Much of this effort and the progressive reforms were, however, lessened during the Samper administration (1994–98) where the armed forces, profiting from Samper's weaknesses and acute crisis of governability, partially recovered control of public order issues. The military's recovery of its former tactical autonomy in public order policy implied the enactment of more repressive decrees and more arbitrary measures, such as the special areas of public order.[533] There were also drafts of reform to remove the disciplinary control of the military from the hands of the Procuraduría and diminish the constitutional control over exceptional decrees.[534] Fortunately, the latter drafts of reforms made no progress. Samper's brief recourse to justice-for-war mechanisms contributed to aggravating the armed conflict and threatened the democratic progress made by the 1991 Constitution. However, they contributed to Samper's military support until the end of his presidential term in August 1998. Samper's recourse to justice for war showed that, in spite of the new constitutional limits to exceptionality, the executive still has ample room to manoeuvre in the use of exceptionality.

In summary, during the period under review, the presence of armed conflict, social upheaval, organised crime and political instability have been used to justify an almost permanent recourse to exceptional legislation. At the same time, this exceptionality is one of the causes of the persistence of armed conflict.[535] Although exceptionality is not the only element that explains the crisis of the Colombian judiciary, nor armed conflict, in the case of the system of justice, exceptionality has minimised the administration of justice's main tasks – not only in the cases where military judges adjudicated civilian justice but, more importantly, when the administration of justice insisted on by the executive ignored the resolution of most conflicts that did not threaten the security of the state or the stability of the incumbent political regime. Clearly, the fact that most public order or political stability problems of the state have been dealt with exceptional criminal law not only accentuates the general inefficiency of the system of justice, but also attempts to go against equality in any access to justice and against impartial adjudication. It has been shown that it is mostly the exceptional crimes that have been subject to the attention of the judges (and not always succesfully), whether military or civil, whereas most common conflicts and crimes have been left unsolved, as shown in Chapter 3. This emphasis on exceptional crimes has inhibited equal access to the system of justice; generally, the repressed litigation hardly ever reaches the system, and the percentage of it that does has little chance of success due to the persistent problems of class justice already discussed. This situation generates more violence from frustrated private parties who are convinced *a priori* that the only effective solution to their conflicts is 'private justice'. Equally pervasive is the fact that exceptionality has allowed a great degree of arbitrariness against civilians and social protesters. This is another cause of violence and undoubtedly a worrying one. In this respect, one could argue that exceptionality has exacerbated many of the problems that make the Colombian criminal justice system a system in crisis. The evidence has clearly shown that exceptionality has been an executive initiative. The faults of the system of justice in relation to the exceptional adjudication of justice are more related to its own weakness, its inefficiency, the generalised fear of witnesses and judges, and the historical judicial dependence on the executive, which impeded it from stopping this executive arbitrariness until the 1991 Constitution. At the present time, the judicial limits to exceptionality in public order matters are all in place and the judiciary is more independent. However, the system of justice needs to solve its other crises in order to limit future executive interferences and arbitrariness.

Justice as an instrument of peace

The evidence shows that criminal law has been used to compensate for the frustrations of failed police control (during the *La Violencia* period) and the impossibility of military annihilation of the enemy, mainly the guerrillas but also the drug traffickers and other forms of organised crime, in the last four decades.[536] In such a panorama, justice-for-war mechanisms have coexisted with ordinary justice. The combination of authoritarian and democratic elements that have informed most judicial policies throughout the period of review are symptomatic of the political and administrative weaknesses of the state. In this respect modern Colombia bears a strong resemblance to eighteenth- and nineteenth-century Italy. Even though a system of justice cannot resolve the essential problems of state and social reconstruction in the middle of a prolonged, armed conflict, systems of justice play an important role in the legitimation of states. Legitimation, however, can only be obtained if the system of justice reaches a certain degree of efficiency, equality, predictability and impartiality. The last three conditions can only be attained if justice is applied to all parties in equal and impartial ways. In addition, all potential criminal actors need to understand that justice will be applied to all, in other words, predictability is called for. I am also arguing that justice-for-war mechanisms – which must be truly exceptional and justified – should be administered equally and impartially for the guerrillas, the paramilitary, the organised criminals, the drug traffickers and the state agents who violate human rights and the International

Law of War. According to the same logic, amnesties and pardons should also be offered and given to all these actors under the same terms and conditions. There is no point in criminalising or condoning the actors of this irregular war in different degrees according to their original status. This means that guerrillas cannot be, by their very nature, the only beneficiaries of amnesties or pardons when there is ample evidence that many guerrilla members constantly commit crimes of atrocity not related to their rebellious or combatant nature.[537] Liberal philosophy, like criminology, which initially differentiated common and political criminals, ends in recent decades with their assimilation. European history, in fact, is full of tensions between the privileged or discriminating treatment of political criminals. Traditionally, the Colombian criminal codes of 1890, 1936 and 1980 allowed for the privileged treatment of the political criminal.[538] This privileged treatment, however, was to change with the 1980 criminal code. In spite of the fact that the 1980 code includes the crime of rebellion, that is to say it recognises political criminals, it restricts privileged treatment of rebels for ferocious, barbaric and terrorist acts. This by no means implies that the political criminal status is extinct; however, the 1980 criminal code qualifies the potential subjects of this special privilege. Nevertheless, precisely because ferocious, barbaric and atrocious crimes have become so widespread, while the conflict escalates and becomes more dirty than it was four decades ago, it is impossible to convict and imprison all the offenders. Indeed, not even the abuse of justice-for-war mechanisms has proven effective in this respect, as the *Justicia sin rostro* results clearly demonstrate.[539] Consequently, an International Tribunal should be established or accepted (such as the International Criminal Court of Rome) for the purposes of judging a representative number of war crimes. In addition, a set of amnesties and pardons for those armed actors who truly enter into peace negotiations with the state should be carried out. Finally, and more importantly, the system of justice needs to be reinforced in those areas where it operates and institutionalised in those areas of the country where it is fragile or non-existent. This reinforcement and institutionalisation, however, can only occur if there is a general degree of trust in the system of justice.

Trust in the administration of justice can only be attained if the system of justice fulfils three main tasks. The first task is to significantly improve the adjudication of the existing repressed litigation. Since exceptionality has minimised the capacity of the system of justice to adjudicate justice for common crimes or conflicts of ordinary citizens, there is a pressing need to restructure ordinary justice (whether this signifies the usage of formal or informal mechanisms of crime or conflict resolution) and make it the general rule for conflict and crime resolution. This is possible if the executive ceases to categorise common crime, political violence and organised criminality in order to give preferential treatment only to crimes in these three categories which carry out attempts against the security of the state and the stability of the incumbent political regime. From the system of justice's point of view, this signifies that it cannot continue to operate inefficiently and partially as it has up until now. However, one would expect that if exceptionality ceases to impose burdens on the judges these would have more time and be under less pressure to adjudicate the existing repressed litigation. Impartiality too could improve if the executive did not interfere in the criminal administration of justice.

The second role of justice is related to armed conflict. In spite of the fact that the judges should view peace processes as eminently political negotiations, a lasting peace can only result if a certain degree of judicialisation of the war occurs. By judicialisation I mean the inclusion of the minimum international human rights guarantees in the peace process. Firstly, the creation of a truth commission in charge of establishing what really happened; secondly, sanctions to some of those responsible for the most atrocious crimes as defined in the 1949 Geneva Conventions and Additional Protocols, and finally, reparation for some of the victims of the war. Colombian history has demonstrated that peace processes which end with amnesties and pardons alone, without these minimum guarantees, can be inconclusive and dangerous. In spite of the fact that amnesties or treaties during the nineteenth century were successful ways of restoring peace between the fighting Liberal and Conservative Parties, the twentieth-century history of amnesties in Colombia has not always been one of success.[540] Perhaps the most quoted example of non-lasting peace amnesties are those resulting from the National Front agreement where amnesties were generously given to the Liberal and Conservative fighting parties to end the period of *La Violencia*, but no truth commission or reparation for the victims ever occurred. Many analysts see this lack of reparation and the forced silence of the victims of *La Violencia* as the origin of the irregular war that Colombia is currently fighting. Indeed, even if this is not the only cause of Colombia's present war, the absence of justice that characterised the National Front agreement was certainly responsible for the formation of guerrilla forces such as the FARC.

The third role of the system of justice is the judicial control of military abuses. The type of military operations that are needed in an irregular war such as that fought in modern Colombia are by nature violent and often imply collateral damage to innocent civilians. There is no war without atrocities. However, a state of war of any kind is no excuse for military abuses. Traditionally, the judicial control over the abuses of the military was precarious. Part of the problem in the past resulted from the military's constant resistance to the disciplinary power of the Procuraduría and, most recently, by the military denial of civilian jurisdiction for military abuses of human rights. In relation to disciplinary control, long ignored by the military due to the fact that the Procurador was an active military officer, there is some progress. Since 1983, only civilians can be appointed as Procuradores for the Military Forces and the Procuraduría has begun to investigate and discipline some military personnel for human rights' violations. However, as often happens with the Procuraduría sanctions, these are more symbolic than effective and in the military case this is particularly true. On the one hand, since the Procuraduría has no hierarchical power over the military, the enforcement of the sanctions is left to the military, which in most cases only transfers the disciplined military personnel to other areas of the country or to another task instead of suspending them from service. On the other hand, the military often ignored the Procuraduría decisions, accusing this institution of being manipulated by NGOs that approve of or support the guerrillas. The criminal investigations against the military have suffered a similar fate. However, a general institutional progress, together with internal efforts by the military have been made since the 1990s to enhance military accountability and better their human rights' record. On the institutional side, the Constitution of 1991 limited military power and explicitly banned the application of military justice to civilians. With regard to the military system of justice, progress has also been made. Firstly, since 1997 the Constitutional Court ruled that in spite of exclusive military jurisdiction – which applies to the armed forces members' service-related crimes – any military violation of human rights should be prosecuted by the *Fiscalía* and judged by ordinary judges.[541] As a response to these judicial demands, the new Colombian Code of Criminal Military Justice is one of the few in Latin America that explicitly excludes from its jurisdiction the crimes of torture, genocide and forced disappearance. In fact, following the 1997 Constitutional Court decision and up until 1999, military jurisdiction had forwarded to the ordinary courts 576 cases of members of the armed forces accused of violations of human rights.[542] Moreover, the Military Code separates military judges from military commanders so that there is no hierarchical dependence of the accused and, hence, military judges can be more impartial. Furthermore, military jurisdiction is controlled by the Procuraduría, which intervenes in every stage of military criminal proceedings. Once more, it is worth pointing out that only a few countries in Latin America admit the intervention of civilian Procuradores in military proceedings.[543] Internally, a massive and ongoing training programme concerning human rights is mandated throughout the armed forces. This signifies that all members of the armed forces receive an average of 90 hours training in human rights. Additionally, up to the end of 1999, 73 000 members of the armed forces have been trained in human rights in combat areas as a result of a training scheme that started in 1994. According to the Ministry of National Defence, 'As a matter of fact, today the Public Force of Colombia is a leader in Latin America in human rights and Humanitarian Law training educational programmes'.[544] These institutional and internal reforms and efforts of the armed forces are starting to show results. Many NGOs have acknowledged a better human rights military record in present-day Colombia. For instance, in its latest report, Human Rights Watch recognised that the public force was implicated in only 2 per cent of the violations of human rights and international humanitarian law, as compared with 15.6 per cent in 1995.[545] Additionally, some foreign experts have expressed satisfaction with the military in this field, as Sir Michael Rose, distinguished General and former British Commander of the United Nations Protection Force in Bosnia, argued after his recent visit to Colombia: 'The measures taken by the Colombians to guarantee human rights are now more rigorous than those adopted by the British in Northern Ireland. The results speak for themselves. Only three percent of the population today support the narco-guerrillas, and complaints against the security forces are well down'.[546] Moreover, the army is the only state institution for which Colombians have a high degree of respect, as most polls in the last decade repeatedly reveal.[547] The dark point for the armed forces, however, is the perceived link of some of the military with the paramilitary groups that operate with great impunity across vast regions of Colombia (see Map 7.1).[548] The expansion of the paramilitary has gone hand in hand with the degeneration of the war. Rose has also acknowledged that, 'It is evident that most of the human rights abuses against the Colombian people are being carried out by the narco-guerrillas and paramilitaries'.[549] These two violent actors, who are indeed very threatening, are subject to ordinary judicial control. This judicial control is still precarious at the level of the paramilitary, and even more so in the case of the guerrilla groups, as Table 7.1 shows.

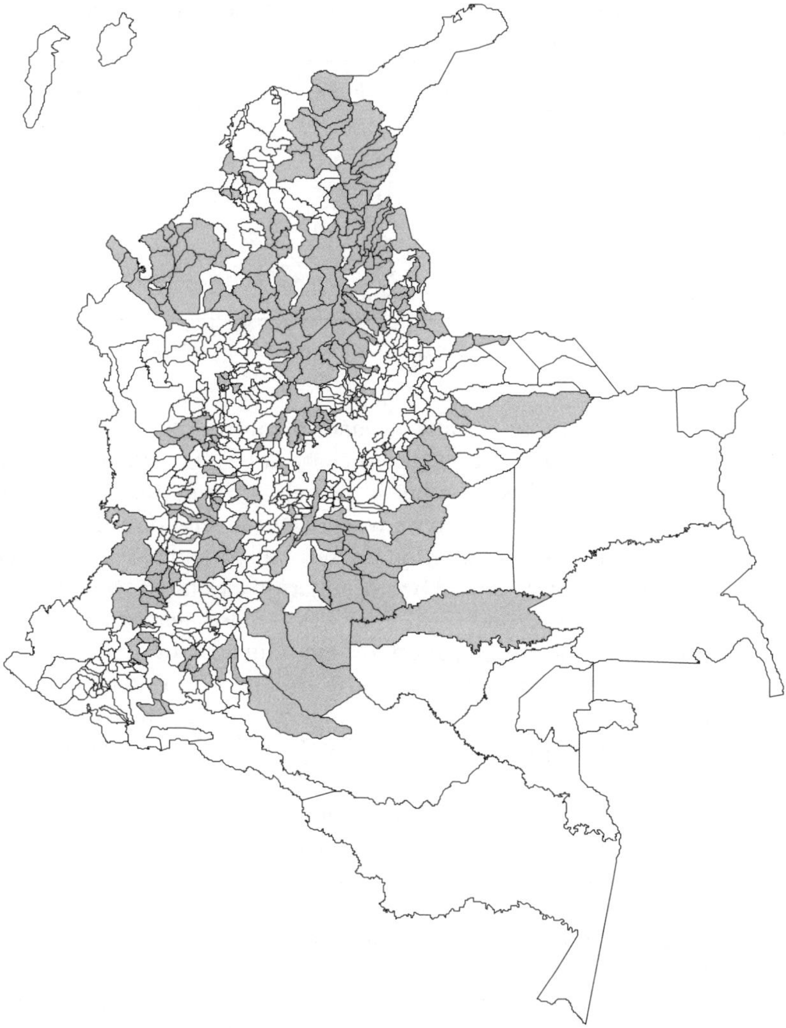

Map 7.1 Paramilitary locations in Colombia

In spite of its precariousness, the judicial control of such threatening actors is important in the sense that it can help to restore trust in the judiciary. As for the case of drug traffickers, however, the Colombian judiciary alone cannot tackle the guerrillas and the paramilitary. A mix of international courts, truth commissions, international co-operation and

Table 7.1 Judicial measures against paramilitary and guerrilla groups for human rights violations, October 2000

Measures	*Against the paramilitary*	*Against guerrillas*
Arrest warrants	309	254
Effective arrests	243	46
Captures	517	137
Charges	311	74
Plea bargains	33	–
Investigations	151	55
Numbers of accused	602	317

Source: Fiscalía General de la Nación. Internal statistics until October 2000.

Special Forces' operations are also needed to control these fast-growing phenomena. The *fiscales* and judges in charge of cases against the paramilitary and the guerrillas, together with their families, need significant protection 24 hours a day, 7 days a week. The capacity of intimidation of these violent actors is internationally recognised and past experience of judicial semi-paralysis caused by intimidation can no longer be tolerated. Significant human and fiscal resources are also needed in order to improve the criminal investigation system. Outside the judiciary, the police's role in crime control needs to be enhanced in order to resolve the failures in the basic collection of evidence and detection of crimes. The success rate in capturing criminals by the police, as well as the military, needs to be improved. Furthermore, prisons need to become safe and efficient: that is to say, prisons should be capable of incarcerating convicts until the end of their sentences. Finally, key witnesses must be protected throughout the criminal process.

While the system of justice in Colombia fails partially because of the insufficiency or underdevelopment of political order, the lack of legitimacy of the said system has exacerbated all the other problems of justice discussed at length in this book. In the long term, however, efficient justice is not enough if minimum conditions of impartiality and equality are not reached in the cases that are prosecuted and judged. Authoritarian solutions, such as those reached via justice-for-war mechanisms, may guarantee some degree of efficiency, even though the few existing statistics are not convincing in this respect – however, violence is likely to continue as a result. While analysing the use and abuse of emergency legislation in Northern Ireland, Walsh concludes: 'The obvious lesson from the foregoing analysis is that the criminal process should not be relied upon to resolve essentially political problems. But it also serves as a warning to any state attracted by the argument that major increases in police powers provide the solution to problems of an increasing crime rate and civil disorder'.[550] The evidence has shown that the search for efficiency, most often resulting from arbitrary measures, has been constant throughout the period of study and yet the system has remained in crisis. Clearly, the search for efficiency must go on, but that efficiency should be such that equality and impartiality are not sacrificed. Only this type of efficiency can achieve legitimacy and restore trust in the system, thereby reducing one of the causes of violence. In this respect, the limits to exceptionality introduced by the 1991 Constitution and the abolition of the *Justicia sin rostro* are all steps in the right direction. Under the present circumstances of irregular war, the system of justice cannot become another arbitrary actor. If a certain degree of equality and impartiality are reached, together with improved general efficiency, the judiciary has the opportunity to play a crucial role in the reconstruction of legitimacy in the state and its institutions. Peace cannot merely be conceived of as the absence of violence. If the armed conflict does finally reach an end in Colombia, it will only be through justice and democracy that a lasting peace can be achieved.

Conclusions

This book has dealt with the capacity, or lack thereof, of modern Colombia's judicial system to administer criminal justice, and with its prospects in the reconstruction of society and its institutions after a prolonged, irregular war. Its first conclusion is that the existing high levels of fear and distrust have inhibited and corrupted the criminal adjudication process. The general absence of efficient and impartial results in criminal investigations and the subversion of criminal justice by both powerful illegal and legal actors, including the executive, have up to now helped feed the different forms of violence that prevail.

Indeed, in the period under review, the executive used the criminal justice system to bolster its fragile autonomy, to help stabilise weak political administrations or to consolidate military efforts in the prolonged armed conflict that characterises modern Colombia. In the process, the executive extensively used and abused state-of-siege decrees and exceptional legislation, and arbitrarily imposed 'duties' on criminal judges, often forcing them to work in ways which subverted the course and fundamental purpose of justice. The results of this exceptionality, however, were generally not successful in their alleged intentions. The judges, overburdened with huge backlogs since the 1960s, were consequently compelled to undermine their own institutions so as to sustain weak incumbent administrations or to consolidate military efforts of the state in the growing and destabilising irregular conflict. One side effect is that the great majority of disputes and crimes which do not directly threaten the stability of the incumbent regime or the security of the state have been ignored and left unsolved. The inefficiency of the Colombian criminal justice system is compounded by its failure to deal with those cases it does prosecute with equity and impartiality. The criminal justice system also suffers from a perverse degree of accessibility, where only the few who can afford a proper defence or 'arrange' a way out, have the privilege of obtaining prompt or impartial justice. In contrast, approximately 50 per cent of those imprisoned have not been convicted. Within this 50 per cent, the great majority are petty criminals coming from the less well-to-do sectors of society, revealing a class system where punishment has generally been for the poor and justice for the privileged few. While these characteristics started to change in the mid-1990s following judicial reform, the changes are still barely perceptible at the statistical level. More research is undoubtedly needed within the different hierarchies of the judiciary in order to understand if judges are still privileging the treatment of the few and to what extent. Establishing positive and negative incentives for judges could help in redressing this situation.

On the other hand, the failure just described tends to lead people to take justice into their own hands, generating further violence and increasing people's distrust in the administration of justice. In other words, the generalised levels of violence and crime that characterise the period under review, together with the inability of the system of justice to resolve most crimes, resulted in a situation whereby the formal institutions of justice administered by the state were increasingly displaced by 'private justice' administered through violence. Those perpetrating the violence were mainly, but not exclusively, drug traffickers, paramilitaries and guerrillas. Intimidation through violence ensures that the 'requests' or impositions of these groups are effectively and rapidly carried out. The constant competition within and among these groups and the increasing inability of the state to control them has meant that 'private justice' is now available as any other market commodity, and can be bought by most ordinary people, not just those who are involved in armed conflict or drug trafficking. Although 'private justice' produces a reign of fear and a threat to lives, for many citizens its effectiveness is in sharp contrast to the inefficiency of the state's administration of justice, making it a preferable option for a significant fraction of individuals who are desperate to settle disputes both at the criminal and civil level.

'Private justice' further inhibits or corrupts the state's system of justice. The capacity of the drug traffickers, the paramilitary, the guerrillas and other armed actors is such that it can impede or corrupt the processes of prosecution and accusation. In the case of prosecution, a judge is often faced with two options: to become a villain by being an accomplice to corruption or a hero who risks sacrificing his life or tranquillity in the name of justice and the common good. Clearly, accusations are also inhibited by fear. Many crimes are never reported, and for those that are, the level of fear involved is such that witnesses, victims and their relatives don't dare to speak up against the perpetrators. It is of course very difficult to establish responsibility for crimes when witnesses are unwilling to come forward. In addition to the intimidation of witnesses, judges themselves became an increasing target for attack in the 1980s. The issue of judges' and witnesses' security was partially resolved during the 1990s with the introduction of *Justicia sin rostro* (faceless judges and secret witness legislation); however, since the abolition of both, most judges who currently deal with dangerous criminals, together with the corresponding key witnesses – the present Special Witness Protection Scheme protects only 2000 witnesses – are again largely unprotected. Consequently, one may conclude that the problem of impunity in criminal justice and corruption in the judiciary should be discussed in the context of widespread fear: fear to accuse and fear to prosecute. It is indeed worrying that, even today, in the mainstream literature on the subject, fear has not been included as one of the most perverse causes that inhibit or corrupt criminal adjudication.

This book also attempts to measure the level of corruption in the judiciary. Surveys, interviews and case studies show that, in spite of the fact that there appears to be a high level of judicial corruption, it is not systemic. The problem of corruption in the judiciary is that in most cases it is hard to determine if judges are the victims or the instigators of judicial corruption. I concluded that the system of justice seems to fail in general in the control of judges' corruption, partially because of the weakness of the system in which it operates, but also as a result of its own inefficiency. I admit, however, that more research into this topic is needed in Colombia and in the region, not only because of the lack of existing empirical data, but also because corruption is a phenomenon that has many origins and hence extremely diverse implications.

Following a general political and judicial crisis in the 1980s, a process of reform was initiated that culminated in the 1991 Constitution which replaced the former one, drawn up in 1886. This new Constitution transformed the structure of the administration of justice, in particular, criminal jurisdiction. New judicial institutions and mechanisms were introduced with the intention of empowering the administration of justice and enhancing the general independence of the judiciary. So far, it has not managed to solve most of the existing problems with the administration of justice, and in some cases it even created new ones; however, it did strengthen the judiciary, in particular the system of criminal jurisdiction, giving it sufficient independence to become an important actor in the reconstruction of society and its institutions. With present-day difficulties in the country tantamount to a permanent state of medium-intensity war, the judiciary has to contribute to the peace process and to the re-establishment of trust or else perish. My final aim was, therefore, to show that the present judiciary has the potential to contribute to peace and the re-establishment of trust in state institutions.

Although the crisis of the Colombian judiciary has grown hand in hand with the irregular war and has aggravated the conflict and contributed to the erosion of state legitimacy, and although the judiciary alone cannot solve the enormous problems facing state building in the current conditions of irregular war, systems of justice have an essential role to play in the legitimisation of states. In spite of the fact that the judiciary is still in crisis and that fear and distrust appear as principal driving factors behind societal relations by the mid-1990s, the judiciary began to make slow but important progress, touching, for example, on former untouchables, such as corrupt political leaders or high-ranking members of organised crime. Of course, claims for progress must be tentative – the strengthening of judicial institutions is still not reflected in changing statistical trends, and the main signs of progress are very recent. More judicial reform and review are undoubtedly needed; in addition, more research is crucial to understand the extent of this progress. In any case, the current judiciary has increased its independence from the executive and has more power over Congress and the military than its predecessors. On the criminal side of the picture, the judiciary now has more effective institutions and mechanisms, offering it a better chance of completing a given criminal investigation. Since 1991 there has also been some progress in the provision of justice for the less well-to-do sectors of society as a result of the creation of the *tutela* instrument, which helped to bring to justice a number of cases that would otherwise never have reached the courts. The *tutela* – which has the capacity to stop or prevent state encroachment on an individual's fundamental rights and liberties – has the virtue, if well adjudicated, to remove a great part of the need to seek a violent solution to conflicts. It has also removed the lawyers' monopoly of conflict resolution.

Although some of the most important problems still persist, it is essential to acknowledge publicly that there has been progress if the judiciary is to begin to rebuild public confidence in its operation and trust in its members. In the end, a stronger judiciary can certainly help to reconstruct trust in the state and to re-establish some of the necessary conditions for a lasting peace. Only a strong state, with a relatively effective and impartial judicial system, can remove the causes of fear. Peace is not only the absence of crime and violence. The system of justice can and should also contribute to re-establishing a sense of fairness and impartiality in societal relations. As Cicero claimed: 'So great a force is justice that not even those who live by ill-doing and crime can manage to exist without some small share of justice'.

Appendixes

Appendix 1 Relevant precepts in the 1886 Constitution

- Supreme Court of Justice: members were elected by direct co-optation (i.e. any vacancy was filled directly by the remaining members of the Supreme Court) for life (i.e. until the legal age of retirement and provisional upon good behaviour). Art. 148 Constitution of 1886.
- *Consejo de Estado*: members were elected by direct co-optation for life (until the legal age of retirement and provisional upon good behaviour). Art. 148 Constitution of 1886.
- Tribunals: Justices of the Tribunals were elected by the members of the Supreme Court of Justice. Art. 156 Constitution of 1886.
- Courts: judges of all courts were elected by members of the Tribunal of their district for a period of two years. Arts 157 and 158 Constitution of 1886.
- *Procurador General*: elected by the House of Representatives from a list of three presented by the President of Colombia, for a period of four years. Art. 144 inc. 1 Constitution of 1886.
- *Contralor General*: elected by the House of Representatives for a period of four years. Art. 59 Constitution of 1886.

Appendix 2 Relevant precepts in the 1991 Constitution

- Supreme Court of Justice: members are elected by indirect co-optation (i.e. members of the Supreme Court themselves select the member vacancies from lists of candidates provided by the Consejo Superior). The period of service of the magistrates is 8 years and there is no re-election. Arts 231 and 233 CN.
- *Consejo de Estado*: members' election and period is exactly the same as that for the magistrates of the Supreme Court of Justice. Arts 231 and 233 CN.
- Constitutional Court: members are elected by the Senate from lists of three presented by the President of Colombia, the Supreme Court of Justice and the *Consejo de Estado*. The period is of 8 years. Art. 239 CN. Note: none of the members of these three High Courts have to belong to the judicial civil service.
- *Fiscal General*: elected by the Supreme Court of Justice from a list of three candidates previously selected by the President of Colombia, for a period of four years and there is no re-election. Art. 249 CN.
- *Consejo Superior*: the members of the disciplinary courtroom are elected by Congress from lists of three candidates sent by the national administration (in Colombia, the national administration, for legal purposes, comprises the President and one or more ministers of the cabinet), for a period of 8 years. The members of the administrative courtroom are elected by the Supreme Court (2 members), the Constitutional Court (1 member) and the *Consejo de Estado* (3 members) for a period of 8 years. Art. 254 CN.

- Tribunals and courts: the selection of these judges is by appointment of the *Consejo Superior de la Judicatura*. The Constitution commands that all remaining public officials, hence the judges, should belong to the civil service. Art. 125 CN.
- *Procurador General*: elected by the Senate from a list of three candidates, one of whom is chosen by the President of Colombia, another by the Supreme Court and the third by the *Consejo de Estado*, for a period of four years. Art. 276 CN.
- *Contralor General*: elected by the Congress from a list of three, made up by one candidate selected by the Supreme Court, another by the Constitutional Court and the last by the *Consejo de Estado*, for a period of four years that coincides with that of the administration of the President of Colombia. Art. 267 CN.

Notes

1 The National Front was an agreement between the two existing rival parties, the Liberals and the Conservatives, to alternate the Presidency and to appoint an equal number of ministers and high-ranking public officials from the opposition party in public institutions, every four years for a period of 16 consecutive years, starting in 1958. This system of political parity was also introduced in the judiciary and in other public offices not covered by the civil service. Some claimed that it politicised the system of justice. For formal and political reasons the National Front lasted in one form or another for more than 16 years; that is, in some public institutions this institutional parity remained until the late 1980s. The purpose of the National Front was to put an end to the violence that affected Colombia between 1945 and 1965, violence that was basically due to sectarian hostility between the dominating Liberal and Conservative parties. The pact was successful in the sense that it stopped the sectarian violence. Viewed from another perspective, the National Front appears to have excluded any other political party or movement from the institutional arena. Those groups who did break through, such as ANAPO or the MRL, had only a short life. It is for these reasons that many analysts blame the National Front for being the main cause of the political crisis in Colombia during the last three decades. For more on the National Front, see Berry *et al.*, 1980 and Hartlyn, 1988.

2 See J. Hartlyn, 1988, p. 2.

3 The procedural definition of democracy does not exclude corrupt democratic regimes. As long as a country is able to hold elections it is still considered to be a democratic regime, whether the government is corrupt or not. Advocates of the procedural definition do not necessarily believe that corruption can be avoided in an electoral system, nor do they address the issue that the electoral system can be used to maintain corrupt elites. Yet when corruption assists elites to manipulate the electoral system, then accountability, which is the very purpose of the electoral system, is nullified. In order to eliminate false claims of democracy, the understanding of what constitutes a democratic regime needs to be extended beyond the procedural definition. It should take into account the potential symbiotic relationship between ruling elites, organised crime and the globalised financial system (Jordan, 1999, p. 19).

4 The FARC – EP (Fuerzas Armadas Revolucionarias de Colombia – Ejército Popular) is a left-wing Marxist guerrilla group that has been fighting against the state for almost five decades. The FARC is historically a peasant guerrilla force driven to processes of colonisation, where they functioned to maintain certain life conditions in some peasant areas and to protect them against exploitation from invaders or the Colombian state. For more on their origins, see Alape, 1989. A good account of the present FARC situation can be found in Prieto, 2000. The FARC was involved in a peace process with the Colombian government which began in August 1998.

5 The ELN (Ejército de Liberación Nacional) is a left-wing Maoist guerrilla group that has been fighting against the state. The ELN follows Guevara's *foquismo*

methods and is more political than the FARC. They were involved in a peace process with the Pastrana administration.

6 See Leal, in F. Leal and L. Zamosc (eds), 1991, p. 28.

7 I would like to make clear that violence in Colombia has not always been motivated by money-related issues. These mostly relate to the drug-related violence that has degenerated into organised crime; see Duhamel and Cepeda, 1997, p. 268.

8 See P. McRae, 1998.

9 See Latorre, 1980, p. 276.

10 The period of *La Violencia* in the mid-twentieth century is considered by most of the literature on the subject to have been the second phase of violence in Colombia, after the nineteenth-century civil wars. This phase commenced in 1945 in the context of high political tension between Liberals and Conservatives and ended around 1965. Some commentators even divide the *Violencia* period into two, an early period from 1945 to 1957, and a later one from 1958 to 1965. A common trait between the course of this war and that of nineteenth-century civil wars is that the ideological management of the wars was exercised in both cases by segments of the ruling class, through political parties. There is also, however, a marked difference which endows *La Violencia* with its ambiguous nature: 'the actual military conduct of the fighting is assumed by the people, and by the peasantry in particular. No single political leader from the oligarchy acted as a military commander during the *Violencia*' – Sanchez, 1985, pp. 790–1. See also Gúzman *et al.*, 1980.

11 See Leal, in F. Leal and L. Zamosc (eds), 1991.

12 See Thoumi, 1999, p. 132.

13 See Bushnell, 1993, p. 226.

14 Some strong labour unions have also played an important role in crucial areas of Colombian politics, for example oil (USO) and education (FECODE).

15 The National Front officially ended in 1974 but the practice of shared office is partly honoured to this day.

16 The Latin American debt crisis of the 1980s did not affect Colombia as it did most Latin American countries since Colombia had a small debt and continued to pay it off throughout the crisis. This relative success of Colombia in moderating the debt crisis probably increased the legitimacy of the system. Yet the general effects of the crisis did cause problems for the Colombian economy.

17 This dramatic transformation of Colombian society is described by Hoskin who argues that during 50 years of the twentieth century, that is between 1925 and 1975, the GDP grew 60.6 per cent, that is, an average of 1.2 per cent per annum, while the population in that same period grew by only 30 per cent (Hoskin, 1994). The growth in the GDP during this 50-year period was higher than that of most industrialised countries between 1870 and 1913 (Urrutia, 1979, p. 11). However, inequality of income also increased dramatically over the same period, a period in which Colombia had a distinctly unfair income distribution. According to some commentators this pattern did not change until the 1980s when the gap in the inequality index lowered to the level of other Latin American countries (Londoño, 1992, p. 51).

18 See Bushnell, 1993, p. 247.

19 Guerrillas' terrorism divided the left in two: the illegal left, that is the guerrillas, and a legal but weak Communist Party.

20 See Duhamel and M.J. Cepeda, 1997, pp. 257–9.
21 The lack of representative support for the guerrillas has inhibited their capacity to provide a viable alternative order. For data on the scant support of the guerrillas, see Lemoine, 1993 and M.M. Cuellar, 2000.
22 Paramilitary groups in Colombia now define themselves as self-defence groups. Most come under the umbrella of AUC (Autodefensas Unidas de Colombia). However, Carlos Castaño, the leader of ACCU (Autodefensas Campesinas de Córdoba y Urabá), currently the most powerful paramilitary nucleus, admits that he has no over-all control of the paramilitary.
23 Leal, in F. Leal and L. Zamosc (eds), 1991, pp. 26–56.
24 See Beetham, 1991, pp. 169–79.
25 The salience of politics stems from the perception that politics is somehow 'superior' to other forms of exchange, for instance, communal, clientelistic or market relations. Exponents of such an argument claim that this salience signifies an acceptance of the moral superiority of the political in those societies where the political is possible, since politics is founded upon a claim to legitimacy which is usually based on principles such as welfare, consent and the common good – see Philp, 1997.
26 M. Philp, 'The Autonomy of the State' (unpublished paper).
27 See Offe, 1974; Przeworski, 1990; and Philp, ibid.
28 The type of opposition that has existed in Colombia is not a straightforward official opposition as that of the United States or Britain. It is a system characterised heavily by co-optation, that is, a system which absorbs dissidents and factions, as was the case of the Luis Carlos Galán Nuevo Liberalismo party.
29 For more on the constitutionality of the Colombian state, see Duhamel and M.J. Cepeda, 1997.
30 Some of these guerrilla groups were formed during the *Violencia* period and continued to operate during the period under consideration, partially as a result of their exclusion from the existing political and judicial arrangements.
31 Henceforth, those legal reforms carried out during the Barco (1986–90) and Gaviria (1990–94) administrations, and incorporated in the Constitution of 1991, will be referred to as the reforms of the 1990s.
32 See Peñate, in M. Deas and M.V. Llorente, 1999.
33 The original ideology, which inspired the two largest left-wing guerrilla groups that exist in modern Colombia, is Marxism in the case of FARC, and Maoism and Guevara's *Foquismo* in the case of the ELN.
34 The guerrillas' drug-traffic-related activities are mainly concerned with the supervision and taxing of the coca crops and coca laboratories. Only recently has there been evidence of direct drug trafficking activities by the FARC guerrillas.
35 Some have even claimed that the 'deficit of legitimacy' of most state institutions made possible the emergence of drug trafficking, guerrillas and the high levels of violence that have existed in the country during the past 20 years. See M. Palacios, in *El Tiempo*, 26 March 1996, p. 9A.
36 See Matthiesen, 2000.
37 See Uprimny, 2001b, p. 374.
38 Ibid., pp. 375–6.
39 The PSJ was a decree enacted during the Gaviria administration which lowered the penalties of the leaders of the Cali Cartel (who were still free at the

time) and other drug traffickers, in return for their surrender and further cooperation with the system of justice.

40 The Consejo de Estado requested De Greiff to leave office upon reaching the age of 65, using debatable legal argument that this was the age of compulsory retirement for public officials of the judiciary. Behind the legal reasons adduced by the Consejo de Estado, the evidence suggested that the forced retirement of De Greiff owed more to his disagreements with the incumbent President of the Republic, Cesar Gaviria, over their differing positions in relation to the surrender of the Cali Cartel leaders (who were at the time still free) and his public declarations to legalise drugs. Gaviria himself was pressurised by the United States government, which wanted tougher policies against the drug dealers.

41 See Uprimny, 2001b, pp. 386–8 and Tokatlián, 1995.

42 See Holmes, 1993.

43 See Beetham, 1991.

44 See Feher, Heller and Markus, 1984.

45 Beetham, for instance, has claimed that Weber's received definition of legitimacy is an 'unqualified disaster', asserting that 'What is wrong with this definition [Weber's definition of legitimacy] is, first, that it misinterprets the relationship between beliefs and legitimacy; and, secondly, that it takes no account of those aspects of legitimacy that have little to do with beliefs at all', Beetham, 1991, p. 11.

46 Beetham's approach to legitimacy presents problems, too, not so much because of a lack of theoretical consistency, but because two of the dimensions of legitimacy in his theory are based on the interpretation of beliefs and values. In societies which lack a strong sense of organic solidarity (Durkheim) such as the Colombian one, it is often hard to identify the values of the ruled and even those of the rulers.

47 See Beetham, 1991, pp. 15–16.

48 See Beetham, 1991, p. 17.

49 Ibid., p. x.

50 The reader who is interested in sources supplying a clearer idea of the country's legitimacy can refer to Lemoine, 1993 and Bermúdez, 1999.

51 In the history of Colombia's independence there have only been two 'official' dictatorships, that of General José María Melo in 1854 and that of General Gustavo Rojas Pinilla from 1953–57.

52 See Deas, 1973, p. 29.

53 See Rouquié, 1984.

54 Some historians explain the absence of popular movements as a result of the relatively small number of people who arrived in Colombia as a result of European migration, in contrast to that of other Latin American countries such as Chile, Argentina and even Venezuela. In the latter, European migration brought socialist and revolutionary thinking that often became the foundation of some of the political parties.

55 Even though clientelism is no longer powerful in the cities, it still determines the composition of Congress and gives important support to Presidential candidates.

56 See Sáez, 1998, pp. 9–10 and Haring, 1963.

57 See Sáez, 1998, p. 13.

58 See Merryman, 1996, p. 111.

59 See Merryman, 1996, p. 116.
60 See Sáez, 1998.
61 *Cooptación* means the election of members of the highest courts, that is the Supreme Court and the Consejo de Estado, by the remaining members, for life or until the legal retirement age, that is the age of 65.
62 See Charria, 1988, p. 40.
63 According to the Constitution, the Supreme Court of Justice had jurisdiction over the military general commanders.
64 See Uprimny *et al.*, 2001a, pp. 38–40.
65 A professional career structure has formally existed in Colombia since 1958. Yet it only started to (partially) operate three decades later, in 1992, after substantial but failed reforms and regulations had tried to implement it in 1958, 1964, 1970, 1986 and 1991.
66 These data come from a survey designed by the Centro Nacional de Consultoría between May and June 1995 on behalf of the Ministry of Justice. The sample covered 711 judges out of the 3245 operating in the country at the time, that is, 21.9 per cent of the total. The methodology of the survey was based upon personal interviews with the judges, who were selected at random in different geographical areas of the country. The survey included judges from 95 of the existing 1000 municipalities.
67 The majority of the members of the Consejo Superior are appointed by Congress and the executive and therefore do not belong to the judiciary. There is already evidence that the non-judicial composition of the *Consejo Superior* has created problems inside the judiciary. Many judges seem reluctant to accept that a majority of the members of the 'integrating court' (that is, the *Consejo Superior*) do not belong to the judiciary. This is reflected in a Supreme Court that refuses to apply the *Consejo Superior* decisions and a *Consejo de Estado* that suspends *Consejo Superior* decisions on the grounds of hierarchical superiority – see Giraldo, 1996, p. 115.
68 See Vélez *et al.*, 1987a.
69 Giraldo *et al.*, 1987, pp. 102–4.
70 Centro Nacional de Consultoría, May and June 1995, *El Tiempo*, 30 July 1995, p. 24A.
71 See Giraldo *et al.*, 1987, p. 105 onwards.
72 See Lara-Bonilla, 1984, p. 87.
73 Following the example of the National Front, the Constitution decreed that there should be political parity in the personnel of all courts. This political parity meant that all collegiate courts, that is the High Courts and tribunals, were to be made up of judges belonging only to the Liberal or Conservative parties on a 50/50 basis. (It is not clear from the literature how this parity was enforced, but viewing the situation in pragmatic terms, it seems that each party made sure that its 50 per cent quota of judicial power was clearly established in most courts.) This measure severely damaged the unity of the judiciary and resulted in its politicisation, something that occurred likewise in Italy between right and left after World War II.
74 See Centro Nacional de Consultoría, May and June 1995.
75 All judges' salaries were raised by 100 to 300 per cent.
76 Informal personal interviews with members of the judiciary during 1999 and 2000.

77 Instituto SER para la Investigación, 1983, pp. 69–70.

78 See 1979 experiment in Giraldo *et al.*, 1987, pp. 97–8. In addition, a sample which randomly contrasts the effects of different proportions of judges in two Colombian cities corroborates the failure of this measure. DANE statistics show that during 1986 and 1987, Tunja, a small regional capital, had nine times more judges per inhabitant than the city of Cali, the third largest city in the country and the capital city of Valle del Cauca where the Cali Cartel operated. Despite this, the percentage of resolved cases per year was considerably lower in Tunja than in Cali – DANE, Boletín Mensual de Estadísticas, 1987.

79 The Instituto SER developed a mathematical model for analysing criminal proceedings that were commenced and completed, together with the output of the system. The conclusions produced by this model demonstrated that even if the number of judges were to be duplicated for a period of ten consecutive years, the accumulated backlog of cases would not be reduced significantly. For more details on this model, see Guzmán and Reyes, 1992, p. 19.

80 *Miami Herald*, International Edition, 4 August 1997, p. 3A.

81 Ministerio de Justicia y de Hacienda, 1985–95.

82 See J. Giraldo and O. Giraldo, 1994, p. 15.

83 Ministerio de Justicia and Ministerio de Hacienda, 1985–95.

84 Other countries such as Italy have experienced the same problem. In 1984, for example, only 0.76 per cent of Italian expenditure went on the administration of justice, a sum that included wages and operating costs for prisons; see Spotts and Wieser, 1986, pp. 157–8.

85 My use of the GNP and total expenditure as bases of reference is reproduced from the sources that I found rather than indicating any specific discrepancy between the two.

86 DANE, Boletín de Estadística 503, 1995, p. 131.

87 Presidencia de la República, 1993, p. 23.

88 For example, before the reforms of the 1990s, the salary of a municipal court judge was 9 per cent of that of a magistrate in the Supreme Court of Justice, the former earning $231,157 pesos, compared with the latter's $2,680,000 pesos per month (*Decretos* 872 y 903 de 1982). Some analysts have argued that the inequality of stipends between judges has perpetuated a class system in Colombian justice. Gúzman and Reyes Alvarado, 1992, pp. 14–15.

89 After a fair analysis of the legal education in Colombia, Pérez, using research carried out by the Ministry of Justice, concluded that most judges and public officials in the judiciary come from low and middle socio-economic levels of society and from universities that she classified as type three. The motives for students from type three universities for studying law included commitment to the profession (21 per cent) while the remainder entered judgeship motivated by the possibility of social improvement and enhanced status within their own socio-economic group. Moreover, 60 per cent of the students of type three universities had part-time jobs. Pérez, 1994, pp. 97–113 and Ministerio de Justicia, 1992b.

90 This situation was partially corrected by the 1990s reforms. Decree 57/1993 reforms the existing wage statute of judges (dating from 1969), which had several technical and administrative anomalies.

91 Vélez *et al.*, 1987a, p. 65.
92 Ibid., p. 65.
93 The CTI is the division of the *Fiscalía* in charge of forensic and criminal investigation.
94 Watanabe, a Brazilian jurist, calls the small daily conflicts, which require an informal and consensual resolution, the 'repressed litigation'. These conflicts usually refer to common crimes committed by ordinary citizens, generally the less well to do sectors of society.
95 See J. Giraldo *et al.*, 1987, p. 81 and Vélez *et al.*, 1987a, pp. 65–6.
96 I say 'in theory' since *fiscal* independence of the judiciary means that it can execute its budget as it wants. However, in practice the final sum depends on the state's *fiscal* availability. In addition, the judiciary does not generate any significant income that might otherwise allow for true *fiscal* independence.
97 Before 1991 the judicial budget was minimal in comparison with state spending on other institutions. In 1987, for example, the judiciary was only allocated 1.9 per cent of the state budget whereas defence spending was 18.3 per cent, and external debt payments were 17.6 per cent (CGR, 1987).
98 Instituto SER para la Investigación, 1978, p. 207.
99 Art. 256(5) CN.
100 The 1979 Constitutional Reform was declared unconstitutional only a few months after being approved by Congress. It has been argued that the 1979 Constitutional Reform failed because of procedural vices, that is to say legal formalisms to reform the law that have nothing to do with the content of the law, in its passage through Congress. However, the evidence suggests that the project failed because it tried to increase executive interference in the administration of justice.
101 In Colombia, for a draft law actually to become law under the 1886 Constitution, it needed to be approved by the two Houses of Congress, and later sanctioned by the President.
102 I have excluded from the above list of reforms other more minor amendments to the criminal statutes carried out in the period under examination.
103 In Colombia there are two categories of statute: ordinary and extraordinary. Ordinary statutes are those produced by Congress in its original and constitutional legislative function, the rule in Colombia being that Congress makes the laws. Extraordinary statutes, on the other hand, are produced by the executive – either through the delegation of Congress or through exceptional legislative powers, for example, state of siege decrees, for which there is provision in the Constitution for granting the executive in times of crisis, such as an internal or external war or a national economic emergency.
104 Under the 1886 Constitution the executive had more powers to legislate than under the 1991 Constitution, specifically by means of state of siege decrees which eventually became permanent legislation. The 1991 Constitution, which was meant to reduce the legislative powers of the executive, abolished the state of siege. However, it introduced a similar provision called *estado de conmoción interior* (state of internal emergency), which allows the executive to continue to act as legislators, albeit with more limitations than before. See Duhamel and M.J. Cepeda, 1997, p. 277 and M. García, 1993, pp. 139–45.

105 See Gallón, 1979. It should be noted that 1958 was the year when the dictatorship of General Gustavo Rojas Pinilla (1953–57), the second dictatorship in Colombia's twentieth-century history, came to an end and democratic elections were restored in the country.
106 See García, 1993, p. 167.
107 Magistrates in the Supreme Court opposed the abuse of exceptionality on many occasions, but the majority decision always prevailed.
108 See Cepeda, 1988 and Pérez, 1994, pp. 54–5.
109 See García and Uprimny, 1999, p. 51.
110 See J. Giraldo *et al.*, 1987, p. 78 and M. García and Uprimny, 1999.
111 See M.J. Cepeda, 1988.
112 See Montenegro, 1994, with reference to a study by Magee, Brook and Joung, 1989.
113 See Table 2.5 for the composition of the National Constitutional Assembly (ANC).
114 Arts 213 and 214 CN.
115 Personal interview, *Fiscal* General, Alfonso Gómez Méndez, 16 August 2000.
116 Art. 13 CN.
117 See Uprimny, 1994, p. 3.
118 Criminal proceedings are divided into three phases: the preliminary phase, the prosecution phase and the judgment phase.
119 See J. Giraldo *et al.*, 1987, p. 112.
120 See Guzmán and Reyes, 1992, pp. 22–3.
121 The statistics are still incomplete so it is difficult to analyse whether this pattern is going to be sustained – *Fiscalía* internal document, Flujo de Procesos Unidades Seccionales y Locales, August 2000.
122 For more information on the details of the preliminary investigations and the nature of the shift in responsibility, see Pérez, 1994, pp. 6–7, Decreto 014 de 1955 and Zea, 1960, pp. 8–9.
123 See Pécault, 1987.
124 Continuing this trend, in 1969, the Supreme Court of Justice ruled that the instruction judges had to be nominated by district tribunals, thus preventing the executive interference of the past.
125 See Pérez, 1994, pp. 28–31.
126 The Judicial Police were then made up of civil servants from DAS (an executive agency), from the National Police and from the military, and they were then specifically assigned to carry out these tasks. Other civil servants from various national bodies could, in case of emergency, exercise the powers of the Judicial Police – see Art. 287 CPP, 1971.
127 See J. Giraldo *et al.*, 1987, p. 115.
128 The Contraloría General was incorporated in 1945 into the 1886 Constitution of Colombia following the effect of the 1923 and 1933 United States Kemmerer Missions. The Contraloría General is to a certain extent equivalent to the United States Tax Court. For more on the origins of the Contraloría, see Drake, 1989.
129 Art. 250 CN.
130 Interviews with several investigators of the CTI, *Fiscalía*, Bogotá, August 2000.
131 *Fiscalía* General de la Nación, Informe de Gestión, 1998–99.

132 Interview with an investigator of the CTI, August 2000.
133 The LABICI (Laboratorios de Investigación Científica) began operating in 1990 thanks to an agreement with the United Nations which provided training and economic support through the UN laboratories in Vienna, Austria.
134 I was able to visit some of the centres and laboratories of the CTI in Bogotá and was impressed both by the installations and equipment as well as some of the personnel in charge (visits to the CTI, August 2000).
135 Details of all training already received is described in *Fiscalía* General de la Nación, Informe de Gestión, 1998–99, pp. 70–2.
136 The prisons are administered by the executive through the INPEC and the Minister of Justice.
137 See Guzman and A.A. Reyes, 1992, p. 45.
138 Law 65/1993.
139 Procuraduría General de la Nación, Primer y Segundo Informe sobre Derechos Humanos, 1990–91.
140 Contraloría General de la República, Auditoría, 1997.
141 *El Tiempo*, 30 April 2000.
142 INPEC is the National Prisons Directorate.
143 *El Tiempo*, 30 April 2000.
144 This percentage has remained fairly stable in the last three decades, even though some analysts put the percentage of those awaiting trial during the 1980s as high as 60 per cent. See, for instance, Nemoga, 1990, p. 180. Recently, new prisons statistics reveal that since the mid-1990s the percentage of prisoners awaiting trial has diminished and is in the order of 43 per cent (Inpec, 2001).
145 See Maier *et al.*, 2000.
146 *El Tiempo*, 30 April 2000.
147 The Defensoría del Pueblo, which as part of the Procuraduría General, is an institution similar to the Scandinavian Ombudsman.
148 Informe de la Alta Comisionada de las Naciones Unidas para los Derechos Humanos en Colombia, April 2000, p. 11.
149 Personal interview, Bogotá, September 1999.
150 Some commentators reacted with cynicism to the escape of James Spencer Springette from the high security prison La Picota while wanted for extradition by the United States. 'Prisoners who remain in jail do so because they do not have enough money to escape, or because they choose voluntarily to do so. Corruption in jails has reached such extremes that if the Rodríguez brothers (bosses of the Cali Cartel) wanted to escape, they would have no problem in doing so ...' Semana, 6–13 March.
151 After a recent riot in one of Bogotá's prisons it was revealed that the main newspaper of the FARC was designed, printed and circulated inside the Modelo prison with the approval of the prison governor. Asobancaria, 3 May 2000.
152 Cambio, 1–6 February 2000.
153 Corte Constitucional, Sentencia T-153 de 1998.
154 *Tutela* is more commonly known as *amparo* in most countries of Latin America. In Anglo-Saxon systems the institution of the writ has many elements of the *tutela*. Writ is an order issued by a court requiring the

performance of a specified act, or granting the authority for it to be done (Black, 1979).

155 The Asamblea Nacional Constituyente (ANC) was a temporary, democratically elected body of representatives from a wide range of social and political forces in Colombia. It was set up in January 1991 for a period of four months (see Table 2.5) with the purpose of reforming the existing Colombian Constitution of 1886 and introducing institutional mechanisms to resolve the political crisis.

156 See Cepeda, 1993, pp. 115–16.

157 The Procuraduría and the Contraloría do not form part of the judiciary, but I include them in the analysis of justice since they both carry para-judicial functions.

158 In fact judicial review has existed in Colombia since 1910 (Acto Legislativo No. 3 de 1910, Art. 41).

159 I should emphasise that the power to exercise judicial review necessarily puts the Constitutional Court above the other two Higher Courts, since judicial review by definition entails the power to adopt political decisions that will become binding (*res judicata*) and have *erga omnes* effects.

160 In Britain, for instance, the Parliament is supreme in the sense that any law that has been enacted by it and has been approved by the Crown becomes the law of the land and cannot be vetoed by any court.

161 See Abraham, 1993, p. 271.

162 See M.J. Cepeda, 1993, p. 124.

163 Art. 239 CN.

164 The limitations were introduced in order to reduce what many called 'the government of judges' which allegedly resulted from the judiciary's excessive independence in the appointment of judges which had existed in Colombia since 1957 when the *cooptación* system and the appointment for life of high court judges were introduced.

165 This new restriction was a response to strong criticism of the *cooptación* system. It was argued that, although *cooptación* made for the independence of judges it generated internal clientelism in the judiciary, since the magistrates of the high courts controlled the appointment of all judges, and also because those who were critical of the stances taken by the high courts were immediately dismissed as potential candidates, thus arresting the natural evolution and dialectical exchange which should characterised a constitutional court (Uprimny, 1997, pp. 80–1).

166 Uprimny, 2001b, pp. 298–9.

167 See M. García and Uprimny, 1999, p. 44.

168 See for example Corte Constitucional, C-995/2000 which is one of the most controversial decisions of the Court on economic matters.

169 Art. 240(5) CN.

170 In some cases, for example, in a ruling taken in 1996, after the assassination of Alvaro Gómez Hurtado, a former Senator and several times Presidential candidate, the Constitutional Court has put restrictions on the constitutional right to freedom of information by banning the identification of witnesses and news reports relating to terrorist acts. The worrying aspect of the Court's stance is not so much the temporary limitation put on freedom of information, but the authoritarian and anti-liberal argument used to justify

this decision, mainly the statement that public order should take precedence over fundamental rights, that is that there are no absolute rights. (Orozco, 1997, pp. 44–51 and Corte Constitucional, C-46, 1996).

171 See Hammergren, 1998, p. 31.

172 See Rosenn, 1974, pp. 812–3.

173 It may be said that judicial review in Colombia, as vested in the new Constitutional Court since 1991, regained the capacity to have substantial, as opposed to merely formal, control of the Constitution that it held during the early part of the twentieth century. Before the 1991 Constitution most analysts agreed that in the hands of the Supreme Court of Justice, the power of judicial review had slowly declined since 1944 as the country lived in an almost permanent state of siege, which was for the most part condoned and endorsed by the Supreme Court of Justice (Dueñas, 1996, pp. 94–7).

174 Respectively Corte Suprema: Sentencias de 5 de 1978, 3 Noviembre de 1981 and 5 de Marzo de 1987.

175 Discurso televisivo del Presidente Barco en *El Tiempo*, 13 January 1988, p. 1A.

176 See M. García, 2001, p. 349.

177 The Constitutional Court through its jurisprudence has established that social rights can be protected via the *tutela* when these rights have a direct connection with a fundamental right. This wide interpretation has given way for a growing number of rights that can be protected via the *tutela*. For more on this, see García, and Rodríguez, 2001.

178 The 1991 Constitution includes a long catalogue of fundamental rights and liberties. Many of these rights are contained in the Universal Declaration of Human Rights, others consist of social, economic and cultural rights and liberties. In fact, some ideals (such as the pursuit of peace) which cannot strictly speaking be classed as rights, are also presented as rights in Art. 22 of the 1991 Constitution (Arts. 11–41 CN).

179 Art. 86 CN and Decree 2591/1991.

180 See Gaviria, 1996.

181 See Barreto, 1996, p. 104.

182 See M. García and Uprimny, 1999, p. 67.

183 See Gaviria, 1996, pp. 47–8 and Cepeda, 1993, p. 71.

184 See M. García, unpublished, quoted in Gaviria, 1996, pp. 48–9.

185 A poll amongst users of the *tutela* in 1996 reveals that 79.1 per cent of its users argue that the *tutela* is a useful mechanism for resolving cases similar to theirs; 77.6 per cent say that it is useful in compensating for the inefficiency of the system of justice, 83.7 per cent consider that it protects people against state arbitrariness, and 83.1 per cent claim that the *tulela* provides social justice. This poll also shows that 92.9 per cent of judges have a positive view of the *tutela* and that they consider it as an efficient mechanism for the protection of the fundamental rights and liberties of the people (Ministerio de Justicia, 1996).

186 The extensive recourse to the *tutela* indicated by these figures is due to the inefficiency of the formal mechanisms of the system of justice, and the still experimental stage of operation of informal or alternative methods of conflict resolution.

187 See Uprimny, 1997, pp. 104–7 and Dueñas, 1996, pp. 92–4.

188 Every *tutela* decision has to be sent to the Constitutional Court for constitutional control purposes. Of these, the Constitutional Court, using well-established control criteria, selects approximately 2 per cent for review (Art. 86 CN and Barreto, 1996, pp. 114–15).
189 See Dueñas, 1996, pp. 94–7.
190 Prescription is a peremptory and perpetual bar to any species of action when a court of law has not decided a proceeding within a set period of time, generally fixed by the law.
191 Corte Constitutional, T-374/1993 and T-397/1993.
192 Amongst the most relevant public examples are those relate to CAJANAL and ISS, two state social security bodies, the EEB, or municipal energy agency of Bogotá and DIAN, which is the internal revenue service and national customs agency.
193 See Barreto, 1996, p. 105.
194 Alfonso Gómez Méndez, the *Fiscal General*. Cambio, 14 August 2000, p. 27.
195 Art. 254 CN.
196 Art. 256 CN. Before the 1991 Constitution this was a duty of the executive which it had neglected for several years.
197 Art. 256 CN.
198 In Colombia, the national government for legal purposes comprises the President and one or more Ministers of the cabinet.
199 Art. 254 CN.
200 In most European countries where it exists, the High Council of the Judiciary's main role is to limit the executive interference in the *fiscal* and administrative affairs of the judiciary.
201 Art. 278 CN.
202 Art. 277 CN.
203 Friendship in Colombia is a valid legal impediment for a judge not to try a particular case.
204 Art. 267 CN.
205 Art. 268 CN.
206 Art. 271 CN.
207 The National Tribunal and the regional courts were the courts responsible for the regional justice or *Justicia sin rostro*, which was abolished in June 1999. Regional justice was exceptionally enacted by the executive at the end of the 1980s to tackle crimes such as terrorism, kidnapping, rebellion, drug trafficking and other high social impact crimes.
208 *Cambio*, 24 April–1 May 2000.
209 The original article 35 of the 1991 Constitution (Art. 35 CN), which was rescinded in 1997, prohibited the extradition of Colombian nationals.
210 At the time Galán was considered to be the most likely candidate to win the 1990 presidential election.
211 There is some controversy surrounding the Extradition Treaty between Colombia and United States. When this treaty was adopted in Colombia it was not actually signed by the incumbent President Turbay, but by his delegate, since Turbay was out of the country at this time – some jurists have claimed that all international treaties have to be signed by the President in order to become binding. It has also been claimed that the absence of Turbay at the time of the signing of the Extradition Treaty was deliberate

because his political campaign had received money from the drug cartels (see Strong, 1995), and Turbay was therefore committed to protecting the interests of the cartels. In fact, the Extradition Treaty was never implemented during the Turbay administration and only in a few cases during the following one, that of Betancur, 1982–86.

212 See Melo, and Bermúdez, 1994, p. 110.

213 These decrees were meant to be provisional since the Constitution of 1886 limited the duration of emergency legislation to three months.

214 See Lee, R.W. III and Thoumi, 1998.

215 Independently of what happened at the ANC, Colombia's polity was and is very vulnerable to illegal drug moneys. The drug traffickers did influence the *Congresito* (little Congress) which followed on from the Constitutional Assembly during the interim period between the two Constitutions. Of particular note was the *Congresito* ratification of the decrees dealing with the Policy of Compliance with the System of Justice or PSJ, which allowed drug traffickers to give themselves up to the judicial authorities in exchange for soft penalties and disproportionate privileges (Lee and Thoumi, 1998).

216 Art. 28 CN.

217 The Constitution of 1886 more sensibly decreed that nobody could be searched or detained without an administrative order.

218 The past record on human rights violations by the Colombian Police supports this fear.

219 See Guzmán, Fals Borda and Luna, 1980.

220 Art. 218 CN.

221 For an analysis of the Colombian Police and its most recent reforms, see Llorente, 1999.

222 Policía Nacional – Revista Criminalidad 1995 and ibid., p. 448.

223 Crime control according to National Police data, consists of judicial police functions, intelligence or information gathering and anti-narcotics control. Most resources are directed towards the latter.

224 This proposition is based on data on the National Police in the journal *Criminalidad*, 1990–95 and DANE as analysed by Llorente, 1999, p. 440. I emphasise that this is only a proposition since police data are not available at local level in the municipalities, but only at departmental level.

225 See Llorente, 1999, pp. 455–6.

226 See Bayley, 1994.

227 Since 1991, police are under exclusive military jurisdiction (*fuero militar*), a situation that in the past granted the armed forces impunity. The 1991 Constitution not only kept the existing *fuero militar* for the military, but also extended it to the police, thus contradicting one of its own ordinances in which it was laid down that the National Police was essentially a civil body. In the light of this Constitutional provision, a judicial reform to the new Constitution expressly ordered that military and police courts should be composed of both active and inactive members of the military and the police (Acto Legislativo No. 2 de 25 Diciembre de 1995). This judicial reform contradicted a Constitutional Court decision of 1995 which had held that active members of the military could not be members of the military courts because the mere fact of there being military hierarchy would inhibit an impartial adjudication.

228 See M.J. Cepeda, 1993.
229 The evidence reveals that not even the most democratic aspects of Justice Reform, such as the *tutela*, originated on the left (Silva, 1997, pp. 77–8).
230 The history of the country since Independence has been shaped by numerous attempts at political agreements between the two traditional parties or factions of these. There have been at least a dozen coalition pacts between the Liberals and the Conservatives, of which the most important is claimed to be that constituted by the National Front. For an account of all the political agreements, see Kline, 1980 and Hartlyn, 1988.
231 The Gaviria administration played an important role in the development and final outcome of the ANC. Gaviria's Minister of Interior, Humberto de la Calle, was personally involved in the daily processes of the ANC – see J. Dugas 1993a and b (cf). See also M.J. Cepeda's comparison of the Gaviria Government's project of Constitutional Reform and the final text of the 1991 Constitution (M.J. Cepeda, 1993).
232 See Hammergren, 1998, pp. 233–4.
233 In 1979 a failed constitutional reform also tried to introduce the accusatorial system of justice.
234 An analysis of the functions of the *Fiscalía* may also shed some light on its role in initiating one of the most serious corruption crisis ever in Colombia with the infamous *Proceso 8000*. *Proceso 8000* is the name given to the criminal proceedings, conducted by the *Fiscalía* to establish the criminal liability of those responsible for the infiltration of drug money from the Cali Cartel into the funding of Ernesto Samper's Presidential campaign in 1994.
235 The role of development agencies in the Colombian 1991 judicial reform was minor compared to their influence in other countries of the region. The United States' aid agency (USAID), for instance, lobbied the 1991 pre-constitutional process in order to push for the introduction of a US-style, accusatorial criminal system. Their lobby didn't really succeed in 1991. Following the Constitutional reform, USAID played a somewhat more important role via its funding to train Colombian *fiscales*, and in the legal regulation of certain aspects of the criminal process. The United Nations PNUD role was even more marginal. Its mission was limited to the funding of external consultants, in particular in the topic of judicial reform. Although comparative law was widely used to reform the judiciary in 1991, and elements of the US accusatorial model were partially adopted the process was coordinated entirely by the Gaviria administration and by members of the 1991 Constitutional Assembly.
236 Art. 250 CN.
237 See Lleras de la Fuente *et al.*, 1992, p. 428.
238 See Uprimny, 1993.
239 The punitive powers of the state have always been feared since the efficiency of a punitive system of justice can come into conflict with the fundamental rights and guarantees of the individual (Zaffaroni, 1986, p. 135).
240 ICAC, 1994, p. 3.
241 Ibid., p. 4.
242 See Uprimny, 1993, p. 13.
243 Art. 249 CN.

244 Before the existence of the *Fiscalía*, each court or tribunal was responsible for a variety of processes which were within its jurisdiction, but there was no body in overall charge of criminal proceedings.
245 See Uprimny, 1993, p. 16.
246 Arts 119, 121 and 250 CPP and Uprimny, 1993.
247 Art. 19, Estatuto Orgánico de la *Fiscalía*.
248 See Zaffaroni, 1986, p. 129.
249 Art. 249 CN.
250 Up to September 1997, the *Fiscalía* had brought charges against 8 public officials, and decisions were expected shortly in 13 other cases which were in the hands of the judges.
251 *Semana*, 18 April 1995, p. 27.
252 *Semana*, 9 May 1995, p. 49.
253 See De Sousa Santos and García, 2001, p. 463.
254 See for example Sáez, 1998; Hammergren, 1998 and Maier *et al.*, 2000.
255 See North, 1990.
256 In fact, the necessity to show results in the administration of justice has determined a judicial policy that privileges efficiency, understood as clearing the judicial backlog of the courts, over the equal access to the system and the increase of justice coverage (justice demand).
257 See Maguire, 1997, p. 139.
258 See Deas, in M. Deas and F. Gaitán, 1995.
259 It is fair to highlight that from the mid-1980s and in particular after the expedition of the 1991 Constitution, research in many aspects of justice is increasing as the growing body of literature reveals. For a sample see Separata de la Revista Estudios Socio-Jurídicos No. 2, 1999.
260 SER is a Colombian private institute for social science research. Unfortunately, many of the SER investigations are not available to the public; of those that were published, only a very limited number of copies were printed.
261 See for example A.A. Reyes, 1990 who when quoting data on the administration of justice, refers to previous works of Giraldo and Velez, 1987, or Pérez, 1994, who refers to all three.
262 The relation between rhetoric and reality in the discourse of justice in Colombia is ambiguous. In many cases the rhetoric may, to a great extent, reflect what a particular group (the political class, the media or people from the legal profession) perceives as reality. The danger of this type of rhetoric is that it is often quoted as fact by the dominant groups, or even the media, and this information remains unchallenged (for example, the expression 99 per cent of impunity). In other cases, the rhetoric does seem to reflect a prevailing opinion among citizens about what they perceive as a reality – such rhetoric is valuable since it reflects the degree of credibility and hence legitimacy that the system has among the people.
263 Evidence of this ongoing rhetoric can be found in Castro and Reyes Echandía, 1978; J. Giraldo *et al.*, 1987; Velez *et al.*, 1987; Reyes, 1989, 1990 and 1992; Guzmán and Reyes, 1992 and Pérez, 1994.
264 Though not all of my data on crimes comes from DANE, most of it does, since, in spite of all warnings, it is still the most reliable source to date.
265 DANE, La justicia Colombiana en Cifras, 1937–94, p. 26.

266 The changes of methodology in the presentation of the data respond to the type of data that was found. Even DANE's data is sometimes presented inconsistently.
267 See Rubio, 1999, p. 139.
268 Before the 1971 Statute each judge was in charge of both the instruction and the judgment of a criminal case.
269 This idea was developed by Rubio, 1999. See also DANE, La justicia Colombiana en cifras, 1937–94.
270 DANE, Boletín Mensual de Estadística, No. 317, 1977.
271 DANE, Estadísticas Judiciales, in Reyes, 1989.
272 DANE, La justicia Colombiana en cifras, 1937–94, p. 32.
273 Note the difference in the statistical data for 1980 in bold in both tables mentioned above (Instituto SER para la investigación and DANE figures). A possible explanation for the differences in the percentage of accumulated proceedings in 1980, and during the decade of the 1980s, could be the fact that the data of the Instituto SER includes the number of atypical ways used to finish a proceeding – in particular, writs of prescription and filing that are explained below – when calculating the judicial backlog, whereas, in the DANE figure, this percentage was based strictly on the sentences that constituted final decisions (*res judicata*).
274 Arts 250(3), 271 and 277 CN.
275 See J. Giraldo, 1996, pp. 110–11.
276 Internal *Fiscalía* statistics, Flujo de Procesos Junio 1997–Junio 2000 and Cambio, 14 Agosto 2000, pp. 18–27.
277 See Spotts and Wieser, 1986, p. 154.
278 See Muñoz-Gómez, 1980, pp. 198–222.
279 A judicial process in Colombia can legally last almost a decade, mainly because of the three judicial instances that most cases go through; that is, initial proceeding, appeal and extraordinary appeal. In addition, in each of these three instances the lawyer of the defendant has the right to contest practically every step (even a procedural one) taken by the *fiscal* or judge in the course of the criminal prosecution and trial.
280 Instituto SER para la Investigación, 1984, pp. 78–116.
281 The 1991 Constitution introduced other ways of finalising a proceeding which are not sentences, but which do resolve the essence of the conflict. One such informal mechanism is the conciliation.
282 This high index of prescription could have resulted from the events that followed the Toma del Palacio de Justicia.
283 Art. 347, Decree 050/1987.
284 Arts 41 and 42, Law 81/1993.
285 The data is based on figures collected by the Instituto Ser para la Investigación published in *Coyuntura Social*, No. 15, November 1996, pp. 47–58.
286 *Fiscalía* General de la Nación. Indices de Gestión 1997–98 and 1998–99.
287 Art. 36 CPP.
288 Personal interviews with *fiscales*, Bogotá, August 2000.
289 The sectional *fiscalías* have jurisdiction over homicides, simple kidnapping, sexual offences, embezzlements and forgeries.
290 Instituto Ser para la Investigación, *Coyuntura Social*, No. 15, November 1996 and J. Giraldo, 1996, pp. 104–5.

291 *Fiscalía* General de la Nación. Informe de Gestión, 1998–1999, p. 54.
292 Instituto SER and Federarrollo, *Coyuntura Social*, No. 15, November 1996, p. 47.
293 Unreported and reported criminality definitions are taken from DANE, La justicia Colombiana en cifras, 1937–94, p. 21.
294 Excerpts of HMIC, *The Sunday Times*, 22 October 2000.
295 See Rubio, 1999, p. 64.
296 Personal Interview with former policeman, Bogotá, August 2000.
297 DANE, 1987, p. 204 and DANE, La justicia Colombiana en cifras, 1996, p. 256.
298 DANE, 1993, p. 515.
299 See Gaitán, in M. Deas and F. Gaitán, 1995, p. 330.
300 Departamento de Planeación Nacional, Justicia y Desarrollo, 1994.
301 See M.M. Cuellar, 2000.
302 DANE, La justicia Colombiana en cifras, 1937–94, p. 103.
303 See Rubio, 1999, pp. 231–3.
304 Excerpts of the Departmento de Planeación Nacional 1998 report. Cambio, 14 August 2000 and personal interview with the Fiscal General, Alfonso Gómez, 16 August 2000.
305 This was not made clear by the Departmento de Planeación Nacional report, a situation that only reinforced the commonly held belief that impunity is in the order of 95 to 99 per cent. Worst of all, Planeación Nacional is one of the most trusted institutions of the Colombian state, making its statements on impunity even more perverse.
306 The *Consejo Superior* asked the Department of Mathematics and Statistics of the Universidad Nacional to construct a probabilistic model to quantify impunity. The sample for this model carried between 1997 and 1998 consists of 3200 households, all the 41 existing *fiscalías locales* and *seccionales* of Bogotá, 66 of the 88 existing municipal courts, and 41 of the existing 55 circuit courts of Bogotá. Social impunity is measured using a household poll with two variables: household victims of crimes which went unreported and household victims of crimes which were reported to the authorities. Judicial impunity is measured by analysing the three phases of criminal proceedings and identifying in each the procedural steps that constitute impunity in the different *fiscalías* and courts of Bogotá. The model classifies as impunity those cases which prescribe and those which are suspended for lack of identification of the culprit in the preliminary phase. In the prosecution phase, prescription and the expiration of legal terms are both considered as impunity. Finally, the model classifies as impunity in the judgment phase cases where acquittal is given as a result of uncertainty of the culprit's responsibility, prescription and *preclusión* (Consejo Superior de la Judicatura y Universidad Nacional de Colombia, 2000, p. 65).
307 The model also showed that the probability of being a victim of a crime in Bogotá, reported or not, is 29 per cent. The predominant crimes are against property (73.7 per cent), followed by crimes against life and personal integrity (7.9 per cent), crimes against the moral integrity and family (6.9 per cent and 6 per cent respectively), offences against personal freedom (4.9 per cent) and finally sexual offences (0.6 per cent). Amongst these offences those that went more unreported were the crimes against the moral integrity (81.7 per cent unreported), followed by those against property

(66.8 per cent unreported). By contrast, the offences that were reported the most were those against life and personal integrity (30.9 per cent unreported). Even though offences against life and personal integrity are the most reported it is very grave that in the capital city 30.9 per cent of these crimes still go unreported.

308 The crimes of more social significance under the jurisdiction of the sectional *fiscalías* and circuit courts are homicide, simple kidnapping, embezzlement, forgery and sexual offences. The local *fiscalías* and municipal courts, which are of inferior hierarchy to the circuit courts, have jurisdiction over crimes against property that does not exceed 50 minimum salaries and crimes that require *querella,* that is denunciation of the victim of the offence. The most significant offences requiring *querella* are incest, bigamy, illegal marriage, absence of alimony, misappropriation of goods, calumny, illegal transference or fraudulent emission of checks, all offences related to the personal integrity of individuals and those described in Art. 29 CPP, Arts 72 and 73 CPP. Since 1995, municipal courts have also had jurisdiction over special misdemeanours such as simple theft, personal injuries, and minor abuses (Law 228/1995).

309 Among the total number of reported crimes (approximately 30 per cent of the crimes are reported in Bogotá according to the Universidad Nacional Model), a large number corresponds to cases where the defendant is unknown. Some analysts have shown that, on average, 20 per cent of the overall proceedings correspond to unknown defendants (Guzmán *et al.*, 1992). Exceptionally, this percentage rose in 1986 when almost 50 per cent of the criminal processes corresponded to unknown defendants (Ortiz, 1990, p. 179).

310 Consejo Superior de la Judicatura y Universidad Nacional de Colombia. 2000, pp. 68–9.

311 Moreover, Colombia has one of the highest homicides rates in the world.

312 Ley 228/1995 and Corte Constitucional C-364/1996.

313 Similar results are reached by an unpublished study of the Universidad de los Andes on property offences made in 2000.

314 See M. García and Uprimny, 1999, p. 40.

315 Consejo Superior de la Judicatura y Universidad Nacional de Colombia, 2000, pp. 52–3.

316 A person who is unable to understand the illegality of his conduct or is unable to act according to his understanding at the moment of committing the offence is *inimputable,* either for psychological immaturity or mental derangement. In addition, those younger than 18 are treated as *inimputables* (Arts 31 to 34 CP). The main causes of justifiability of a crime are the strict fulfilment of a legal duty or right and personal defence, provided these are proportional to the aggression (Art. 29 CP).

317 See Maguire, 1997, p. 173.

318 Consejo Superior de la Judicatura y Universidad Nacional, 2000, pp. 52–3.

319 See Guzmán and Reyes, 1992, p. 45.

320 The most recent statistics revealed that in July 2000 there were 55 000 prisoners.

321 See Inpec, 1997.

322 See Montenegro, 1994.

323 See Guzmán and A.A. Reyes, 1992, p. 46.

324 See Nemoga, 1990, p. 180.
325 See Inpec, 2000.
326 Ministerio de Justicia, 1992a.
327 See Sandoval, in L. Guzmán and A.A. Reyes, 1992, p. 59.
328 E. Caballero, *El Espectador*, 6 January 1979.
329 Universidad Nacional, CID, 1989.
330 DANE, Anuarios de Justicia de 1971 a 1975 y Tabulados de Justicia: de 1976 a 1993.
331 See Maguire, 1997, p. 174.
332 See Losada and Velez, 1981.
333 The sample included 504 individuals from the main four cities of the country and was carried out between 12 and 14 June 1992 by the Centro Nacional de Consultoría; see Lemoine, 1993, p. 264.
334 See Centro Nacional de Consultoría, August 1997.
335 See Losada and Vélez, 1981.
336 A 1997 survey shows that among the poorer sectors of society lawyers are either not easy to find or are considered 'undesirable'. In fact, only 8 per cent of less well-to-do individuals admit to having used a lawyer to settle a civil dispute (Cuellar, 2000, p. 594).
337 These claims come from my own experience as a former law student providing legal aid, but also from informal interviews with colleagues and members of the judiciary. One of the first experiences that struck me as a legal aid lawyer was the case of a petty thief (he had stolen a pair of blue jeans) who had been waiting trial for 3 years while in prison. Desperation led him to study and learn by heart the criminal code to the point, that when we met, he gave me all the arguments that legally justified his immediate release from prison. All he needed was a lawyer.
338 President Carlos Lleras Restrepo, Ministerio de Justicia, 1964, p. 341.
339 See Betancur, 1978, p. 225.
340 See Gaitán, in M. Deas and F. Gaitán, 1995, p. 403.
341 The sample included 699 individuals from Bogotá, Medellín, Cali and Barranquilla and was carried out on 1 and 2 July 1992 (Centro Nacional de Consultoría en Lemoine, C., 1993).
342 The sample included more than 1000 individuals from each country and was carried out between September and November 1979 (International Public Opinion 1980–81, p. 512, in C. Lemoine, 1993, p. 222).
343 In terms of questionnaires, this is not a good question since it asks about two potentially unrelated things.
344 The survey by the Centro Nacional de Consultoría was carried out between May and June 1997 in many rural and urban areas of Colombia. The sample included 3000 individuals, of which there were 250 judges, 250 teachers, 250 members of the armed forces and 250 inhabitants from the most violent areas of the country. The survey was done using personal interviews and detailed questionnaires. Technical details and samples of the questions are available in Cuellar. The survey was coordinated and analysed by M.M. Cuellar, 2000, pp. 47–137.
345 See M.M. Cuellar, 2000.
346 According to the 1997 survey, the necessity for criminal justice is higher for those with middle and high income, than for those with low income.

This necessity is particularly high for offences against life and personal integrity.

347 At the level of civil disputes the situation is very similar; 44 per cent of the population does nothing when a civil conflict arises: 36 per cent perceives justice as ineffective because of excessive procedures or ignorance as to how to proceed, whereas 9 per cent, does not do anything out of fear of reprisal or because they believe threats to be more effective (Cuellar, 200, p. 597).

348 Judges were obviously the least critical of their own inefficiency – 23 per cent in contrast with 35 per cent of the total population.

349 Personal Interview, Bogotá, 16 August 2000.

350 In this operation, 5000 members of the military took the *barrios* of the Comuna Nororiental of Medellín with the objective of dismantling the *sicarios* bands that were at the service of the Medellín Cartel (Salazar and Jaramillo, 1996, pp. 98–101).

351 *El Mundo*, Medellín, 18 April 1990, p. 7.

352 Even though we cannot tell from the way the question was posed whether the victims reported these crimes, the data related to subsidiary questions gives an idea of the high degree of unreported homicides.

353 These include personal injuries, domestic violence and sexual crimes.

354 'Private justice' is defined in this survey as life threats, homicides and kidnapping.

355 See Vélez *et al.*, 1987b.

356 Ibid., p. 15.

357 The 1997 survey reveals that for the judges theirs is the most respected profession. However, for the general public, and even for the teachers (who themselves are respected by judges), the judges' profession is one of the least respected (Cuellar, 2000, pp. 489–90).

358 See Losada and Vélez, 1986.

359 See Vélez *et al.*, 1987b, p. 46.

360 Evolución de la Percepción de los Dirigentes sobre la Corrupción, 1991 and 1994. The sample included 50 people related to industrial and commercial activities and also some high public officials and ex-officials of state institutions. The synthesis of these surveys was published in Cepeda (comp.), 1997, pp. 149–64.

361 Centro Nacional de Consultoría, August 1997. The sample included 1378 people from 35 municipalities and cities interviewed personally in August 1997 (374 of those interviewed came from the most violent municipalities of Colombia).

362 The opinions of the judges were collected through a written questionnaire sent out to judges and clerks (a different one to each). The sample included judges and clerks from most departments of Colombia and from all hierarchical levels of the judiciary. Additional interviews were carried out in eight courts in Bogotá to check some of the evidence collected through the questionnaires. In those regions and courts where the questionnaires were not answered, face-to-face interviews were carried out in order to fulfil the minimum quotas per region and per hierarchical position which were required by the sample. For more details on the sample, see Vélez *et al.*, 1987b, pp. 141–5.

363 Ibid., p. 50.

364 *Latin American Weekly Report*, 31 October 1980, p. 2.
365 Ibid.
366 It is interesting to point out that the most critical judges are not a homogenous group – they include judges from Bogotá, magistrates of the district tribunals, graduates of private and public universities and, not surprisingly, those who have been personally threatened (Vélez *et al.*, 1987b, p. 52).
367 Ibid., pp. 60–1.
368 Ibid., p. 62.
369 A document taken from a member of the Ochoa family (Medellín Cartel) arrested in 1987 was leaked to the Press in January 1988; it suggested that dozens of leading politicians and public figures were in the payroll of drug barons. The alleged recipients of payoffs from the Medellín Cartel included high-ranking officials in the Ministry of Justice, former judges and a number of attorneys (*Latin American Weekly Report*, 21 January 1988, p. 8).
370 The 1997 survey reveals that the crime that makes judges feel the most insecure is kidnapping (23 per cent), followed by homicide (21 per cent). In comparison with the general population, 19 per cent fear kidnapping and 13 per cent homicide. Moreover, the judges' fear of violence against them is exemplified in the percentage who are afraid to ride on a bus, 43 per cent, compared with 22 per cent for the general population and 20 per cent for the armed forces (M.M. Cuellar, 2000, p. 668).
371 Although I was asked by this judge to send my student ID, the day before the interview she decided not to see me, allegedly out of fear. I had to ask my original contact to make up a short questionnaire, and some of the questions that I prepared were left unanswered.
372 I note here that, to date, in 44.9 per cent of these homicides or threats there is no one identified as culprit.
373 See Bonilla and Villa, 1992.
374 The Toma del Palacio de Justicia (the takeover of the Justice building) was a tragic episode where many of the magistrates and clerks of the then two highest Tribunals of the country, that is the Supreme Court of Justice and the Consejo de Estado, were killed in a confusing operation of armed confrontation between the left-wing guerrillas, members of the M-19 and the Colombian military. The M-19 violently took over the Justice building and, using the magistrates as hostages, demanded a public trial of the President of Colombia, Belisario Betancur. The guerrillas accused Betancur's administration of double-crossing in peace talks and of oppression by the 'leading class' and 'high military officials'. However, their most telling demand was that the Supreme Court magistrates decide 'here and now' whether Colombia should continue to surrender not only its national resources but also 'through an unpopular extradition treaty' the jurisdiction over Colombian nationals, which they regarded as 'a mortal blow against national sovereignty'. This latter claim led most analysts to argue that drug traffickers were behind the Toma del Palacio. See Strong, 1995, p. 146. The military tried to rescue the hostages and stop the insurgent movement from pursuing their goals. The fatal confrontation of the two and the excessive military force left most magistrates of the Supreme Court dead, together with their staff and an unknown number of guerrilla members who were inside the building. The building itself was left in ruins, and in many people's

minds the image of a military tank entering the small door of the Palacio de Justicia remains.

375 See Bonilla and Villa, 1992.

376 I found no record of the number of assassinated judges in the Ministry of Justice, nor as part of any other official statistic.

377 For more on the Italian case, see Stille, 1996.

378 See Bagley, 1989, p. 11.

379 *El Espectador*, 3 July 1999, p. 1A.

380 See Cuellar, 2000.

381 This data coincides with survey results that show that 2 per cent of judges accept the use of 'private justice'.

382 Decreto legislativo 1855 de 1989.

383 See Nemogá, 1996.

384 Mico is an expression used in Colombia to describe pieces of legislation that are introduced in a statute in a clandestine manner, having no relation to the topic that the specific statute regulates.

385 Corte Constitucional, C-392/2000, 6 April 2000.

386 It should be added that it is indeed significant that the Constitutional Court decision that abolished the Special Justice Statute was adopted by 5 votes to 4.

387 *El Espectador*, 4 April 2000, p. 5A and *El Tiempo*, 4 April 2000, p. 2C.

388 The Comisión Andina de Juristas is an NGO (Non Government Organisation) that acts as a watchdog for human rights violations. In Colombia, it has a reputation of being pro-guerrilla, and consequently anti-right-wing.

389 See Bonilla and Villa, 1992.

390 See Rubio, 1999.

391 In June 1998, when he was still running for the presidency, Andrés Pastrana announced that if he were elected he would order military forces to withdraw from a portion of territory in the sub-Amazon region around San Vicente del Cagúan, in order to guarantee the FARC leadership safety so that the government peace negotiations with the group could begin. The demilitarised zone, referred to as the *zona de despeje*, included five municipal districts, each one with less than a few hundred thousand inhabitants, but each with as much territory as a small European country. The extension of the *despeje* adds up to 26 250 square miles – the size of Switzerland. San Vicente, which sits on the edge of the *despeje* closest to Bogotá, was the centre for the peace talks. The FARC guerrillas, who for all practical purposes already controlled the rolling countryside around it, were allowed free rein in San Vicente from December 1998, when withdrawal of the military began, until the beginning of 2002 when the talks ended.

392 Manuel Marulanda declarations, *El Espectador*, 3 March 1999, p. 1A.

393 See Brecht, 1960, p. 108.

394 This evidence was found between 26 August and 10 September 1997 in the Procuraduría Delegada para la Vigilancia Judicial in Bogotá where I studied more than 30 cases of 'inefficiency' by judges in the administration of justice that were decided between 1990 and 1996.

395 The Supreme Court of Justice, in a decision of 1990, defined what was meant by unjustified delay in the administration of justice. In this decision, the Court held that to defer deliberately or wilfully procrastinate over

a decision, thus exceeding the legal term in judicial proceedings, was an unjustified delay (Supreme Court of Justice, 10 July 1990).

396 Most of the 30 cases that I reviewed involved instances of inefficiency by clerks or office secretaries rather than inefficiency by judges or *fiscales*. It was hard to judge from the evidence whether the delays were justified or not.

397 Tribunal Superior de Orden Público, 1992.

398 Procuraduría Delegada para la Vigilancia Judicial, 6 June 1996.

399 Personal interviews with two public officials of the Procuraduría para la Vigilancia Judicial, 2 September 1997.

400 This claim is corroborated by data from the Consejo Superior analysed below, which reveals that in fact a large number of lawyers have been penalised for corruption-related causes and is also corroborated by my case study. Moreover, the 1997 survey shows that lawyers are generally not respected, not even by judges (Cuellar, 2000, p. 490).

401 Personal interview with a member of the Procuraduría, 2 September 1997.

402 Personal interview with an official of the Procuraduría Delegada para la Vigilancia Judicial, 2 September 1997. The person interviewed constituted a very valuable source of information: firstly, because he was one of the few members of the system of justice to talk openly about corruption in the judiciary (he had worked for more than a decade in the Procuraduría), but also because I had known him from the time when I worked in the Procuraduría and hence I believe he trusted me.

403 A public office approach defines corruption as '... behavior which deviates from the formal duties of a public role because of private regarding (personal, close family, private clique) pecuniary or status gains; or violates rules against the exercise of certain types of private-regarding influence. This includes such behavior as bribery (use of reward to pervert the judgment of a person in a position of trust); nepotism (bestowal of patronage by reason of adscriptive relationship rather than merit); and misappropriation (illegal appropriation of public resources for private-regarding uses' (Nye, 1989, p. 966).

404 This perception coincides with the general public view of corruption in more than 10 surveys carried out during the 1990s.

405 The lack of accountability for the actions of the state and its agents has been characteristic of Colombia's political system.

406 This was, however, a unilateral decision of the Consejo Superior, something I was told by a member of the Consejo Superior in June 1998. I don't know what the reaction of the Procuraduría was, nor what is happening in practice.

407 Indeed, most members of the judiciary and the Procuraduría come from the same universities and have similar backgrounds (Pérez, 1994, p. 98).

408 These were the only available statistics on corruption that the Procuraduría could supply, at least until 1994.

409 Procuraduría General de la Nación. Informe sobre Corrupción, 1994.

410 Consejo Superior de la Judicatura, Informe de la Labor jurisdiccional disciplinaria, 1992–96.

411 The percentage of penalised members of the judiciary by the Consejo Superior de la Judicatura has had a tendency to increase. In 1995, the number of disciplined members was 253 (ibid.).

412 Personal interview with a Magistrate of the Consejo Superior de la Judicatura, Sala Disciplinaria, 1 April 1997.

413 Consejo Superior de la Judicatura, internal document, 1999. The non-technical way in which these statistics were presented and processed makes me slightly apprehensive about the future of judicial statistics in the charge of the Consejo Superior. It could also reflect a lack of interest from the Consejo Superior in showing their performance to outsiders.
414 Consejo Superior de la Judicatura, 1993, p. 146.
415 This decision of the Consejo Superior is very worrying since it accepts judges' and clerks' negligence as an excuse for their disciplinary responsibility.
416 The ordinary jurisdiction comprises criminal, civil and labour matters.
417 Contraloría General de la República. Auditoría, 1997.
418 Up to 1991, corruption as a crime was defined by the law (Código Penal de 1980) as peculation, extortion, abuse of power or authority, illegal enrichment, prevarication (breach of duty), and fraud in public documents. This legal approach is used in the Externado investigation.
419 See Cancino, 1994.
420 I consider that the results of this research will allow only a general view of the incidence of corruption of judges since the research has three limitations. First, it does not involve a systematic study of all cases of corruption of judges in the period 1980–91. Second, the Externado investigation only includes those cases of corruption of judges that reached the stage of extraordinary review by the Supreme Court of Justice, that is, after each of the decisions analysed had been ruled on by the first instance judge and had gone through appellate jurisdiction or second instance. Thirdly, the cases included as corruption are often cases of judicial delay which should not be classified as corruption.
421 A delay of 8 years is certainly a cause of major concern for the administration of justice. It could even be claimed that the chronic inefficiency of the system constitutes a form of corruption.
422 The 'reparto' (allotment) of cases that reach the courts is supposed to be done following impartial procedures. It is known that lawyers manipulate these procedures in order to have their cases heard by friendly judges or by those judges who are easily intimidated.
423 Under the title 'Evil lawyers' it is claimed that lawyers are profiting from the weakness and inefficiency of justice. Recently it was shown that penalties imposed on corrupt lawyers do not deter them from continuing to carry out corrupt deals. 'Out of 107 sanctioned lawyers in the last three years, 39 have relapsed. Some lawyers have such a hard skin that they are not affected by their reputation or disciplinary status. These lawyers have converted litigation into a market for the opportunists' (*Cambio*, 6–13 March 2000).
424 Consejo Superior de la Judicatura, Informe de la Labor jurisdiccional disciplinaria, 1992–96.
425 It should be noted that not all of the 42 cases of corruption were punished by the Supreme Court; some were prescribed, and others that were clearly established were closed indefinitely because of formalities.
426 The 1968 and 1986 survey results are quoted in Losada and Vélez, 1986.
427 The survey did not specify whether this meant that judges had accepted or merely been offered a bribe (Vélez *et al.*, 1987b, p. 40).
428 I have found only one study that deals directly with judicial corruption in Colombia: see Cancino, 1994.

429 In fact, one of the few surveys that mentioned justice in the 1980s shows that the courts are perceived as the least corrupt state institutions (Centro Nacional de Consultoría, March 1984, in Lemoine, 1986).
430 Estudio sobre percepción de la justicia, 1995. The survey's main objectives were to diagnose the perception of the efficiency, access and impartiality of the administration of justice in Colombia. The sample included 4903 people (non-public officials) from the 7 biggest cities of the country between the ages of 18–60; 1200 users of the system in Bogotá, Medellín and Cali and 50 experts; it was carried out during February and March 1994.
431 This survey is important because it is one of the few of its kind (only recently DANE – the official body in charge of statistics – has initiated a similar survey) and also because it included the views of the general public, a group of experts in the field, and a broad percentage of users of the system of justice. The survey included many open questions, a feature that makes it even more valuable since it includes qualitative as well as quantitative data.
432 By users of the system I mean those individuals who had already been involved in judicial proceedings as defendants, victims and so on.
433 This suggests that the system of justice also suffers from the problem of having an unfavourable image.
434 Opinion of a criminal lawyer writing in Estudio sobre Percepción de la Justicia, 1995.
435 These differentiations are based on a theory from Taylor, 1982.
436 Ibid., p. 18.
437 Testimony of a judge, who had been in the judiciary for 9 years, writing in Estudio sobre Percepción de la Justicia, 1995.
438 Testimony of a judge who had been in the judiciary for 17 years, ibid.
439 Personal interview with a former *fiscal sin rostro*, Bogotá, 10 September 1997.
440 Ibid.
441 Evidence from the 1997 survey supports this claim when it shows that the wealthiest are those who mostly use 'private justice' (Cuellar, 2000).
442 Testimony of a *fiscal* who has been in the *Fiscalía* since its creation in 1992 (Estudio sobre Percepción de la Justicia, 1995).
443 Estudio de Opiniones y Percepciones de la Justicia en Colombia, Resumen Ejecutivo, 1995, p. 5.
444 The 1994 survey also revealed that public opinion in Colombia depended primarily on the media, so that it was very difficult to differentiate between the two.
445 Since those interviewed could select between one or more options the percentage adds up to more than 100 per cent.
446 See Frears, 1988, pp. 307–8.
447 Estudio de Opiniones y Percepciones de la Justicia en Colombia, Resumen Ejecutivo, 1995, p. 9.
448 See Caballero, 1996.
449 Testimony of a judge writing in Estudio sobre percepción de la justicia, 1995.
450 Ibid.
451 The 1997 survey divides these sectors into teachers, judges, armed forces and the rest of society.
452 See Cuellar, 2000, pp. 569, 577, 580 and 586.

453 See Buscaglia and Dakolias, 1999, p. 2.

454 Ibid., p. 3.

455 A recent example has been the case of a *juez sin rostro* (faceless judge) in charge of hearing the case charges for cocaine trafficking to Costa Rica against Miguel Rodríguez (one of the main Cali Cartel leaders now imprisoned). The *juez sin rostro* heroically rejected several attempts at pressurizing him, and turned down a bribe of $1000 million pesos allegedly made by one of his hierarchical superiors (a Magistrate of the *Tribunal Nacional*, Carlos H. Sánchez) for him to clear Miguel Rodríguez. Instead, the judge convicted Rodríguez, handing down a 24-year jail sentence and sued the corrupt magistrate who was sacked by the *Consejo Superior de la Judicatura* in a speedy disciplinary procedure (Consejo Superior de la Judicatura, Judgment, 12 March 1998).

456 Testimony of the Minister of Justice, *El Tiempo*, 19 January 1997, p. 11A.

457 Decertification is a process whereby the Congress of the United States of America imposes a sanction on a country which in its view does not fulfil certain democratic requirements. It is a political decision that can lead to economic sanctions.

458 This principle orders that the most favourable law to the accused should always prevail (Art. 29 CN).

459 Código Unico Disciplinario. Ley 200 de 1995.

460 Personal interview with a Magistrate of the Consejo Superior de la Judicatura, 1 April 1997.

461 Not surprisingly, the author of the 1995 Disciplinary Statute, the former Procurador General, is currently preventatively detained accused of illegal enrichment.

462 Consejo Superior de la Judicatura, Judgment, 12 March 1998.

463 Personal interview with a Magistrate of the Consejo Superior de la Judicatura, Sala Disciplinaria, 1 April 1997.

464 *El Tiempo*, 19 January, 1997, p. 1A.

465 See Vélez *et al.*, 1987 and Estudio sobre Percepción de la Justicia, 1995.

466 See Merrill, 1989, p. 126.

467 I divide these periods, partially using McRae's chronology (McRae, 1998).

468 See Krauthausen and Sarmiento, 1991, p. 32.

469 Most of the violence of the second and third phases described in this chapter is perpetrated by the Medellín Cartel. The Cali Cartel was 'tolerated' by the state until the beginning of the 1990s. The different degree of involvement of the two cartels is summed up in a phrase in the British *Guardian* newspaper, where, in an interview, one of the Cali leaders claims: 'we don't kill judges, we buy them'.

470 See Medina, 1990, pp. 20–3. For example, the kidnapping by guerrillas of the sister of one of the leaders of the Medellín Cartel, Marta Ochoa, marked the birth of MAS – Muerte a Secuestradores (Death to the Kidnappers' paramilitary), one of the first paramilitary organisations of the drug traffickers.

471 Enraged by Minister Lara's assassination, President Belisario Betancur (1982–86) announced the initiation of extradition of Colombian nationals to the United States. Days after Belisario's offensive a group of drug traffickers, headed by Jorge Luis Ochoa and Pablo Escobar (later known as the 'extraditables'), made what would be their first attempt at negotiation with

the government. They met in Panama city with *Procurador* Carlos Jiménez Gómez and ex-President Alfonso López Michelsen and proposed the dismantling of their illegal activities in exchange for a ban on extradition of Colombian nationals. The dialogues did not progress and the Betancur administration extradited a few Colombians, the most notorious being Carlos Ledher, who was at the time an internally discredited member of the Medellín Cartel, *El Mundo*, Medellín, 8 July 1984 and Salazar and Jaramillo, 1996, pp. 70–1.

472 Thoumi, 1995 and Salazar and Jaramillo, 1996 provide a partial list of the victims.

473 The FARC creation of the UP, Unión Patriótica – a legal party that would soon be contending in national elections – was a way of opening the FARC to the part of the country that was not rural. 'But a campaign of terror against the Unión Patriótica, and against the left in general, was unleashed simultaneously with Betancur's offer of peace'. In 1988, when Colombians were first allowed to elect their own mayors, the Unión Patriótica participated, and won eighteen mayoralties out of about a thousand. Thirteen of these mayors were subsequently assassinated, often after having been forced to resign. No one has ever been charged with these murders, but it is widely assumed that members of the military, which has historically operated more or less independently of the chief executive, and sometimes at loggerheads with it, played a role. In 1991, on the same day that a national convention charged with drafting a new constitution held its first session, the FARC headquarters ... was at long last bombed and overrun by the army – a worthy military goal whose timing was evidently political. For all practical purposes, the Unión Patriótica (UP) was now dead, peace talks had been definitely suspended, and the FARC was on an all-out war footing again. By 1992, 3500 UP militants and leaders of the legal party, including two presidential candidates, had been assassinated (although only a handful of those murders have ever been brought to trial). The guerrillas had lost nearly all of their urban, better-educated, politically minded leaders ...' Prieto, 2000.

474 Corte Suprema de Justicia, 5 December 1986. The motivation of the Supreme Court of Justice's decision is clearly procedural. It argued that the Extradition Treaty was unconstitutional, due to the fact that it was signed by an interim acting President instead of the Colombian President who was abroad at the time. Some even argue that Turbay left the country purposely not to sign the Extradition Treaty since his administration was compromised with the drug traffickers (Strong, 1995).

475 *Latin American Weekly Report*, 31 October 1980, p. 2.

476 As shown elsewhere, judges belong to the sector of the population who carry more weapons (Cuellar, 2000).

477 Galán was one of the first individuals to publicly denounce the penetration of the drug traffickers into the state and the power of their corruption.

478 Corte Suprema de Justicia, Sentencia 7 October 1989.

479 Latinamerica Press, September 7, 1989, p. 1.

480 Since constitutional reform had been blocked twice during the Barco administration, he introduced reforms to the system of justice through extraordinary emergency decrees. Most of his proposed reforms to the system of justice materialised later in the 1991 Constitution.

481 The abuse of the executive in the drafting of criminal law for the purposes of consolidating its military success is what I call justice as an instrument of war.
482 The main reason for restoring extradition was the Barco administration conviction that the Colombian system of justice was incapable of convicting drug traffickers: see Melo and Bermúdez, 1994, p. 110.
483 The *Justicia sin rostro* is part of the Regional Justice which originated in a series of exceptional decrees enacted during the Barco administration, mainly the Statutes for the Defence of Democracy and Justice and Decree 474/1988.
484 Decree 2700/1991.
485 See Lee and Thoumi, 1998.
486 See Thoumi, 1999 and McRae, 1998.
487 Legal technicalities and practical problems have inhibited the expropriation of drug traffickers' property and goods regulated by Law 333/1996. Until 1999, only one definite judgment had been enforced while many others await definite judgment (*Fiscalía*. Informe de Gestión, 1998–99, pp. 150–2).
488 *El Tiempo*, 26 May 2000, Sección Judicial.
489 Since the reestablishment of extradition, the 1991 CPP provisions have allowed the extradition of three Colombian nationals in 1998 and 1999 (*Fiscalía* Internal Statistics on effective extraditions).
490 See Nemogá, 1996.
491 *El Tiempo*, 6 April 2000, p. 11A.
492 As I mentioned in Chapter 4, other actors tried also without success to limit or annul the Statute.
493 *El Tiempo*, 6 April 2000, p. 11A.
494 Briefly, the organisation and strategy of Colombian drug traffickers has changed dramatically since the mid-1990s due to national and international facts. At the national level, the dismantling of the two main cartels, Medellín in 1993 with the shooting of Pablo Escobar by an Elite Police Force, and Cali since 1995 with the imprisonment of the Cali Cartel leaders, changed the organisation of drug dealers from vertical and oligopolistic cartels to more horizontal organisations of many independent drug traffickers. Secondly, the advent of globalisation made organised crime a truly transnational organisation as opposed to a mere assortment of national arm's-length trading relations. The drug trafficker's present strategy is characterised by the establishment of affiliates 'cells' abroad, like multinational corporations, corrupt relations with foreign leaders, transnational strategic alliances, and legitimate investments in foreign countries (see Lee III, R.W., 1999).
495 The 1991 CPP ordered that extradition would not proceed when the same crime for which extradition was sought had been prosecuted or judged in Colombia (Art. 565 CPP).
496 Concepto de la Corte Suprema de Justicia, 8 August 2000. This opinion is in accordance with a 1999 decision of the Constitutional Court that held that any *extraditables* prosecuted or even convicted in Colombia could still be extradited (*El Tiempo*, 21 June 2000, Sección Judicial). Following this Constitutional Court decision, 'El Caracol' was extradited to the United States.
497 Ibid.
498 Art. 17, 1980 CP.

499 *El Tiempo*, 16 July 2000, Sección Judicial.
500 The Supreme Court of Justice is in charge of the approval or denial of a government petition of extradition. According to the 1991 CPP, the Court has to ground its decision on the formal validity of the evidence for extradition (Art. 558 CPP).
501 Art. 558 CPP.
502 *El Tiempo*, 16 July 2000, Sección Judicial.
503 Obscure proposals of this kind have occurred before, without success; see M.A. López, 1988. In fact, during the administration of Alfonso López (1978–82), the Banco de la República (Central Bank) established the *ventanilla siniestra* which allowed the repatriation of dollars without asking for their origins, i.e. a clear government consent to launder drugs money.
504 See Thoumi, 1999, p. 133.
505 Orozco, 1992, p. 226.
506 See Kaldor, 1999, p. 2. The political nature of Colombia's 'new war' derives from the fact that violence has political roots – it is not merely a conflict of law and order.
507 See Davis, 1988, p. 4.
508 See Umaña Luna, 1980 and Silva, 1997, p. 47.
509 In theory, political crime as a designation of a class of crimes denotes offences which are incidental to and form a part of political disturbances. It might also be understood to include offences consisting of an attack upon the established political order of things in the country where committed, and even to include offences committed to obtain any political object. In general, political crime is any crime directed against the government, for example, treason, sedition, rebellion. It includes any violent political disturbance, without reference to a specific crime (Black's Law Dictionary, 1979, p. 1043).
510 See Gallón, 1979, p. 10.
511 See Gallón, 1979 and Orozco, 1992.
512 In 1968, a Constitutional reform to the 1886 Constitution established the prohibition of the executive to legislate on economic matters using state of siege decrees and introduced a constitutional control of any state of siege decree by the Supreme Court of Justice. Since the system of justice was not independent of the executive, however, the constitutional control was weak and the executive continued exceptional legislation, with practically no constitutional restrictions, until 1991.
513 Original article 28 of the 1886 Constitution, later with the 1968 Constitutional reform Art. 121.
514 See Gallón, 1979.
515 Gallón, 1979, p. 63.
516 Silva, 1997, p. 67.
517 Decree 1699/1964.
518 See Leal, 1992. It is worth noting that military operations were circumscribed to identified rural and urban areas since the army was still very small in number.
519 See Gallón, 1979, p. 66.
520 Decrees 593, 605, 611, 636, 637 of 1970.
521 See Silva, 1997.

522 For more on the criticism, see Orozco, 1992, pp. 173–5.
523 For an account of the Consejo de Estado's main decisions that impose torts on the state, see Silva, 1997, pp. 45–47 and 69.
524 See Pécaut, 1989, p. 320.
525 See Orozco, 1992, p. 173.
526 For more on the development of the Toma del Palacio, see Behar, 1988.
527 Corte Suprema de Justicia, Sentencias 18 de Diciembre 1986 y 5 Marzo de 1987.
528 For more on the ambiguities on the Antiterrorism Barco Statute, see Orozco, 1992, pp. 54, 174–7.
529 Corte Suprema de Justicia, 4 October 1988.
530 There are at least 40 decrees that governed the *Justicia sin rostro*; see Némoga, 1996, pp. 183–4.
531 See Orozco, 1992, 56–7.
532 Arts 212–215 CN and Art. 121 Constitution of 1886.
533 These are geographic areas of the country where some of the rights and liberties of the individuals are reduced or suspended temporarily so that the military can operate more 'freely'.
534 See Leal, 1996, pp. 40–2.
535 See García and Uprimny, 1999.
536 See Orozco, 1992.
537 This topic, which falls outside the scope of the book, is amply corroborated by the simple reading of recent press reports which almost daily describe the barbarity and degeneration of the guerrillas' criminal behaviour, at present only comparable to that of the paramilitary.
538 Consequently most peace negotiations between the state and the different armed actors have been intimately related to this privileged treatment (Orozco, 1992, p. 52).
539 For the reader who is interested in the results of the *Justicia sin rostro* as compared to the ordinary criminal jurisdiction, see Nemoga, 1996, pp. 35–55.
540 For more on twentieth-century amnesties, see Molano, 1978 and Umaña Luna, 1980.
541 Corte Constitucional, C-358/1997.
542 Ministry of National Defence, March 2000.
543 Ministry of National Defence, October 2000.
544 Ibid., p. 26.
545 Human Rights Watch, *Informe Anual*, 2000, p. 19.
546 M. Rose, 'How the West has Wrecked Colombia'. *The Times*, 15 December 2000.
547 The Napoléon Franco 1999 opinion poll showed that 69 per cent of those surveyed had a positive opinion of the Army; 25 per cent had a negative opinion. The only institution more popular than the Army was the Church, with 77 per cent and 18 per cent respectively. The third most popular institution was the Unions, with only 39 per cent positive opinion and 43 per cent negative (Napoléon Franco y Cía, August 1999). Similar results are found in the Cuellar 1997 poll (Cuellar, 2000, pp. 79–81).
548 Several recent documents with new data have tried to disprove these links; see Ministry of National Defence, ibid., 2000.
549 M. Rose, ibid.
550 See Walsh, 1983, p. 129.

Bibliography

Official documents

Memoirs and discourses

Barco, V. *Discursos 1986–1990*. Vol. I (Bogotá: Presidencia de la República, 1990).

Castro, J. *Memorias del Ministro de Justicia* (Bogotá: Imprenta Nacional, 1974).

Del Plebiscito a la Asamblea Constitucional. *Informe del Presidente Virgilio Barco*. Vol. VIII, Vol. II, 1990.

Lara Bonilla, R. *Memorias al Congreso* (Bogotá: Ministerio de Justicia, 1984).

Zea, G. *Memorias del Ministro de Justicia* (Bogotá: Imprenta Nacional, 1960).

Government documents, books and pamphlets

Camacho, A. 'Violencia Urbana: Cali y Medellín,' *Medellín Alternativas de Futuro* (Medellín: Consejería Presidencial para Medellín y su area Metropolitana, 1992).

Comisión de Estudios sobre la Violencia. *Colombia: Violencia y Democracia* 4th edn (Bogotá: IEPRI, Universidad Nacional, 1995).

Comisión Interamericana de Derechos Humanos. 'Derechos Humanos en Colombia', Segundo Informe (Bogotá, 1994).

Consejo Superior de la Judicatura. 'Informe de la Labor Jurisdiccional disciplinaria 1992–1996' (Bogotá, 1996).

Consejo Superior y Universidad Nacional. *Modelo Probabilístico para cuantificar la impunidad* (Bogotá: Imprenta Nacional de Colombia, 2000).

Contraloría General de la Républica. 'Resultados de la Auditoría Organizacional y de Gestión practicada al Consejo Superior de la Judicatura' (Bogotá, 1997).

DANE. *Anuarios de Justicia de 1971 a 1975* (Bogotá, 1976).

——*Boletín Mensual de Estadística*, No. 317, Diciembre 1977.

——*Boletín Mensual de Estadística*, No. 380, Marzo 1983.

——*Boletín Mensual de Estadística*, No. 410, Mayo 1987.

——*Tabulados de Justicia de 1976 a 1993* (Bogotá, 1993).

——*Las Estadísticas Sociales en Colombia*, Primera Edición (Bogotá, 1993).

——*La Justicia Colombiana en Cifras, 1937–1994* (Bogotá, 1994).

——*Boletín Mensual de Estadística*, No. 503, Febrero 1995.

——*Encuesta Nacional de Hogares* (Bogotá, 1995).

Departamento Nacional de Planeación. *Justicia y Desarrollo* (Bogotá, 1994).

Echandía, C. 'El Conflicto Armado y las Manifestaciones de la Violencia en las Regiones de Colombia', *Serie Aportes para la Paz*, Tomo I, Presidencia de la República, Observatorio de Violencia (Bogotá, 1999b).

Fiscalía General de la Nación. 'Informe de Gestión, 1997–1998' (Bogotá: Imprenta Nacional de Colombia, 1998).

——Informe de Gestión, 1998–1999 (Bogotá: Imprenta Nacional de Colombia, 1999).

Fiscalía General de la Nación. Oficina de Derechos Humanos, 'Criminal measures against paramilitary and guerrillas' (Bogotá, 15 November 2000).
Gaceta del Congreso, Año III, No. 48 (Bogotá: Imprenta Nacional, 10 Mayo 1994).
Gaviria, C. 'La Corrupción no es un camino sin regreso'. *La Corrupción al Descubierto* (Bogotá: Imprenta Nacional, 1994).
Inpec. (Instituto Nacional y Penitenciario) 'Población Reclusa agrupada según delitos: 1990–1995' (Bogotá: Oficina de Planeación, 1995).
——'Número de Internos años 1991 a 1997' (Bogotá, 1997).
——Estadísticas Población Carcelaria, 1990–2000 (Bogotá, 2001).
Instituto Ser de Investigación. *Justicia Penal, Juicio y Reforma* (Bogotá: Fescol y CGN, 1983).
Ministerio de Defensa. 'The Public Force and Human Rights in Colombia' (Bogotá: Imprenta Nacional, March 2000).
——'The New Military Criminal Justice in Colombia' (Bogotá: Imprenta Nacional, October 2000).
Ministerio de Gobierno. 'Moralización de la Administración Pública' (Bogotá: Imprenta Nacional, 1993).
Ministerio de Justicia. 'Población Reclusa Agrupada por delito' (Bogotá: Unidad de Evaluación de Proyectos, Dirección Nacional de Prisiones, 1992a).
——*El Ejercicio del Derecho y Educación legal* (Bogotá: Universidad Nacional, 1992b).
——'Incidencia Social de la Acción de Tutela, Resumen Ejecutivo' (Bogotá, 1996).
Ministerio de Justicia y Ministerio de Hacienda. 'Cálculos Gasto Público en la Justicia, 1985–95' (Bogotá, 1995).
Montenegro, A. 'Justicia y Desarrollo'. *Seminario Justicia y Desarrollo* (Bogotá: Departamento de Planeación Nacional, 1994).
Oficina de Investigaciones Especiales. 'La punición del enriquecimiento ilícito como forma de lucha contra la criminalidad económica' (Bogotá: Ponencia para el Noveno Congreso de las Naciones Unidas sobre Prevención del delito y tratamiento del delincuente, Febrero 1994).
Oficina en Colombia del Alto Comisionado de las Naciones Unidas para los Derechos Humanos. 'Informe sobre Derechos Humanos del 1 Enero al 31 Diciembre 1999' (Bogotá, April 2000).
Ortiz, E. 'Criminalidad y Gestión judicial según las estadístiscas del DANE: información de avance 1990', *Boletín de Estadísticas* No. 453 (Diciembre 1990).
Pérez, O.L. 'Seguridad Ciudadana: Pactos y Violencias. Sector Justicia y Política de Criminalidad, 1958–1993' (Bogotá: Misión Ciencia, Educación y Desarrollo, Mayo 1994).
Policía Nacional. *Criminalidad 1993* (Bogotá: Imprenta Fondo Rotatorio de la Policía Nacional, 1993).
Presidencia de la República. *La Revolución Pacífica de la Justicia* (Bogotá: Ministerio de Justicia, 1991).
——Seguridad para la Gente. Segunda Fase de la Estrategia Nacional contra la Violencia (Bogotá, 1993).
——'Costos del Conflicto Armado' (Bogotá: Oficina del Alto Comisionado para la Paz, 1994).
Procuraduría General de la Nación. 'Primer y Segundo Informe sobre Derechos Humanos 1990–91' (Bogotá, 1991).
——'Informe sobre Corrupción', Revista Procuraduría (Bogotá, 1994).

Registraduría General del Estado Civil. *Estadísticas Electorales*, Vol. I (Bogotá, 1990).
Sarmiento, A. *et al.* 'La violencia y las variables sociales' (Bogotá: Departamento de Planeación Nacional).
Universidad Nacional – CID. 'Plan de Desarrollo y Rehabilitación del Sistema Penitenciario Nacional' (Bogotá: Imprenta Nacional, 1989).

Codes, Laws and Decrees

Codes

Código Penal 1980 or CP 1980 (Criminal Code).
Código de Procedimiento Penal 1971 (Former Criminal Procedure).
Código de Procedimiento Penal 1991 or CPP 1991 (Criminal Procedure).
Constitución Nacional 1886 (Former National Constitution).
Constitución Nacional 1991 or CN (National Constitution).

Laws

Ley 16/1968 (Judicial Civil Service and Judicial School).
Ley 17/1975 (Transfers crimes against property and personal injuries to the Police Inspectorates' jurisdiction).
Ley 22/1977 (Modifies the criteria to identify property crimes).
Ley 2/1984 (Jurisdiction of municipal courts).
Ley 100/1984 or CP 1980 (Criminal Statute).
Ley 38/1989 (Fiscal Independence of the Judiciary).
Ley 30/1987 (De-criminalisation of some criminal conducts and fiscal and administrative independence of the judiciary).
Ley 77/1989 (Pardon granted by President Virgilio Barco to the M-19 guerrillas).
Ley 23/1991 (Anti-judicial backlog law).
Ley 65/1993 (Prison Statute).
Ley 190/1995 (Anticorruption Statute).
Ley 200/1995 (Unified Code of Conduct).
Ley 228/1995 (Transfers misdemeanours to the municipal judges jurisdiction).
Ley 270/1996 (Justice Statute).
Ley 333/1996 (Regulates drug traffickers' property confiscation).
Ley 504/1999 (Special Justice Statute).

Decrees

Decreto 1775/1926 (Preliminary Investigation and instruction of all criminal proceedings by the National Police).
Decreto 014/1955 (Preliminary investigation in criminal proceedings).
Decreto 11/1959 (Limits the amnesty granted during the Alberto Lleras administration).
Decreto 12/1959 (Assigns special justice to instruction judges).
Decreto 1699/1964 (Transfers certain crimes to military jurisdiction).

Decreto 1817/1964 (Prison Statute).
Decreto 893/1966 (Legalisation of private defence groups).
Decreto 2267/1969 (Criminal Instruction).
Decreto 250/1970 (Judicial Civil Service and Judicial School).
Decretos 593, 605, 611, 636, 637/1970 (Empowers military jurisdiction).
Decreto 409/1971 (1971 CPP).
Decreto 2195/1976 (Permits arrest of any suspect, the latter being amply defined).
Decreto 2578/1976 (Allows for the arrest of any person suspected of any crime).
Decreto 01/1978 (Transfers ordinary crimes to military jurisdiction).
Decreto 70/1978 (Gives the armed forces a licence to kill for offences committed while controlling drug trafficking operations and other high impact crimes).
Decreto 1450/1984 (Confers jurisdiction to the police over certain crimes).
Decreto 3664/1986 (Statute for the Defence of Democracy).
Decreto 050/1987 (Discards criminal investigation where the accused is unknown).
Decreto 180/1988 (Anti-terrorist Statute).
Decretos 181 y 182/1988 (Part of the Statute for the Defence of Democracy).
Decreto 1857/1989 (Part of the Statute for the Defence of Democracy).
Decreto 815/1989 (Illegality of former private defence groups or paramilitary).
Decreto 1150/1989 (Reforms the public administration).
Decreto 1855/1989 (Security fund for the judiciary).
Decretos 99, 390, 1676 y 2790/1990 (Statute for the Defence of Justice).
Decreto 1895/1989 and 2266/1991 (Reforms to illegal enrichment statute).
Decreto 2591/1991 (*Tutela*).
Decreto 2699/1991 (Organic Statute of the *Fiscalía*).
Decreto 2700/1991 (Conciliation).
Decreto 1872/1992 (Financial Organic Statute).
Decreto 57/1993 (Increases judges' salaries).
Decreto 356/1994 (Creates private security associations known as *Convivir*).
Decreto 324/2000 (Creates an elite military force to fight the paramilitary).

Other Statutes

Acto Legislativo No. 3, 1910 (Judicial reform to the 1886 Constitution which amongst other things, introduced judicial review).
Acto Legislativo No. 2, 1995 (Judicial reform that mandates military courts to be composed of active or retired members of the military).
Plebiscitum of 1957 (Ratified the National Front Pact).
Protocols I and II of 8 June 1977 additional to the Geneva Conventions of 12 August 1949.
Proyecto de Ley 184/1994 (Tried to annul illegal enrichment new legislation).

Judicial proceedings

Corte Suprema de Justicia

Sentencia 5 Mayo 1978 (Unconstitutionality of President Alfonso López P. 1977 Constitutional Reform).

Sentencia 3 Noviembre 1981 (Unconstitutionality of President Julio Cesar Turbay 1979 Constitutional Reform).
Sentencia 18 Diciembre 1986 (Precedents for the abolition of military jurisdiction).
Sentencia 5 Marzo 1987 (Abolition of military jurisdiction).
Sentencia 4 Octubre 1988 (Anti-terrorist statute interpretation).
Sentencia 7 Octubre 1989 (Declares extradition of Colombian nationals unconstitutional).
Sentencia 10 Julio 1990 (Defines 'justified delay' in the administration of justice).
Sentencia 8 Agosto 2000 (Allows any *extraditable* prosecuted or convicted person in Colombia to be extradited).

Corte Constitucional

Sentencia T-374 and 397/1993 (*Tutelas* on right of life).
Sentencia C-46/1996 (Constitutionality of state of siege decree 1902/1995).
Sentencia C-364/1996 (Re-judicialisation of certain offences).
Sentencia C-358/1997 (Mandates that any human rights violation by the military would be prosecuted in the civil courts).
Sentencia T-153/1998 (*Tutela* that ordered a plan for the construction and reparation of Colombia's prisons).
Sentencia C-392/2000 (Abolition of Special Justice).

Other tribunals

Tribunal Superior de Orden Público, Proceso A 27/91, 17 Febrero 1992.
Consejo Superior de la Judicatura, Fallo 12 Marzo 1998 (Destitution of magistrate who extorted a judge responsible for Miguel Rodríguez Orejuela's trial).

Books

Abraham, H.J. *The Judicial Process* (Oxford and New York: Oxford University Press, 1993).
Alape, A. *Las Vidas de Pedro Antonio Marin. Manual Marulanda Velez. Tirofijo* (Bogotá: Planeta, 1989).
Arendt, H. *Between Past and Future. Eight Exercises in Political Thought* (New York: The Viking Press, 1976).
Arlacchi, P. *Mafia, Peasants and Great States* (Cambridge: Cambridge University Press, 1983).
Bayley, D.H. *Police for the Future* (New York: Oxford University Press, 1994).
Barry, B. *Justice as Impartiality. A Treatise on Social Justice,* Vol. II (Oxford: Clarendon Press, 1995).
Behar, O. *Noches de Humo. Como se planeó y ejecutó la Toma del Palacio de Justicia* (Bogotá: Planeta Colombiana Editorial, 1988).
Beccaria, C. *On Crimes and Punishments* (Indianapolis, IN: Helckett Publishing, 1986).
Beetham, D. *The Legitimation of Power. Issues in Political Theory* (London: Palgrave Macmillan, 1991).

Bejarano, J.A. (ed.) *Construír la Paz* (Bogotá: Cerec, 1990).

Benhams', G. *Book of Quotations. Proverbs and Household Words* (London and Sidney: George Harrap and Company, 1948).

Benjamin, W. *One Way Street and Other Writings* (London: Lowe and Brydone Printers, 1979).

Bergquist, C., Peñaranda, R. and Sanchez, G. (eds). *Violence in Colombia. The Contemporary Crisis in Historical Perspective* (Delaware, DE: Scholarly Resources, 1992).

Betancur Cuartas, J. *La Constituyente. Itinerario de una Propuesta* (Bogotá: Tercer Mundo Editores, 1978).

Black, H.C. *Black's Law Dictionary* (St. Paul, MN: West Publishing, 1979).

Bornstein, S.E. 'The Greenpeace Affair and the Peculiarities of French Politics'. *The Politics of Scandal. Power and Process in Liberal Democracies* (New York and London: Holmes and Meier, 1988).

Borrero, A. 'Estado y Violencia'. *Construír la Paz* (Bogotá: Cerec, 1990).

Brecht, B. *Life of Galileo*, Sc. 13 trans. (London: D.I. Vesey, 1960).

Bretch, B and Knowles, E. (eds) *The Oxford Dictionary of Phrase, Saying and Quotations* (Oxford and New York: Oxford University Press, 1997).

Bushnell, D. *The Making of Modern Colombia: a Nation in Spite of Itself* (Berkeley and Los Angeles, CA: The University of California Press, 1993).

Cancino, A.J. *Corrupción Administrativa y Delincuencia Judicial* (Bogotá: Editorial ABC Ltd, 1994).

Castro, J. *La Justicia en Colombia* (Bogotá: Imprenta Patriótica, 1975).

——*Control sobre la moralidad y eficiencia administrativas. Aproximaciones al Ombudsman* (Bogotá: Planeta, 1976).

Castro, J. and Reyes Echandía, A. *Propuestas de Reforma Judicial* (Bogotá: Temis, 1978).

Cepeda Ulloa, F. 'Poder Judicial y Estabilidad Democrática'. *La Modernización de la Justicia en Colombia* (Bogotá: Uniandes, 1986).

——Una Colombia Nueva: la Visión Política de Barco. *EI Gobierno Barco. Política, Economía y Desarrollo Social en Colombia, 1986–1990* (Bogotá: Fedesarrollo y Fondo Cultural Cafetero, 1994).

—— *La Corrupción en Colombia* (Bogotá: Tercer Mundo Editores, 1997).

Cepeda, M.J. 'El Poder de los Jueces en el Nuevo Sistema de Separación de Poderes'. *Introducción a la Constitución de 1991. Hacia un Nuevo Constitucionalismo* (Bogotá: Imprenta Nacional, 1993).

Charria, A. *Plebiscito, referendum o dictadura?* (Bogotá: Impresores Iberoamericanos, 1988).

Chubb, J. and Vannicelli, M. 'Italy a Web of Scandals in a Flawed Democracy'. *The Politics of Scandal. Power and Process in Liberal Democracies* (New York and London: Holmes and Meier, 1988).

Coleman, C. and Moynihan, J. *Understanding Crime Data* (Buckingham and Philadelphia: Open University Press, 1999).

Cuellar, M.M. *Colombia: Un Proyecto Inconcluso. Valores, instituciones y capital social*, Vols I and II (Bogotá: Universidad Externado de Colombia, 2000).

Dahl, R. *Democracy in the United States: Promises and Performance* (Boston, MA: Houghton Mifflin, 1981).

Damaska, M. *The Faces of Justice and State Authority* (New Haven and London: Yale University Press, 1986).

Davis, J.A. *Conflict and Control: Law and Order in Nineteenth Century Italy* (Houndmills and London: Macmillan Education, 1988).
Deas, M. *Del Poder y la Gramática y otros ensayos sobre historia, política y literatura Colombianas* (Bogotá: Tercer Mundo Editores, 1993).
——'Canjes violentos: Reflexiones sobre la violencia Política en Colombia'. *Dos Ensayos Especulativos sobre la violencia en Colombia* (Bogotá: Tercer Mundo Editores, 1995).
Deas, M. and Ossa, C. *El Gobierno Barco. Política, Economía y Desarrollo Social en Colombia, 1986–1990* (Bogotá: Fedesarrollo y Fondo Cultural Cafetero, 1994).
Deas, M. and Gaitán, F. *Dos ensayos especulativos sobre la violencia en Colombia* (Bogotá: Tercer Mundo Editores, 1995).
Deas, M. and Llorente, M.V. *Reconocer la Guerra para contruír la Paz* (Bogotá: Uniandes, 1999).
De Soussa Santos, B. and García, M. *El Caleidoscopio de las justicias en Colombia.* Vols I and II (Bogotá: Siglo del Orden Editores, 2001).
Drake, P.W. *The Money Doctor in Los Andes. The Kemmerer Missions, 1923–1933* (Durham and London: Duke University Press, 1989).
Duhamel, O. and Cepeda, M.J. *Las Democracias. Entre el Derecho Constitucional y la Política* (Bogotá: Tercer Mundo Editores, 1997).
Dugas, J. 'La Constitución Política de 1991: Un Pacto Político Viable?' *La Constitución Política de 1991: un Pacto Político Viable* (Bogotá: Fondo Editorial Cerec, 1993a).
——'El desarrollo de la Asamblea Nacional Constituyente'. *La Constitución Política de 1991: un Pacto Político Viable* (Bogotá: Fondo Editorial Cerec, 1993b).
Echandía, C. 'Expansión territorial de las guerrillas Colombianas'. *Reconocer la Guerra para construir la Paz* (Bogotá: Uniandes, 1999a).
Elster, J. *The Cement of Society: a Study of Social Order* (Cambridge: Cambridge University Press, 1989).
Escobar Sierra, H. *La Constituyente: reforma nacional* (Bogotá: Temis, 1991).
Escobar, J.F. *La Crisis de las Leyes en Colombia* (Cali: Feriva Ltda, 1990).
Fanon, F. *The Wretched of the Earth* (Harmondsworth: Penguin, 1963).
Farer, T. *Transnational Crime in the Americas* (New York and London: Routledge, 1999).
Friedman, W. *Law in a Changing Society* (London: Stevens and Sons, 1959).
Gaitán, F. 'Una indagación sobre las causas de la violencia en Colombia'. *Dos Ensayos Especulativos sobre la violencia en Colombia* (Bogotá: Tercer Mundo Editores, 1995).
Gallón, G. *Quince Años de Estado de Sitio en Colombia, 1958–78* (Bogotá: Editora Guadalupe, 1979).
Gambetta, D. (ed.) *Trust Breaking and Co-operative Relations* (London: Blackwell, 1988).
——*The Sicilian Mafia. The Business of Private Protection* (Cambridge, MA: Harvard University Press, 1993).
García, M. *La Eficacia Simbólica del Derecho. Exámen de Situaciones Colombianas* (Bogotá: Uniandes, 1993).
——'Constitucionalismo Perverso. Normalidad y Anormalidad Constitucional en Colombia: 1957–1997'. *Caleidoscopio de las Justicias en Colombia* (Bogotá: Siglo del Orden Editores, 2001).
García, M. and Rodriguez, C. 'Justicia Cosntitucional: la acción de tutela'. *Caleidoscopio de las Justicias en Colombia* (Bogotá: Siglo del Orden Editores, 2001).

García, M. and Uprimny, R. 'El Nudo Gordiano de la Justicia y la Guerra en Colombia'. *Armar la Paz es desarmar la Guerra* (Bogotá: Fescol, 1999).
Giraldo, J. 'La Administración de Justicia en Los Estados Unidos'. *La modernización de la Justicia en Colombia* (Bogotá: Uniandes, 1986).
Giraldo, J., Reyes, A. A. and Acevedo, J. *Reforma de la Justicia en Colombia* (Bogotá: Instituto Ser de Investigación, 1987).
Giraldo, J. *et al. Justicia y Sistema Político* (Bogotá: IEPRI y Fescol, 1997).
Gutierrez, F. 'Gestión del Conflicto en entornos turbulentos. El caso Colombiano'. *Conflicto y Contexto* (Bogotá: Tercer Mundo Editores, 1997).
Guzmán, M. and Reyes Alvarado, A. *El Proceso de Modernización de la Justicia en Colombia* (Bogotá: Instituto Ser de Investigación, 1992).
Guzmán, G., Fals Borda, O. and Luna, E. *La Violencia en Colombia*, Vols I and II, Novena Edición (Bogotá: Carlos Valencia Editores, 1980).
Hammergren, L.A. *The Politics of Justice and Justice Reform in Latin America. The Peruvian Case in Comparative Perspective* (Boulder, CO: Westview Press, 1998).
Haring, C.H. *El Imperio Español en América* (México: Alianza Editorial Mexicana, 1990).
Hart, H.L.A. *The Concept of Law* (Oxford: Clarendon Press, 1994).
Hartlyn, J. *The Politics of Coalition Rule in Colombia* (Cambridge: Cambridge University Press, 1988).
Heher, F., Heller, A. and Markus, G. *Dictatorship over Needs* (Oxford: Blackwell, 1984).
Hine, D. 'Italy: Parties and Party Government under Pressure'. *Political Parties: Electoral Change and Structural Response* (Oxford: Basil Blackwell, 1987).
——*Governing Italy: The Politics of Bargained Pluralism* (Oxford: Oxford University Press, 1993).
Hoskin, G. 'Los partidos tradicionales: Hasta donde son los responsables de la crisis política.' *Al Filo del Caos: La crisis política en Colombia en los años 80* (Bogotá: Tercer Mundo Editores, 1991).
——'La administración Barco: Del Caos Político a una salida ambigua'. *El Gobierno Barco. Política, Economía y Desarrollo Social en Colombia: 1986–1990* (Bogotá: Fedesarrollo, 1994).
Huntington, S.P. *Political Order in Changing Societies* (New Haven and London: Yale University Press, 1968).
Instituto Ser de Investigación. *Fundamentos empíricos para una reforma de la Justicia Penal* (Bogotá, 1978).
Jaffe, L.L. *English and American Judges and Lawmakers* (Oxford: Clarendon Press, 1969).
Jordan, D.C. *Drug Politics: Dirty Money and Democracies* (Norman, OK: University of Oklahoma Press, 1999).
Kafka, F. *The Process* (London: Penguin, 1994).
Kaldor, M. *New and Old Wars. Organized Violence in a Global Era* (Cambridge: Polity Press, 1999).
Kline, H. 'The National Front: Historical Perspective and Overview'. *Politics of Compromise: Coalition Government in Colombia* (New Brunswick and New Jersey: Transaction Books, 1980).
Krauthausen, C. and Sarniento, F. *Cocaina & Co.: un Mercado Ilegal por Dentro* (Bogotá: Tercer Mundo Editores, 1991).
Koretze, R. *América Latina II. La Epoca Colonial* (Bogotá: Siglo Veintiuno Editores, 1995).

Kotkin, S. and Sajos, A. (eds). *The Political Corruption of Transition: a Handbook* (Princeton, NJ: Princeton University Press, 2001).

La Palombara, J. *Democracy Italian Style* (New Haven, CT: Yale University Press, 1987).

Latorre, M. 'Colombia: Una Sociedad Bloqueada?' *Política y Elecciones* (Bogotá: Uniandes, 1980).

Leal Buitrago, F. and Zamosc, L. (eds). *Al Filo del Caos. Crisis Política en la Colombia de los años 80* (Bogotá: Tercer Mundo Editores, 1991).

Leal, F. 'Estructura y Coyuntura de la Crisis Política'. *Al Filo del Caos. Crisis Política en la Colombia de los años 80* (Bogotá: Tercer Mundo Editores, 1991).

——'Alcances y Dilemas de la Crisis Política'. *Tras las Huellas de la Crisis Política* (Bogotá: Tercer Mundo Editores, 1996).

Lemoine, C. *Las Fuerzas de la Opinión* (Bogotá: Centro Nacional de Consultoría, 1993).

Levi, M. 'Violent Crime'. *The Oxford Handbook of Criminology* (Oxford: Clarendon Press, 1997).

Llorente, M.V. 'Perfil de la Policía Colombiana'. *Reconocer la Guerra para construír la Paz* (Bogotá: Uniandes, 1999).

Linz, J. and Valenzuela, A. (eds). *The Failure of Presidential Democracy. The Case of Latin America*, Vol. 2 (Baltimore and London: The Johns Hopkins University Press, 1994).

Lleras de la Fuente, C. *et al.* (eds). *Interpretación y Génesis de la Constitución de Colombia* (Bogotá: Cámara de Comercio, 1992).

Lleras Restrepo, C. *Constituyente o Congreso?* (Bogotá: Ancora Editores, 1990).

Losada, R. and Vélez, E. *Identificación y participación política en Colombia* (Bogotá: Editorial Presencia, 1981).

Londoño, J. 'Had Kuznets Visited Colombia'. *The Colombian Economy: Issues of Trade and Development* (Boulder, CO: Westview Press, 1992).

MacFarlane, L.J. *Violence and the State* (London: Nelson and Sons, 1974).

Maier, J.B.J., Ambos, K. and Woischnik, J. (coords). *Las Reformas Procesales Penales en América Latina* (Buenos Aires: Ad-hoc, 2000)

Maguire, M., Morgan, R. and Reiner, R. *The Oxford Handbook of Criminology*, 2nd edn (Oxford: Clarendon Press, 1997).

Maguire, M. 'Crime Statistics, Patterns, and Trends'. *The Oxford Handbook of Criminology*, 2nd edn (Oxford: Clarendon Press, 1997).

McRae, P. *Impact of the Illegal Narcotics Trade on Economic and Legal Institutions in Colombia* (Mississippi, MS: Historical Text Archive, 1998).

Matthiesen, T. *El Arte Político de Conciliar. El Tema de las Drogas en las Relaciones entre Colombia y Estados Unidos, 1986–1994* (Bogotá: Fescol, Cerec y Fedesarrollo, 2000).

Mayhew, P. 'Researching the State of Crime: Local, National and International Victim Surveys', in R.D. King and E. Wincup (eds). *Doing Research on Crime and Justice* (Oxford: Oxford University Press, 2000).

Medina, C. *ELN: Una Historia contada a dos voces* (Bogotá: Rodríguez Quintero Editores, 1996).

Melo, J.O. 'Comentarios sobre ponencias anteriores'. *Construír la Paz* (Bogotá: Cerec, 1990).

Melo, J.O. and Bermúdez, J. 'La Lucha Contra el Narcotráfico: Exitos y Limitaciones'. *El Gobierno de Barco* (Bogotá: Fedesarrollo y Fondo Cultural Cafetero, 1994).

Merryman, J.H. *The Civil Law Tradition: an Introduction to the Legal Systems of Western Europe and Latin America*, 2nd edn (Stanford, CA: Stanford University Press, 1985).
Molano, A. *Trochas y Fusiles* (Bogotá: El Ancora, 1996).
Némoga, G.E. *Estado y Administración de Justicia en Colombia* (Bogotá: Ediciones Ciencia y Derecho, 1990).
——*Justicia sin Rostro. Estudio sobre la Justicia Regional* (Bogotá: UNIJUS, 1996).
Nelken, D. 'Stopping the Judges'. *Italian Politics: the Stalled Transition* (Boulder, CO: Westview Press, 1996).
Nino, C. *Un país al margen de la ley. Estudio de la anomia como componente del subdesarrollo argentino* (Buenos Aires: Emecé Editores, 1993).
North, D. *Institutions, Institutional Change and Economic Performance* (Cambridge: Cambridge University Press, 1990).
Offe, C. *Disorganized Capitalism: Contemporary Transformations of Work and Politics* (Cambridge: Polity Press, 1985).
Oquist, P. *Violencia, Conflicto y Política en Colombia* (Bogotá: Biblioteca Banco Popular, 1978).
Orozco, I. *Combatientes, rebeldes y terroristas. Guerra y Derecho en Colombia* (Bogotá: Temis, 1992).
——'Administración de Justicia. Sistema Político y Democracia'. *Justicia y Sistema Político* (Bogotá: IEPRI y Fescol, 1997).
Ots y Capdequi, J.M. *Las Instituciones del Nuevo Reino de Granada al Tiempo de la Independencia* (Madrid, Consejo Superior de Investigaciones Científicas. Instituto 'Gonzalo Fernandez de Oviedo', 1958).
Palacios, M. *Entre la Legitimidad y la Violencia. Colombia 1875–1994* (Bogotá: Grupo Editorial Norma, 1995).
Pardo, R. 'Democratización, guerrilla y narcotráfico. Reflexiones sobre la violencia contemporánea'. *Construír la Paz* (Bogotá: Cerec, 1990).
Pearce, J. *Colombia: Inside the Labyrinth* (London: Latin American Bureau, 1990).
Pécaut, D. *Política y Sindicalismo en Colombia* (Bogotá: Ediciones la Carreta, 1973).
——*Orden Y Violencia. Colombia 1930–1954*, Vols I and II (Bogotá: Siglo Ventiuno Editores and Cerec, 1987).
——*Crónica de dos décadas de Política Colombiana 1968–1988* (Bogotá: Siglo Ventiuno Editores, 1989).
Peñate, A. 'El Sendero Estratégico del ELN: Del idealismo guevarista al clientelismo armado'. *Reconocer la Guerra para contuír la Paz* (Bogotá: Cerec, 1999).
Philp, M. 'Political Corruption, Democratization and Reform'. *The Political Corruption of Transition: a Handbook* (Princeton, NJ: Princeton University Press, to be published 2001–2).
Pizarro, E. *Insurgencia sin Revolución. La guerrilla Colombiana en una perspectiva comparada* (Bogotá: Tercer Mundo Editores, 1996).
Przeworski, A. *The State and the Economy under Capitalism* (New York: Harwood Academic, 1990).
Putnam, R.D. *Making Democracy Work. Civic Traditions in Modern Italy* (Princeton, NJ: Princeton University Press, 1993).
Rangel, A. 'Las Farc-EP: Una mirada actual'. *Reconocer la Guerra para construir la Paz* (Bogotá: Cerec, 1999).

Raz, J. *The Concept of a Legal System. An Introduction to the Theory of a Legal System* (Oxford: Clarendon Press, 1980).
—— (ed.). *Authority* (Oxford: Blackwell, 1990).
Rensselaer, W.L. III. 'Transnational Organized Crime: an Overview'. *Transnational Crime in the Americas* (New York and London: Routledge, 1999).
Reyes Alvarado, A. *Justicia y Criminalidad* (Bogotá: Instituto Ser de Investigación, 1989).
——*Comentarios sobre la administración de justicia en Colombia* (Bogotá: Instituto Ser de Investigación, 1990).
——*Evaluación del Sistema Judicial Penal de 1987 a 1991* (Bogotá: Instituto Ser de Investigación, 1992).
Rico, J.M., Salas, L., Gutiérrez, E. and Cruz, C. *La Justicia Penal en Costa Rica* (San José: Educa, 1988).
Rico, J.M. and Salas, L. *Independencia Judicial en América Latina: Replanteamiento de un tema tradicional* (Miami: Centro para la Administración de Justicia, Universidad de la Florida, 1990).
Rouquié, A. *El Estado Militar en América Latina* (Bogotá: Siglo Veintiuno Editores, 1984).
Rubio, M. *Crimen e Impunidad. Precisiones sobre la violencia* (Bogotá: Tercer Mundo Editores, 1999).
Ryan, A. 'Introduction', in *Justice* (Oxford: Oxford University Press, 1993).
Salazar, A. *No Nacimos pa' semilla* (Bogotá: Corporación Región y Cinep, 1990).
——*Mujeres de Fuego* (Medellín: Corporación Región, 1993).
Salazar, A. and Jaramillo, A.M. *Medellín: Las Subculturas del Narcotráfico* (Bogotá: Cinep, 1996).
Samper, J.M. *Derecho Público Interno de Colombia*, Vols I and II (Bogotá: Biblioteca Banco Popular, 1974).
Shklar, J. 'The Liberalism of Fear'. *Liberalism and Morality* (Cambridge, MA: Harvard University Press, 1989).
Sintura, J.F. *La Fiscalía: una realidad Jurídica en Colombia* (Bogotá: Ediciones Jurídicas Gustavo Ibañez, 1993).
Silva, G. *Será Justicia? Criminalidad y Justicia Penal en Colombia* (Bogotá: Universidad Externado de Colombia, 1997).
Spotts, F. and Wieser, T. *Italy: a Difficult Democracy* (Cambridge University Press, 1986).
Stille, A. *Excellent Cadavers. The Mafia and the Death of the First Italian Republic* (London: Vintage, 1996).
Strong, S. *Whitewash. Pablo Escobar and the Cocaine Wars* (Basingstoke: Palgrave Macmillan, 1995).
Struensee, E. and Maier, J.B.J. 'Introducción a las Reformas Penales en Latino America'. *La Reformas Procesales Penales en América Latina* (Buenos Aires: Ad-hoc, 2000).
Taylor, M. *Community, Anarchy and Liberty* (Cambridge: Cambridge University Press, 1982).
Thoumi, F.E. *Political Economy and Illegal Drugs in Colombia* (Boulder, CO: Lynne Rienner, 1995).
——'The Impact of the Illegal Drug Industry in Colombia'. *Transnational Crime in the Americas* (London: Routledge, 1999).

Tokatlián, J.G. *Drogas, dilemas y dogmas. Estados Unidos y la narcocriminalidad organizada en Colombia* (Bogotá: Tercer Mundo Editores, 1995).
Uprimny, R. 'La Judialización de la Crisis Política'. *Tras las Huellas de la Crisis Política* (Bogotá: Tercer Mundo Editores, 1996).
——'Administración de Justicia'. *Sistema Político y Democracia* (Bogotá: IEPRI and Fescol, 1997).
——'El "laboratorio" Colombiano: Narcotráfico, Poder, y Administración de Justicia'. *El Caleidoscopio de las justicias en Colombia*, Vol. I (Bogotá: Siglo del Hombre Editores, 2001b).
Urrutia, M. *Cincuenta Años de Desarrollo Económico Colombiano* (Bogotá: La Carreta, 1979).
Valencia, C. 'La Modernización de la Justicia Penal mediante el desarrollo organizacional'. *Modernización de la Justicia en Colombia* (Bogotá: Uniandes, 1987).
Valencia, D. and Giraldo, J. *et al.* 'Derechos Humanos, reforma penal y violencia en Colombia'. *Derecho penal, terrorismo y legislación* (Bogotá: Universidad Nacional, 1991).
Velásquez, F. *Derecho Penal* (Bogotá: Temis, 1995).
Vélez, E., Gómez, P. and Giraldo, J. *Jueces y Justicia en Colombia* (Bogotá: Instituto Ser de Investigación and Cerec, 1987a).
Vélez, E., Gómez, P. and Rodríguez, P. *Informe Metodológico. Estudio sobre aspectos socio-económicos y organizacionales de la justicia Colombiana* (Bogotá: Instituto Ser de Investigación and Cerec, 1987b).
Walsh, D.P.J. *The Use and Abuse of Emergency Legislation in Northern Ireland* (London: Russell Press, 1983).
Whitehead, L. 'International Aspects of Democratization'. *Transitions from Authoritarian Rule. Comparative Perspectives* (Baltimore and London: The Johns Hopkins University Press, 1986).
Zaffaroni, E. *Sistemas Penales y Derechos Humanos en América Latina. Informe Final* (Argentina: Ediciones de Palma, 1986).

Journals

Barreto, M. 'Aspectos constitucionales de la acción de tutela', *Revista de Teoría del Derecho y Análisis Jurídico*, 7 (1996).
Binder, A. 'Principios Fundamentales del Proceso Penal Acusatorio', *Justicia y Derechos Humanos*, No. 18 (1993).
Cepeda, M.J. 'La práctica Jurídica Colombiana: una visión crítica', *Revista de Derecho Privado*, No. 4, Vol. II (1988).
De los Rios, H. and Ruiz, J. 'La violencia urbana en Medellín en los años 80', *Revista Universidad de Antioquia*, No. 221 (1994).
Deas, M. 'Algunas Notas sobre la historia del caciquismo en Colombia', *Revista de Occidente*, No. 27 (1973).
Dueñas, O.J. 'La Contrareforma Sueña con golpear la "herejía" de la tutela', *Revista Teoría del Derecho y Análisis Jurídico*, No. 7 (1996).
Gaviria, C. 'La tutela como instrumento de paz', *Revista Teoría del Derecho y Análisis Jurídico*, No. 7 (1996).
Goldstock, R. 'Organized Crime and Corruption', *Corruption and Reform*, 7 (1993).

Hammergreen, F. 'Reforma Judicial en Latinoamérica: premisas para el cambio', *Revista Debates*, Vol. II, No. 4 (1998).
Leal, F. 'Estados de sitio', *Análisis Político*, No. 15, January–April (1992).
Lee, R. and Thoumi, F.E. 'El Nexo entre las organizaciones criminales y la política en Colombia', *Ensayo y Error*, 4, April (1998).
Lynch, D.O. 'Lawyers in Colombia: Perspective on the Organisation and Allocation of Legal Services', *Texas International Law Journal*, Vol. 13, Spring (1978).
Merryman, J.H. 'The French Deviation', *The American Journal of Comparative Law*, Winter (1996).
Muñoz, J.A. 'La duración del proceso penal', *Derecho Penal y Criminología*, Vol. VI, No. 15 (1980).
Nelken, D. 'The Judges and Political Corruption in Italy', *Journal of Law and Society*, Vol. 23, No. 1, March (1996a).
North, D. 'No sólo de macroeconomía vive el hombre', *Estrategia Económica y Financiera*, June (1996).
Nye, J.S. 'Corruption and Political Development: a Cost–Benefit Analysis', *American Political Science Review*, No. 61, June (1967).
Pécaut, D. 'Presente, pasado y futuro de la violencia', *Análisis Político*, No. 30 (1997).
Philp, M. 'Politics, Market and Corruption', *Innovation*, Vol. 2, No. 4 (1989).
——'Defining Political Corruption', *Political Studies*, XLV (1997).
Pocock, J.G.A. 'Machiavelli, Harrington and English Political Ideologies in the Eighteen Century', *William and Mary Quarterly*, 3d. ser. 22 (1965).
Roldán, H. 'La Justicia Colombiana y la construcción de consensos en al comunas de Medellín. Caso del Barrio Moravia', *Justicia y Desarrollo*, Vol. II, No. 10, December (1999).
Rojas, D. 'Tutela contra providencias judiciales', *Pensamiento Jurídico*, No. 7 (1996).
Sánchez, G. 'Violence in Colombia: New Research, New Questions', *Hispanic American Historical Review*, Vol. 65, No. 4, November (1985).
Rosenn, K.S. 'Judicial Review in Latin America', *Ohio State Law Journal*, Vol. 35 (1974).
Rubio, M. 'Perverse Social Capital: Some Evidence from Colombia', *Journal of Economic Issues*, Vol. 33, No. 3, September (1997).
Sáez, F. 'La Naturaleza de la Reforma Judicial en América Latina: consideraciones estratégicas', *Revista Debates*, Vol. II, No. 4 (1998).
Uprimny, R. 'Fiscal General o General Fiscal? Nuevo Procedimiento Penal y Derechos Humanos en Colombia', *Revista del Colegio de Abogados Penalistas del Valle*, Nos 29 and 30 (1995).
——'Informalización de la Justicia', *Pensamiento Jurídico*, No. 1 (1994a).
——'Justicia y resolución de conflictos: la alternativa comunitaria', *Pensamiento Jurídico*, No. 1 (1994b).
Uprimny, R., Rodríguez, C. and García, M. 'Más allá de la oferta y la demanda: análisis socio-jurídico de la justicia Colombiana a comienzos del Siglo', *Justicia y Desarrollo*, Vol. IV, No. 18, November (2001a).
Valencia Villa, H. 'De las guerras constitucionales en Colombia, capítulo LXVIII: un informe sobre la reforma Barco', *Análisis Político*, No. 6, January–April (1989).

Young, J. 'Radical Criminology in Britain: The Emergence of a Competing Paradigm', *British Journal of Criminology*, Vol. 28, No. 2 (1988).
Zambrano, W. 'Les Droits des citoyens vis-à-vis de l'administration. Le cas de la Colombie', *Revue Internationale de Droit Comparé*, No. 2 (1992).

Newspapers and magazines

Associated Press (United States).
Boletín El Miliciano (Medellín, Colombia).
Cambio (Colombia).
El Espectador (Colombia).
El Mundo (Medellín, Colombia).
El Tiempo (Colombia).
Latin America Weekly Report.
Le Monde (France).
Miami Herald, International Edition (United States).
New York Times (United States).
Número (Colombia).
Semana (Colombia).
The Guardian (United Kingdom).
The Economist (United Kingdom).
Time Magazine (United States).

Personal interviews

1993

Bogotá

Magistrate of the Consejo de Estado, July.
William Zambrano and Cesar Caballero, members of Misión para la Moralización, August.
Rodrigo Uprimy, Conjuez, Corte Constitucional, August.
Ana María Ruan, Procuradora Delegada para la Contratación Administrativa, Procuraduría General de la Nación, August.
Asesora Despacho Procurador General, Procuraduría, September.
Eduardo Wills, Ex-Director of Misión para la Moralización, September.
Gustavo de Greiff, Fiscal General de la Nación, September.
Diego Niño, Director Policía Judicial, September.
Coordinadora Unidad de Planeación, PNR, Bogotá, September.
Member of the PNR, Bogotá, September.

Barranquilla

Personero de Barranquilla, August.
Personero Delegado en lo Penal, Personería de Barranquilla, August.
Delegada en Asuntos Policivos, Personería de Barranquilla, August.
Personero en servicios Públicos, Personería de Barranquilla, August.
Student of ESAP, Barranquilla, August.

Cali

Coronel Policía, Secret Service, September.
Jorge Eliecer Delgado Fajardo, Director Cárcel varones Villahermosa, September.
Felipe López, Director Regional de Fiscalías, September.
Fiscal Seccional Administración Pública, Fiscalía, September.
Fiscal 42, Unidad de Investigaciones Especiales, Fiscalía Regional de Cali, September.

1994

Bogotá

Ernesto Carrasco, Jefe OIE, Procuraduría, August.
Several clerks of the OIE, Procuraduría, August.
Members of the Procuraduría Delegada para Vigilancia Judicial, August.

1995

Bogotá

Colombian Senator, Congress, July.
Alexandra Baquero, Procuradora Delegada para Asuntos Presupuestales, Procuraduría, August.
Claudia Balcázar, Procuradora Provincial para la Contratación Administrativa, Procuraduría, August.
Miguel Silva, General Secretary of the Presidency of Colombia, September.

1996

Bogotá

Two Criminal Circuit Judges, September.
Clerk, División de Estadísticas, Consejo Superior de la Judicatura, November.
Clerk, Division de Información Judicial, Ministerio de Justicia, November.
Pedro Nel Ospina, Former Director of DIAN, December.

1997

Bogotá

Rudolf Hommes, Ex-Minister of Public Finances, January.
Myriam Donato, Magistrate and President of the Disciplinary Room, Consejo Superior de la Judicatura, April.
Clerk of the Procuraduría Delegada para la Vigilancia Judicial, Procuraduría, July.
Alfredo Fuentes, Director Fundación para la Excelencia en la Justicia, July.
Cristina Motta, Directora del Cijus, Universidad de los Andes, July.
Professor of Law, Universidad de los Andes, July.
Several Private lawyers in litigation, July.
Research associate of Fedesarrollo, August.

Coordinator of FES in charge of the 1995 survey on the perception of the system of justice, August.
Two Clerks of the Ministry of Justice, September.
Two lawyers of the Procuraduría Delegada para la Vigilancia Judicial, Procuraduría, September.
Former *Fiscal sin rostro*, Fiscalía General de la Nación, September.
Fiscal from the Centro de Información sobre actividades delictivas, *Fiscalía*, September.
Many *fiscales*, *Fiscalía*, September.
Fiscal sin rostro in charge of the *Proceso 8000*, interview through a third person, September.

2000

Bogotá

Fiscal General de la Nación, Alfonso Gómez Méndez, August.
Assistant to the Dirección Nacional de Fiscalías, *Fiscalía*, August.
Oficial de Derechos Humanos, Oficina del Alto Comisionado de Naciones Unidas para los Derechos Humanos, August.
Several members of the CTI *Fiscalía*, August.
British Journalist reporting on the armed conflict in Colombia, September.
Government negotiator in FARC Peace Process, September.
Journalist who has been several times in the DMZ, September.

Monographs, theses, unpublished papers and private documents or letters

Bagley, B.M. 'Colombia under Siege' (University of Miami: Paper presented at the International Symposium on Money Laundering, October 26–28, 1989).
Bermúdez, J. 'Battles for Public Opinion: Mass Media, Political Scandal and Presidential Popularity in Colombia (1994–96) and Venezuela (1989–93)', PhD Thesis (Oxford University, 1999).
Buvinic, M., Morrison, A. and Shifter, M. 'La Violencia en América Latina y el Caribe', BID, 1999.
BID. 'Informes de Consultoría de Países Latinoamericanos', 1994.
Consejo Superior de la Judicatura. 'Sistema Nacional de Estadísticas, SINEJ', Documento interno (Bogotá: 1997).
Corporación Excelencia en la Justicia. 'Indicadores del Area de la justicia en Colombia' (Bogotá, 1996).
Fajnzylber, P., Lederman, D. and Loayza, N. 'What causes Violent Crime', Office of the Chief Economist. Latin America and the Caribbean Region (The World Bank, 1998).
FARC Comando Central de los Héroes de Marquetalia, Trial document, May 2000.
Fiscalía General. 'Paramilitares Capturados de 1997–1998', Documento interno, 1998.
—— 'Internal Statistics on effective extraditions', 1999.
—— 'Flujo de Procesos, Unidades Seccionales y Locales', July 1999 to July 2000.

García, M. 'Incidencia Social de la Acción de tutela' (Bogotá: Uniandes, 1996).
Giraldo, J. 'La Defensa de las personas de escasos recursos económicos' (Bogotá: Instituto Ser de Investigación, 1980).
Giraldo, J. and Giraldo, O. 'Consultoría Banco Interamericano de desarrollo-BID', (Bogotá, 1994).
Human Rights Watch. 'Informe Anual', 2000.
ICAC. 'Inquisitorial Systems of Criminal Justice and the ICAC: a Comparison' (Hong Kong: November 1994).
Jaramillo, A.M. 'Milicias Populares en Medellín: entre la guerra y la paz' (Medellín: Corporación Región, 1994).
López M.A. 'Parábolas del retorno' (Bogotá: Tercer Mundo Editores, 1988).
UC-ELN. 'Poder Popular y nuevo Gobierno. Conclusiones del Segundo Congreso' (Ediciones Colombia Viva, sin lugar de edición, 1990).

Index

Note: emboldened page ranges indicate chapters